Jacques Pépin's Kitchen

ENCORE WITH CLAUDINE

Jacques Pépin's Kitchen

ENCORE WITH CLAUDINE

JACQUES PÉPIN

Photographs by Tim Turner

Design by Madeleine Corson

Illustrations by Jacques Pépin

BAY BOOKS

SAN FRANCISCO

PRODUCTION OF THE PUBLIC TELEVISION SERIES
JACQUES PÉPIN'S KITCHEN IS MADE POSSIBLE BY GENEROUS GRANTS FROM
BRAUN INC   CAMBRIA WINERY & VINEYARD
ANOLON COOKWARE   NEAR EAST FOODS   OXO INTERNATIONAL

First Paperback Edition Published 2002 By Bay Books

Copyright 1998 by Jacques Pépin

Illustrations Copyright 1998 by Jacques Pépin

Photographs Copyright 1998 by Tim Turner

Bay Books Is An Imprint Of Bay/Soma Publishing, Inc.

444 De Haro St., No. 130, San Francisco, CA 94107.

Publisher: James Connolly

Art Director: Jeffrey O'Rourke

Editorial Director: Clancy Drake

Book Designer: Madeleine Corson Design

Copy Editor: Joan Nielsen

Proofreader: Leah Stewart

Photographer: Tim Turner

Photography Coordinator: Tina Salter

Photography Chefs: Vincent Nattress and Laura Ammons

Prop Stylist: Carol Hacker

Props Provided By: Barbara Chambers/Spencer House

Food Provided By: Fresh Fish Company, Green Leaf Produce,

Provini Veal, Straus Family Creamery, Superior Farms

Menu Illustrations By: Jacques Pépin

The Publishers Wish To Thank The Following For Thier Contributions To This Book's Photography:

Draeger's Market; New On Sang Poultry Co., Inc.; Caffe Centro; Tallia Hillel

Library Of Congress Cataloging-in-Publication Data

Pépin, Jaques

Jacques Pépin's kitchen: encore with Claudine/ by Jacques Pépin:

photographs by Tim Turner: design by Madeleine Corson Design

p. cm.

"Companion to the public television series."

Includes index.

ISBN 0-912333-86-3

1. Cookery. 2. Menus. 3. Jacques Pépin's kitchen (Television program)

I. Jacques Pépin's kitchen (Television program)

II. Title

TX714.P457 1998

641.5 – DC21   98-19862

CIP

ISBN: 0-912333-86-3(hardcover)

ISBN: 1-57959-521-9(paperback)

Printed In China

10 9 8 7 6 5 4 3 2 1

Distributed By Publishers Group West

to Tonton Richard.
Bringing the family together at the table was
one of his greatest pleasures. His love, laughter and
joy of life will forever be missed.
Claudine

to my brother Bichon, with love
Jacques Pépin

CONTENTS

NOTE ON NUTRITIONAL INFORMATION:
ALL NUTRITION ANALYSES ARE BASED
ON ONE SERVING.

RECIPES BY COURSE

SIDE DISHES

Bean Sprout Salad 151

Beet Salad with Pecans 230

Bread Galettes on Salad Greens 38

Broccoli Velvet Puree 73

Stuffed Butternut Squash 135

Carrots with Orange and Dill 177

Glazed Carrots with Olives 94

Cauliflower *Salmis* 65

Spicy Celery with Garlic 238

Celeriac Puree 111

Stew of Spring Vegetables 60

Eggplant Ragout 170

Stew of Eggplant and Chinese Sausage 86

Endive with Tarragon Oil 253

Endive, Radicchio, and Walnut Salad 128

Gratin of Leeks 247

Skillet Lettuce "Packages" 220

Potato Slabs Raclette 200

Spinach with Pignola Nuts and Croutons 267

Essence of Tomato "Petals" with Tarragon Oil 209

Corn-and-Ham-Stuffed Tomatoes 48

Sautéed Turnip Greens 188

Noodles and Peas 146

Orzo with Arugula Sauce 102

California Arborio Rice and Pecans 118

Wild Rice with Pignola Nuts and Peas 159

DESSERTS

Apples Grandma 154

Apple Rounds with Calvados Glaze 49

Apricot Compote 95

Apricot *Feuilleté* 221

Apricot and Hazelnut Biscotti 210

Cantaloupe Sherbet 112

Banana-Mint Ice Cream with Rum-Raisin Sauce 40

French Vanilla Ice Cream 138

Berries *Rafraîchis* 268

Bread Pudding Soufflés
with Chocolate-Bourbon Sauce 121

Cherry Compote 103

Top-Crust Cherry Pie 189

Pecan-and-Armagnac-Stuffed Dates 231

Orange Cubes in Orange "Baskets" 61

Candied Grapefruit, Orange, and Lemon Chips 87

Grapes and Raisins in Citrus Juice 129

Baked Peaches with Almonds 172

Peaches in Red Wine 249

Roast Caramelized Pears 162

Pears in Chocolate 201

Pineapple in Apricot Sauce 68

Rhubarb and Berry Nectar with Mint 147

Quick Almond and Plum Cake 257

Plum Cobbler 239

Vincent's Almond Shortbread Cookies 139

Individual Chocolate Nut Pies 76

Phyllo Tart with Fruit *Salpicon* 180

MISCELLANEOUS

Basil Oil 56

Tarragon Oil 256

Berry Jam 270

Corn Panbread 171

Small Light Country Loaves 31

Cucumber-Yogurt Relish 110

Horseradish and Cottage Cheese Dip 217

ACKNOWLEDGMENTS

Our new television series, *Jacques Pépin's Kitchen: Encore with Claudine,* for which this book is the companion, is, perhaps, the most complex series we've done so far – yet it has come together very well. This was only possible because everyone associated with the taping of this series of twenty-six shows and the production of this book did a really good job. In my estimation, we probably had the best team effort we've ever had. ✲ The essential person on the series is my daughter, *Claudine,* who, I am proud to say, does an incredible job of just being natural. She was much more comfortable this time around, not only in front of the cameras but in the kitchen and dining room, and it was an absolute joy to work with her. As in the last series, she is the bridge between me and the audience, and she connects with our viewers even better this time than she did in the last series, exhibiting what I can only describe as real class. ✲ I want to thank *Peter Stein,* the executive producer of the series. Peter is truly where our series begin: he makes certain that we carry through our ideas well, and I thank him for his invaluable support. ✲ Thanks to *Peggy Lee Scott,* able producer on this and my last three series. As the essential liaison between everyone involved in the shows, she organized all the minutest details and brought the whole thing together. ✲ *Tina Salter,* coordinating producer, proved once again that she is the best possible person to coordinate activities between the kitchen and the set. She was, as always, efficient and gracious to all of us. ✲ Our director, *Brian Murphy,* was not only fun to work with but great to be with out on the town after the tapings. We all benefited from Brian's knowledge, and he lent great style to the shows. ✲ Thanks, also, to: *Leslee Newcomb,* our makeup artist, who did so well with Claudine and me that we look better than we ever do in real life; the associate producer, *Caroline Hockaday,* who did her job well – filling in where she was needed with no questions asked and a pleasant smile – and then kindly drove us here and there and back to our hotel; *Heidi Gintner,* our food stylist, who worked diligently throughout to make all the food look great, as well as *Lorraine Battle,* who produced incredible flower arrangements and gave generously of her knowledge to make us all look good.   ↓   I am particularly indebted to the back kitchen, which I truly believe was the best we ever had under the direction of *Vincent Nattress,* who served us well as chef and kitchen manager. With Vincent at the helm, everything ran smoothly and efficiently; his team exemplified not only speed and style, but an abiding cheerfulness and willingness to do whatever was necessary to make the shows move forward. My sincere thanks to Vincent's staff: *Laura Ammons,* who returned from Australia to work with us again and did a great job; *Mike Pleiss,* a dear, long-time friend, who fit his fine

work for us in between overseas business trips; *Joseph Strebler,* who graciously lent his expertise when we were making bread or dough and always had a smile; *Christine Swett,* always happy and ready to help where she was needed; *Douglas Keane,* who, between his job at Jardinière and helping in our kitchen, must have worked twenty hours a day but always with great enthusiasm; and *Julia Lee,* smiling, happy, and so nice to work with.   ↓   I also want to thank all the students from *Contra Costa College,* who so ably served as interns in the kitchen under *Paul Poumirau's* fine direction. ⋎ Each series culminates in a book, the production of which is an enormous and difficult undertaking. For their extensive work on *Jacques Pépin's Kitchen: Encore with Claudine,* I thank: *Norma Galehouse,* my assistant and alter ego, who did much of the hard work on this book, organizing all the material with her usual dedication; my wife, *Gloria,* who tested all of the recipes included here in the last year or so and unfailingly advised me, often suggesting ideas for new recipes; *James Connolly,* the publisher of Bay Books, who did such a great job on my two previous books that I was

delighted to be able to work with him again on this one; *Clancy Drake,* the managing editor of Bay Books, for being so exacting and helpful, and for working so diligently – even to the extent of doing the dishes for us during the shooting of photographs for the book; *Madeleine Corson,* the designer of the book, whose stylish design and layout please me enormously; *Laura Pensiero,* nutritionist, for her expert nutritional analyses and health notes; *Tim Turner,* who, working quickly and well, did all the photography for this book in just ten days. In his terrific pictures, Tim captures precisely what we did on the show; and the copy editor, *Joan Nielsen,* and proofreader, *Leah Stewart*, for their meticulous attention to detail. ⋎ There were many other people – some known to me, some not – who were involved in the production of the book as well as the show, and I want to thank all of them for making these two projects possible.

Jacques Pépin

INTRODUCTION

With better knife skills under her belt and more confidence in the kitchen, Jacques Pépin's favorite student is back for more. In *Encore with Claudine,* the new television series from the popular French chef, daughter Claudine Pépin joins her father for a second round of cooking lessons featuring a fresh repertoire of recipes.

Viewers who met Claudine during the previous series, *Cooking with Claudine,* will notice the progress. She's more hands-on now, more involved with the recipes, more sure of herself around the stove. But then, the audience probably is, too. In both series, Claudine asks the questions that viewers would if they could, making these shows as educational and motivational as a private class with Jacques.

"People told me they watched *Cooking with Claudine* with their daughters," says Jacques, who hopes the interest won't stop there. If viewers actually go into the kitchen and cook together, the Claudine shows will have achieved their aim: to persuade people of the value of cooking with and for one's family.

In *Encore with Claudine,* Jacques does on camera what he has always done at home, encouraging his daughter's hand in meal preparation. "The process can't start too early," says Jacques, who remembers lifting a five-year-old Claudine so she could stir the pot. "She 'made' dinner then," recalls Jacques, "and she'd tell her mother, 'I made it.' So she felt part of it and wanted to taste it."

Working parents may struggle with making time for these activities, but there are easy ways to get children involved, says the chef. Even if youngsters merely sit at the kitchen table doing their homework as a parent cooks, they are absorbing the rhythms, smelling the food, learning the sights and sounds of a meal in progress.

The thirty-year-old Claudine hasn't lived with her parents for years, but she still relishes a meal at their house — not only because her father's wine cellar is better than hers, but because she enjoys being his cooking sidekick. She cleans up after him ("I'm my mother's daughter on that front," says Claudine), solicits his help in deciphering dishes she's tasted, and prods him for tips and explanations — the same role, in fact, that she plays on the set.

"The series works because it's realistic," says Claudine, who enjoys cooking but does it infrequently, in part because she has lived a graduate student's existence for the past few years. She may have grown up with a French chef for a father, but she still stands in her Boston kitchen wondering how to trim the broccoli rabe or whether she can freeze

the soup. "There's always that one little step I have to call home for," she admits.

In *Encore with Claudine,* Jacques guides his redheaded daughter through more accomplishments in the kitchen. His twenty-six new menus illuminate basic skills, such as trimming an artichoke down to its bottom and cleaning salad greens, as well as more advanced techniques, such as how to bone and stuff quail. But as always, Jacques is less interested in teaching show-off dishes than in teaching Claudine and viewers how to cook with economy — how to make wholesome, satisfying meals without a great investment of time or expense.

That's how Jacques and wife Gloria cook on their own, and it's the guiding principle during the year or more that Jacques works on a book's recipes. "My concern is to create something people can do at home," says Jacques. "I'm very pragmatic that way. I know people want something light and healthful, but something a bit different and new, too. These are the same concerns I have for my own family."

But unlike those of us who struggle for fresh ideas and come up empty, Jacques finds solutions. We wander the grocery store hoping for inspiration; Jacques walks through and sees possibility. For *Encore with Claudine,* each menu started with a trip to the market — a conventional supermarket like any his readers and viewers might patronize. The day's best offerings came home with him and metamorphosed into a meal, to be tasted and criticized with friends and family, then revised and recorded.

In the Pépin home, ethnic ingredients add spice and variety. The classically trained French chef embraces the Asian and Latin foods that are redefining American cooking; ingredients like Chinese chili sauce, rice stick noodles, cilantro, and salsa. His eggplant stew with Chinese sausage and his mushroom pâtés with tomatillo sauce — both in *Encore with Claudine* — reflect his forty-year immersion in our melting-pot culture.

Jacques' culinary evolution hasn't escaped his mother, herself a former chef. "She comes here and tastes my food and says, 'It's good, but it's not French,'" he says with a laugh.

Novelty for novelty's sake doesn't amuse him, however. He shakes his head over young chefs who consider themselves creative because they've combined ingredients that no one has ever combined before. His own cooking, although he would never say so, pairs adventure with restraint and reveals an open-mindedness rarely attributed to French chefs. Jacques himself refers to his style as a *cuisine d'opportunité —*

a way of cooking that makes the most of what's available.

And what's available these days is, frankly, amazing, says the chef. The cornu-
copia at the typical American supermarket astounds him and provides his rebuttal to

the widespread notion that nobody cooks anymore.

"Maybe I'm an optimist," says Pépin, "but I see more
and more incredible supermarkets every year. Years ago, you
had two types of salad greens; now there are fifteen. Leeks,
shallots, different types of potato, tropical fruits – it's all there
now. Dozens of oils, vinegars, mustards… if no one is cooking,
what's happening to all of it? At the end of the week, a dump truck comes and throws
it out? There's no question somebody's cooking. That stuff goes somewhere."

Pépin's market-driven style takes advantage of this bounty, but never
squanders it. Like many French chefs who trained in kitchens where nothing is tossed
before squeezing every centime out of it, he can't bear waste. Jacques knows (and
shows us) how to make a tasty side dish from braised lettuce, how to stretch a costly
rack of lamb by making timbales from the trimmings, how to transform stale bread
into a puffy soufflé or bread *galettes*.

He doesn't waste motions, either. "If you're organized," says Jacques, "you can
minimize the drudgery of cooking, from chopping garlic to washing pots. Say you need
some chopped onion for soup and some pureed tomato for a pasta sauce. If you puree
the tomato in the food processor first, you have to wash it before you do the onion. If
you do the onion first, you save yourself a trip to the sink."

Viewers who watch Jacques long enough can't help but absorb some of these strategies that make cooking easier. Claudine certainly has. Chief among her new good habits is a devotion to sharp knives, a professional priority that many home cooks dismiss. "Sharpen your knives," she says, "and see what a whiz you become in the kitchen."

She has also learned to read a recipe through before launching into it, a practice that every cooking teacher preaches and most novices ignore until their haste causes calamity. "It's like the student who races to answer all five exam questions before realizing that, at the bottom of the test, it says, 'Pick two,'" says Claudine.

But, as even Jacques acknowledges, it takes practice to get organized. People who complain that they don't have time to cook would find, if they cooked more often, that it doesn't take much time. "It's a vicious circle," he admits. "The more you know, the less time it takes to put a good meal on the table. But if you never cook, you never master the routines that make it easy."

In France, he watches his sister-in-law produce dinner with no-nonsense efficiency. She works all day, then stops at the market on the way home for provisions. Before she even changes out of her business clothes, she goes into the kitchen, gets out the pressure cooker and starts the veal stew. Then she changes, sets the table, adds the vegetables to the veal, makes a salad, and has a meal on the table in short order.

"It becomes a ritual, and if you understand it, you'd be surprised how much you can do in minimal time," says the chef. "But people who haven't learned the rhythms of cooking don't know what to do first. They'll make the whole pasta sauce before thinking to put the water on to boil."

In *Encore with Claudine,* Jacques shares the techniques and time-management skills that seem so natural to a professional cook. "The show is substantial in that sense. We give a lot of information," says the inveterate teacher, whose content-heavy cooking series are so popular that some stations air two shows a day.

In the competitive world of TV chefdom, where entertainment often outweighs education, an observer might conclude that Pépin and his producers are consciously choosing another path. Jacques denies it. "We're not trying to make it different," he claims. "We're just trying to be ourselves and have a natural show."

To that end, he and Claudine decline to rehearse the shows. "I am not an actor," says Pépin. "It's not like if I do a show once, I will do it better the next time. In fact, it's probably the opposite. If I say something funny in rehearsal, I wouldn't want to say it again."

The two value the spontaneity of their dialogue and don't want to ruin it with a rehearsal or script. The uncertainty generates some tension, but it's a constructive tension that keeps everybody alert. "The producers are a bit concerned about what we're going to say," acknowledges Jacques, "but we don't know ourselves."

What Jacques does know is that his good-natured assistant has matured in the two years since the last series. Claudine is a more competent and imaginative cook now, says her father, and she brings her own creativity to the show. She's the one who suggested doing a kosher menu appropriate for her Jewish friends. And she's responsible for the expanded wine selection on the new series. Although wine has always been on the Pépin table, at home and on TV, Claudine is showing a blossoming passion for the subject.

Acknowledging her progress, the producers of *Encore with Claudine* have freed her up a little. In the first series, they told her to look only at her father, not at the camera – perhaps to emphasize her novice's role. "I was the big unknown," admits Claudine, who is unknown no more. Even a bus driver recognized her, although he apparently confused her with another TV cook (he called her Julia).

Viewers who enjoy *Encore with Claudine* will treasure the companion book for its clear recipe presentation and for Jacques' helpful notes. The twenty-six menus exemplify his signature blend of practicality and pleasure, whether the context is a weekday dinner or a weekend feast. Even his celebration menus, such as a graduation party with shrimp and rack of lamb, never lure home cooks beyond what they can reasonably do.

In one menu, Jacques remembers his fellow chef and brother, Claudine's favorite uncle, with a dinner *tonton* Richard would have loved: fillet of sole in artichoke bottoms, a spicy rib roast, and a flaky apricot pastry. In others, he revives French classics like leek gratin and salmon *grenobloise*; crosses borders with Italian tomato soup with basil oil and Chinese noodles with dried mushrooms; and nods to contemporary fashion with scallop and potato napoleons and arugula salad with salmon cracklings.

In short, *Encore with Claudine* is Jacques at his educational best, encouraging us to try the new, to respect the old, and, above all, to take pleasure in cooking for family and friends. With Claudine at his side to elicit his considerable wisdom, the lesson is as easy to swallow as that apricot pastry.

A Note on Menus and Wines

When I prepare a menu at home, I go to the market first. More often than not, the ideas I have of what I want to cook change when I look at the produce – its price, availability, quality, and so forth. So dictating a menu to someone else is, to a certain extent, against my own way of cooking; it can seem overly rigid to tell people what dishes to serve together, and what wines should accompany the meal. Yet I believe that it is important to give some guidelines so that people do not become perplexed when putting dishes together in a menu or choosing a wine. Just remember these are only guidelines, and you can use as many or as few of them as you like.

In this book, as on my television series, I have presented the dishes together in menus of three, four, or five dishes, with suggested wines to serve with the menus. However, I know that very often people choose one dish or another from a menu, rather than preparing all the dishes together. This is as it should be. Any of the dishes in this book can be enjoyed by themselves or rearranged into countless different menus, depending on any number of factors: the availability and price of the ingredients; the time you have for cooking; the mood of your eating partner; or what you yourself feel like eating on that particular day.   The possibilities are even more open when you are selecting wines. With each menu, I suggest specific wines to serve at the table; often both a red and a white, and sometimes a dessert wine as well. In many cases, there are also wines and spirits that I use in the kitchen to prepare the dishes themselves. In my kitchen at home, I will often open a bottle of wine, enjoy a glass as an aperitif while I am cooking, and use half a cup or so in one of the dishes I am preparing. As with the arrangement of dishes into menus, I feel that giving you a peek at the wines that Claudine and I consume with each meal will help you to choose similar wines that will complement specific dishes. These suggested wines give only a glimpse of the immense range of wines available at different prices today. ✧ Salads, too, are usually part of most meals at our house; so unless there is already a salad incorporated into the menu, I would recommend adding one to your meal. Finally, cheeses are more often than not served in lieu of dessert at our table, and enjoyed with red wines. ✧ Although there is nothing wrong with following the advice of the experts, feel free to follow your own taste and experiment with combinations of food and wine. The wine you choose can follow the theme of the menu – more expensive wines for classic menus, such as our Graduation Party (page 260), for example, and less costly ones for more casual menus, such as Everyday Cooking (page 78), or Cuisine Bon Marché (page 88). ✧ The idea is, more than anything else, to have fun. Read the menus and the wine suggestions for guidance or inspiration, then give the food your own touch, and simply enjoy it with your friends and your family.

Great Sandwich Party

CUCUMBER AND MINT SOUP

SMALL LIGHT COUNTRY LOAVES

SANDWICH ASSORTMENT

BREAD *GALETTES* ON SALAD GREENS

BANANA-MINT ICE CREAM WITH
RUM-RAISIN SAUCE

Claudine loves the country bread that we buy in the shop next to her grandmother's house in France; light and airy, it makes delicious sandwiches. I wanted to show Claudine how to reproduce that bread, then transform the loaves into sandwiches, all in the style of *pan bagna,* a sandwich specialty of the south of France. ⩔ I make four large, main-dish sandwiches, each with a different filling: one contains vegetables, one ham, one fish, and one cheese. These sandwiches are great made ahead, as the filling soaks into the bread and flavors it. At serving time, each sandwich is cut into four pieces, and a piece from each is served to each of the four guests. ⩔ This outdoor menu begins with a cold cucumber and mint soup, which is served before the sandwiches. Then, as a bonus, I make bread *galettes* from leftover bread and serve them on salad greens. The salad makes a great lunch dish, and showing Claudine how to make good use of a stale baguette teaches her economy in the kitchen. ⩔ The menu ends with banana-mint ice cream served with a rum-raisin sauce. Since you don't need an ice-cream machine for this dessert, it couldn't be easier to prepare. Frozen banana slices are simply pureed in a food processor with a bit of honey, sour cream, and a few mint leaves until creamy. The rum-raisin sauce makes a nice addition, but the ice cream is good on its own, too.

White
CA SAL DI
SERRA,
VERDICCHIO

Red
CAMBRIA,
JULIA'S
VINEYARD,
PINOT NOIR

Cucumber and Mint Soup

TOTAL TIME

20 minutes

YIELD

4 servings (6 cups)

NUTRITION

112 calories

6 g protein

3 g fat

.6 g saturated fat

2 mg cholesterol

950 mg sodium

14 g carbohydrate

1 g dietary fiber

Cucumbers and mint
are good sources
of vitamin C. Yogurt
provides substan-
tial calcium.

This refreshing summer soup is made from peeled and seeded cucumbers that I puree raw in a food processor along with some garlic and mint — an herb that grows profusely in my garden each summer. Yogurt, olive oil, cider vinegar, salt, and Tabasco sauce round out the ingredients in this make-ahead dish.

2 CUCUMBERS (2 POUNDS TOTAL), PEELED, SEEDED, AND COARSELY SLICED

¾ CUP (LOOSELY PACKED) MINT LEAVES

3 CLOVES GARLIC, PEELED

1¼ CUPS COLD WATER

1½ CUPS REGULAR OR NONFAT YOGURT

1 TABLESPOON VIRGIN OLIVE OIL

2 TABLESPOONS CIDER VINEGAR

1½ TEASPOONS SALT

10 DROPS TABASCO HOT PEPPER SAUCE

1. Place the cucumber slices in the bowl of a food processor with the mint, garlic, and ½ cup of the cold water. Process until pureed; the mixture will be granular. (For a smoother-textured mixture, puree in a conventional blender or with a handheld immersion blender.)

2. Transfer the puree to a bowl, and mix in the yogurt, olive oil, vinegar, salt, Tabasco, and remaining ¾ cup of water. Chill.

3. Stir before serving.

Small Light Country Loaves

A favorite at my house, this is bread like you find in the French countryside – airy (with large holes inside) and full of flavor. The dough is extremely soft and so is not worked by hand until after the second proofing, when it is formed into a ball, divided into four pieces, and placed on a lined baking pan. The bread and liner then are slid out of the pan and onto a bread stone for baking. The 2 teaspoons of yeast in the recipe can be reduced to 1½ or even 1 teaspoon in full summer or in areas where there is great humidity, as yeast develops more rapidly and gives you more extending power in these conditions.

TOTAL TIME
About 7 hours

YIELD
4 loaves

NUTRITION
(PER LOAF)
460 calories
14 g protein
1 g fat
.2 g saturated fat
0 mg cholesterol
1169 mg sodium
96 g carbohydrate
4 g dietary fiber

4 CUPS ALL-PURPOSE FLOUR (1 POUND, 5 OUNCES), WITH 1 TABLESPOON RESERVED FOR DUSTING THE TOPS OF THE LOAVES

2 TEASPOONS INSTANT GRANULATED YEAST

2 TEASPOONS SALT

2 CUPS COOL WATER

1. Place all the bread dough ingredients in the bowl of a food processor, and process the mixture for 15 seconds.

2. Transfer the dough to a bowl, cover it with plastic wrap, and let it rise for about 3½ hours at room temperature (60 to 70 degrees).

3. Release the dough from the sides of the bowl with your fingers, and press it firmly into the center of the bowl, repeating this procedure until all the dough is deflated and in a ball again.

4. Cover the dough again with plastic wrap, and let it rise for 2 hours. Then deflate the dough as described in the previous step, and form it into a ball. Moisten your hands, and break the dough into 4 pieces of about equal size.

5. Arrange the pieces of dough so they are equally spaced on a cookie sheet lined with parchment paper or a nonstick baking mat. Moisten your hands again, and press on the dough pieces to flatten them. Place an inverted roasting pan over the cookie sheet to simulate a proof box and so prevent the dough from crusting on top as it rises. Let the dough rise for 45 minutes.

(CONTINUED)

32

6. Meanwhile, preheat an oven with a bread stone on the center rack to 425 degrees.

7. After the dough has risen for 45 minutes, remove the roasting pan, and dust the tops of the loaves with the reserved flour. Firmly holding the sides of the liner, slide it and the loaves carefully onto the hot bread stone. Using a spray bottle filled with tap water, mist the interior of the oven a few times, then quickly close the door to create steam. Repeat this misting process after 2 or 3 minutes, and bake the bread for a total of 35 to 40 minutes.

8. Slide the loaves and liner onto a wire rack. Let the loaves cool for 10 to 15 minutes, then remove the liner. Continue to cool the loaves on the rack until they are at room temperature.

A Variation: Small Light Country Loaves with Mixed Grains

½ CUP MIXED GRAINS (SEE NOTE, BELOW)

2 TABLESPOONS WATER

To the original recipe ingredients, add the mixed grains and 2 tablespoons of water. Proceed as instructed in the original recipe.

Note: Mixtures of up to 10 grains — including oats, millet, bulgur, etc. — can be purchased at most supermarkets. Or, you can choose an assortment of your favorite grains at a health food store for use in this recipe.

Sandwich Assortment

These four large sandwiches are made with the Small Light Country Loaves (page 31). Although each guest can be served an entire sandwich of one variety, I recommend quartering the various sandwiches and serving each guest a section from each. Ideal for picnics, the sandwiches are very good made a few hours ahead but also keep well overnight if refrigerated.

❧   ❧   ❧   ❧   ❧   ❧   ❧   ❧   ❧

VEGETABLE SANDWICH

1 SMALL LIGHT COUNTRY LOAF (PAGE 31)

1½ TEASPOONS VIRGIN OLIVE OIL

1½ TEASPOONS RED WINE VINEGAR

1 CUP (LOOSELY PACKED) ARUGULA LEAVES, WASHED AND DRIED

5 HALF-INCH-THICK SLICES TOMATO

⅛ TEASPOON FRESHLY GROUND BLACK PEPPER

18 PITTED DRIED OIL-CURED OLIVES, COARSELY CHOPPED (¼ CUP)

4 VERY THIN SLICES RED ONION, SLICED WITH A VEGETABLE PEELER TO ASSURE THINNESS (ABOUT 1 OUNCE)

1. Split the bread loaf horizontally, and place the two halves crust side down on the table. Sprinkle both bread halves with the olive oil and vinegar.

2. Arrange the arugula leaves on one bread half, and add the tomato and pepper. Keep layering, adding the olives and, finally, the red onion slices. Cover with the other bread half, and press on the sandwich to help combine the flavors of the various filling ingredients.

3. Cut the sandwich into wedges, and serve. (Note: The sandwich will have more flavor if made an hour ahead.)

(CONTINUED)

TOTAL TIME

About 40 minutes

YIELD

Each recipe yields 1 sandwich; serving size ¼ sandwich

NUTRITION

155 calories

4 g protein

4 g fat

.5 g saturated fat

0 mg cholesterol

647 mg sodium

26 g carbohydrate

1 g dietary fiber

CHEESE SANDWICH

1 SMALL LIGHT COUNTRY LOAF (PAGE 31)

2 TABLESPOONS RED SALSA

3 OUNCES SOFT GORGONZOLA CHEESE

1 CUP (LIGHTLY PACKED) WATERCRESS LEAVES, WASHED AND DRIED

½ CUP PECAN HALVES

8 VERY THIN SLICES CUCUMBER, SLICED WITH A VEGETABLE PEELER TO ASSURE THINNESS (ABOUT 2 OUNCES)

3 OUNCES SLICED SWISS CHEESE

⅛ TEASPOON FRESHLY GROUND BLACK PEPPER

1 MUSHROOM (1 OUNCE), WASHED AND THINLY SLICED

1. Split the bread loaf horizontally, and place the two halves crust side down on the table. Sprinkle 1 tablespoon of the salsa on the surface of each bread half. Spread the Gorgonzola on one bread half, and press the watercress into the cheese.

2. Layer on the pecan halves, and arrange the cucumber slices and the Swiss cheese slices on top. Sprinkle with the black pepper, and add the mushroom slices.

3. Reassemble the loaf, and press on the sandwich to help combine the flavors of the various filling ingredients.

4. Cut the sandwich into 4 wedges, and serve within 1 to 2 hours.

(CONTINUED)

NUTRITION 35

338 calories

14 g protein

19 g fat

7 g saturated fat

29 mg cholesterol

690 mg sodium

28 g carbohydrate

2 g dietary fiber

Watercress is a good source of vitamins C and K, folate, beta-carotene, magnesium, and potassium. Cheese provides substantial calcium.

Sandwich Assortment (page 33)

36

NUTRITION

198 calories

14 g protein

4 g fat

1 g saturated fat

79 mg cholesterol

625 mg sodium

25 g carbohydrate

1 g dietary fiber

Tuna and anchovies

are very good

sources of omega-3

fatty acids.

FISH SANDWICH

1 SMALL LIGHT COUNTRY LOAF (PAGE 31)

4 OUNCES DRAINED CANNED TUNA
   (PACKED IN WATER)

¼ CUP (LIGHTLY PACKED) FRESH CILANTRO LEAVES

6 ANCHOVY FILLETS (PACKED IN OIL)

1½ TEASPOONS ANCHOVY OIL (FROM CANNED
   ANCHOVIES, ABOVE)

⅛ TEASPOON FRESHLY GROUND BLACK PEPPER

1 LARGE CLOVE GARLIC, PEELED AND SLICED WITH
   A VEGETABLE PEELER INTO 12 THIN SLICES

1 HARD-COOKED EGG, SLICED (SEE NOTE BELOW)

3 TO 4 LEAVES LETTUCE, WASHED AND DRIED

1. Split the bread loaf horizontally, and place the two halves crust side down on the table. Spread the tuna on one bread half, and cover it with the cilantro leaves. Add the anchovy fillets, and sprinkle on the anchovy oil and the pepper. Arrange the garlic slices on top, then add the egg slices and the lettuce leaves.

2. Reassemble the loaf, and press on the sandwich to help combine the flavors of the various filling ingredients.

3. Cut the sandwich into 4 wedges, and serve within the next 2 hours.

Note: To hard-cook an egg, bring 2 cups of water to a boil in a small saucepan. Using a thumbtack or pushpin, make a small hole in the rounded end of each egg. Lower the egg gently into the boiling water, and add additional boiling water, if needed, to cover the egg completely. Bring the water back to a very gentle boil, and cook the egg for 8 to 9 minutes. Drain off the water, and shake the pan vigorously to crack the shells of the eggs. Then add ice to the pan, and let the eggs cool completely in the ice.

HAM SANDWICH

1 SMALL LIGHT COUNTRY LOAF (PAGE 31)

1½ TEASPOONS DIJON-STYLE MUSTARD

1½ TEASPOONS MAYONNAISE

3 RADISHES, THINLY SLICED (1½ OUNCES)

8 LEAVES FRESH BASIL

4 OUNCES SLICED HAM, PREFERABLY HONEY-BAKED

⅛ TEASPOON FRESHLY GROUND BLACK PEPPER

1½ CUPS (LOOSELY PACKED) MESCLUN SALAD
GREENS, WASHED AND DRIED IF NECESSARY

1. Split the bread loaf horizontally, and place the two halves crust side down on the table. Spread one of the bread halves with the mustard and the other half with the mayonnaise.

2. Cover one bread half with the radish slices, and arrange the basil leaves on top. Layer on the ham, and sprinkle the ham with the pepper. Finish with the mesclun leaves.

3. Reassemble the bread loaf, and press on the sandwich to make the bread adhere to the filling and help combine the flavors of the various filling ingredients.

4. Cut the sandwich into 4 wedges, and eat within the next 2 hours.

179 calories

11 g protein

3 g fat

1 g saturated fat

16 mg cholesterol

691 mg sodium

25 g carbohydrate

1 g dietary fiber

Bread Galettes on Salad Greens

TOTAL TIME
30 to 40 minutes

YIELD
4 servings

NUTRITION
223 calories
6 g protein
17 g fat
2 g saturated fat
106 mg cholesterol
800 mg sodium
13 g carbohydrate
2 g dietary fiber

Each serving
provides more than
20% of the daily
value for vitamin C
and folate.

Since I deal with bread elsewhere in this menu, I'm including this economical recipe for what I consider to be an excellent use for leftover bread. I saturate stale bread with water, then mix it with a variety of vegetables and herbs — in this instance, mushrooms, zucchini, onion, garlic, and chives because that was what I had on hand. With the addition of eggs, these ingredients are transformed into little pancakes or galettes that go beautifully with salad greens.

BREAD GALETTES

2½ OUNCES STALE BREAD, PREFERABLY FROM A BAGUETTE, CUT INTO 1-INCH PIECES (2 CUPS)

½ CUP LUKEWARM WATER

1 LARGE MUSHROOM (ABOUT 1½ OUNCES), WASHED AND COARSELY CHOPPED

1 PIECE ZUCCHINI (2 OUNCES), CUT INTO ¼-INCH PIECES (½ CUP)

2 TABLESPOONS CHOPPED ONION

1½ TABLESPOONS CHOPPED FRESH CHIVES

1 CLOVE GARLIC, PEELED, CRUSHED, AND CHOPPED (½ TEASPOON)

¼ TEASPOON SALT

¼ TEASPOON FRESHLY GROUND BLACK PEPPER

2 EGGS

2 TABLESPOONS CANOLA OIL

SALAD

2 TABLESPOONS EXTRA VIRGIN OLIVE OIL

2 TEASPOONS RED WINE VINEGAR

⅛ TEASPOON SALT

¼ TEASPOON FRESHLY GROUND BLACK PEPPER

4 CUPS (LOOSELY PACKED) CLEANED MESCLUN SALAD GREENS

1. Place the bread pieces in a bowl, add the water, and squeeze the bread lightly to saturate it with the water. Add the mushroom, zucchini, onion, chives, garlic, ¼ teaspoon each salt and pepper, and the eggs, and mix well. (The ingredients should be well combined but not like a puree.) Yield: About 2 cups.

2. Heat the canola oil in one large or two smaller skillets. Using about ½ cup of the bread mixture for each of four pancakes, spoon it into the skillet(s), and press down on it with a fork to make pancakes that are about 5 inches in diameter and ½ inch thick. Cook the pancakes for about 5 minutes over medium to high heat, then flip them over, and cook them on the other side for 5 minutes. Transfer the pancakes (or galettes) to a warm plate, and set them aside while you make the salad.

3. In a bowl large enough to hold the salad greens, mix together the olive oil, vinegar, ⅛ teaspoon salt, and ¼ teaspoon pepper. Add the mesclun to the bowl, and toss well to coat the leaves with the dressing.

4. To serve, divide the salad among four plates, and place a bread galette on top or alongside the greens on each plate. Serve.

We use old bread at home for savory dishes as well as sweet ones. You can make bread-and-butter pudding, which is my mother's favorite dessert; or you can do what we do here, which is to use it for galettes with vegetables.

Banana-Mint Ice Cream with Rum-Raisin Sauce

TOTAL TIME

*10 minutes prepa-
ration time, about
5 hours freezer time*

YIELD

4 servings

NUTRITION

*332 calories
3 g protein
9 g fat
5 g saturated fat
19 mg cholesterol
28 mg sodium
62 g carbohydrate
2 g dietary fiber*

This is a great dessert to prepare when you have several overripe bananas languishing in your fruit bowl. It's an easy recipe: slice the bananas, freeze them on a tray, then puree them in a food processor along with some honey, mint, and sour cream. Store this almost instant ice cream in the freezer for several hours before serving it with a delicious sauce made of peach preserves, orange juice, rum, and raisins.

ICE CREAM

3 RIPE BANANAS (ABOUT 1½ POUNDS), PEELED

¼ CUP HONEY

6 TO 8 MINT LEAVES

¾ CUP SOUR CREAM

RUM-RAISIN SAUCE

¼ CUP PEACH PRESERVES

¼ CUP ORANGE JUICE

1 TABLESPOON DARK RUM

¼ CUP GOLDEN RAISINS

4 STRIPS FRESH MINT (OPTIONAL)

1. *For the Ice Cream:* Cut the bananas into ½-inch slices, and arrange them in a single layer on a cookie sheet. Place in the freezer for at least 2 hours.

2. Remove the bananas from the freezer, and allow them to soften slightly at room temperature for a few minutes. Place the bananas (still frozen but not solidly hard) in the bowl of a food processor, and add the honey, mint, and sour cream. Process for at least 1 minute, until the mixture is smooth and creamy. Yield: About 3½ cups.

3. Transfer the ice cream mixture to a bowl, cover, and place in the freezer for several hours, until solidly frozen.

4. *For the Rum-Raisin Sauce:* In a small bowl, mix the preserves, orange juice, and rum together until smooth. Stir in the raisins.

5. At serving time, spoon the ice cream into bowls, and coat with the sauce. Decorate each serving with a mint strip, if you like.

Special Celebration

GLOSSY YELLOW PEPPER SOUP
WITH ASPARAGUS GARNISH

TOURNEDOS OF BEEF IN MUSHROOM, MUSTARD,
AND RED WINE SAUCE

CORN-AND-HAM-STUFFED TOMATOES

APPLE ROUNDS WITH CALVADOS GLAZE

———

An elegant soup begins this casual but sophisticated menu. With a base composed primarily of yellow bell pepper pieces that are cooked, pressed through a food mill, then processed until smooth and glossy, the soup is served with a garnish of sliced asparagus. ✷ Our rich and luscious meat main dish features tournedos of beef – small pieces of well-trimmed fillet of beef weighing about 5 ounces each. The tournedos are cooked with shiitake mushrooms and served with a concentrated, savory sauce made from the meat and mushroom cooking juices, red wine, and a little mustard for flavor. ✷ To accompany the meat, we serve stuffed tomatoes. This dish consists of halved and seeded tomatoes that are cooked briefly cut side down in a skillet, then turned over and topped with a mixture of corn kernels

Red
STONESTREET,
CABERNET
SAUVIGNON

White Dessert
MARC BRÉDIF,
NECTAR

and ham. ✷ We finish with apple desserts, each of which resembles a whole apple. Consisting of a round of thinly rolled dough that is topped with apple slices and baked, each "apple" is coated with a flavorful glaze and presented with its pastry "stem" and "leaves" positioned appropriately alongside on the plate.

Glossy Yellow Pepper Soup with Asparagus Garnish

TOTAL TIME

About 1 hour

YIELD

4 servings

NUTRITION

237 calories

5 g protein

13 g fat

4 g saturated fat

16 mg cholesterol

662 mg sodium

27 g carbohydrate

2 g dietary fiber

Peppers are a terrific source of vitamin C (more than 400% of the daily value per serving in this recipe). When combined, asparagus and peppers contribute 25% of the daily value for folate.

This elegant soup is the perfect opener for a formal dinner. Essentially a puree of yellow peppers garnished with spears of asparagus, the soup's gloss and creamy texture are achieved by emulsifying the mixture with a handheld immersion blender before it is served.

8 OUNCES ASPARAGUS, PREFERABLY LARGE STALKS WITH TIGHT HEADS, FOR GARNISH

2½ CUPS WATER

3 YELLOW PEPPERS (1⅓ POUNDS), HALVED, STEMMED, SEEDED, AND CUT INTO 1-INCH PIECES

1 LARGE POTATO (9 OUNCES), PEELED AND CUT INTO 1-INCH PIECES

1 LARGE ONION (8 OUNCES), PEELED AND CUT INTO 1-INCH PIECES

3 CLOVES GARLIC, PEELED

1 TEASPOON SALT

1½ TEASPOONS SUGAR

¼ TEASPOON FRESHLY GROUND BLACK PEPPER

2 TABLESPOONS UNSALTED BUTTER

2 TABLESPOONS EXTRA VIRGIN OLIVE OIL

1. Peel the lower third of the asparagus stalks, and discard the trimmings. Cut the asparagus on the bias into slices about ¼ to ½ inch thick. (You should have about 1½ cups.) Bring ½ cup of the water to a boil in a saucepan, and add the asparagus pieces. Bring the water back to a boil, and boil the asparagus for 30 seconds. Drain, reserving the cooking juices, and set the cooked asparagus pieces aside in a bowl.

2. Place the yellow peppers, potato, onion, garlic, salt, sugar, and pepper in a large saucepan, and add the remaining 2 cups of water. Bring to a boil, add the reserved asparagus cooking juices, cover, and reduce the heat to medium. Cook the mixture for 30 minutes, then push it through a food mill fitted with a fine screen to remove the skin of the yellow peppers.

3. Add the butter and oil, and emulsify the mixture with a handheld immersion blender until it is smooth and creamy in appearance. Add the reserved asparagus, heat through, and serve.

Tournedos of Beef in Mushroom, Mustard, and Red Wine Sauce

TOTAL TIME
About 1 ¼ hours

YIELD
4 servings

NUTRITION
384 calories
30 g protein
17 g fat
7 g saturated fat
99 mg cholesterol
582 mg sodium
19 g carbohydrate
1 g dietary fiber

Small, well-trimmed tournedos of beef are sautéed and served here on croutons in the classical manner. A light but flavorful sauce, made by incorporating reconstituted shiitake mushrooms, red wine, and mustard into the meat drippings and mushroom soaking liquid, lends a modern touch to this old favorite.

1 OUNCE DRIED SHIITAKE MUSHROOMS (6 TO 8 MUSHROOMS)

1 CUP HOT TAP WATER

1 TEASPOON CANOLA OIL

4 SLICES BREAD

2 TABLESPOONS UNSALTED BUTTER

4 COMPLETELY TRIMMED BEEF FILLET STEAKS, EACH ABOUT 5 OUNCES AND 1¼ INCHES THICK

½ TEASPOON SALT

½ TEASPOON FRESHLY GROUND BLACK PEPPER

½ CUP RED WINE

2 TABLESPOONS KETCHUP

1 TABLESPOON COLMAN'S DRY MUSTARD

1. Preheat the oven to 400 degrees.

2. Place the mushrooms in a small bowl, cover them with the hot water, and set them aside to soak for at least 1 hour.

3. Meanwhile, spread the oil lightly over the surface of a cookie sheet. Using a round cookie cutter about 3 inches in diameter, cut a round crouton from each of the 4 slices of bread. Press the croutons lightly into the oil on the tray, then turn them over so they are oiled on both sides. Bake the croutons in the 400-degree oven for about 7 minutes, until they are nicely browned on both sides and crisp. Set the croutons aside.

4. After the mushrooms have soaked for at least an hour, drain them, reserving the soaking liquid (about ½ cup) in a bowl. Remove and discard the stems from the mushrooms, and cut the mushroom caps into ½-inch pieces. (You should have about ¾ cup.) Transfer the soaking liquid to another bowl, pouring it slowly and discarding the sandy residue in the bottom of the original bowl. Set the liquid aside.

5. At cooking time, heat the butter in a skillet. Sprinkle the tournedos with ¼ teaspoon each of the salt and pepper, and place them in the skillet. Arrange the mushroom pieces around them in the skillet, and sauté the tournedos over medium to high heat for about 2½ minutes on each side. Transfer the tournedos to a warm platter, and set them aside to rest in a 170-degree oven while you make the sauce.

6. To the liquid and mushrooms in the skillet, add the reserved mushroom liquid along with the wine, ketchup, dry mustard, and remaining ¼ teaspoon each salt and pepper. Bring the mixture to a boil, and boil it gently for 3 to 4 minutes, until the sauce thickens slightly. (You should have about 1 cup of sauce.)

7. Place a crouton in the center of each of four warmed dinner plates, and place a tournedo on top of each crouton. Coat the meat with the sauce, and spoon some of the sauce around the meat. Serve immediately.

Tournedos of Beef (these pages) and Corn-and-Ham-Stuffed Tomato (page 48)

Corn-and-Ham-Stuffed Tomatoes

TOTAL TIME

About 15 minutes

YIELD

4 servings

NUTRITION

166 calories

6 g protein

8 g fat

1 g saturated fat

8 mg cholesterol

498 mg sodium

19 g carbohydrate

2 g dietary fiber

Tomatoes and corn are good sources of vitamin C, providing more than 40% of the daily value per serving.

This colorful dish, served as a meat accompaniment in this menu, also makes a great first course and is perfect as the main course for a summer luncheon. It features large tomatoes that are halved, seeded, and cooked cut side down until their flesh begins to caramelize, then turned over and topped with a mixture of sautéed corn, ham, and chives.

2 TABLESPOONS VIRGIN OLIVE OIL

2 LARGE TOMATOES (ABOUT 8 OUNCES EACH)

1¾ CUPS CORN KERNELS (CUT FROM ABOUT 2 EARS OF CORN)

2 SLICES HAM (2 OUNCES TOTAL), CUT INTO JULIENNE STRIPS (½ CUP)

¼ CUP ½-INCH PIECES OF FRESH CHIVES

½ TEASPOON SALT

¼ TEASPOON FRESHLY GROUND BLACK PEPPER

1. Heat 1 tablespoon of the oil in a skillet (not nonstick) until it is very hot. Meanwhile, cut the tomatoes in half crosswise and, holding them cut side down, squeeze them gently over a bowl to remove the seeds. (The extracted seeds and juice can be reserved for later use in a stock.)

2. Place the seeded tomatoes cut side down in the hot oil in the skillet, and cook them over high heat for 5 to 6 minutes, until they begin to caramelize on the cut side. Transfer the tomatoes to a gratin dish, arranging them cut side up next to one another.

3. Add the remaining tablespoon of oil to the skillet you used to cook the tomatoes, and add the corn kernels. Sauté the corn over high heat for 4 minutes, stirring it and scraping the bottom of the pan occasionally. Add the ham, chives, salt, and pepper, and cook for 1 minute.

4. Spoon some of the corn and ham mixture into the tomato halves, and place the remainder of the mixture around the tomatoes. Serve immediately.

Apple Rounds with Calvados Glaze

A new twist on the classic apple tart, these individual desserts consist of apple slices baked on thin, round pieces of dough. Served with a strategically arranged "stem" and some "leaves" of cooked dough alongside, each finished dessert resembles an apple. A glaze of apricot preserves mixed with a little Calvados intensifies the flavor of the apples and gives them a polished look.

DOUGH

¾ CUP (4 OUNCES) ALL-PURPOSE FLOUR

½ STICK (2 OUNCES) UNSALTED BUTTER, CUT WHILE FROZEN INTO ½-INCH SLICES

1 TEASPOON SUGAR

1 SMALL PINCH SALT

2 TABLESPOONS COLD WATER

GARNISH

2 GOLDEN DELICIOUS APPLES (ABOUT 14 OUNCES TOTAL)

1 TABLESPOON SUGAR

CALVADOS GLAZE

3 TABLESPOONS EXCELLENT QUALITY APRICOT PRESERVES

2 TEASPOONS CALVADOS (APPLE BRANDY) OR, IF UNAVAILABLE, COGNAC

1. *For the Dough:* Place the flour, frozen butter pieces, sugar, and salt in the bowl of a food processor. Process for 5 to 10 seconds, just until the mixture looks granulated. Add the cold water, and process for another 5 seconds. The mixture will not have gathered together by then; pour the contents of the bowl onto a piece of plastic wrap, and press it together into a ball.

2. Roll the ball of dough between 2 sheets of plastic wrap until it is very thin (about ⅛ inch) and measures about 8 by 10 inches. Using a cookie cutter about 4 inches in diameter, cut out 4 circles of dough, and place them on a cookie sheet lined with a nonstick baking mat or parchment paper.

3. With the leftover dough, cut 8 oval shapes to make leaves, each about 2½ inches long and 1½ inches wide. Mark the leaves with the dull edge side of a knife blade to imitate the veins of a leaf. Then, make apple stems by rolling 4 small pieces of dough to form cylinders or sticks, each about ¼ inch thick and 2 inches long. Place the stems and leaves on the cookie sheet with the dough circles. (Use any leftover dough to make a free-form cookie to eat at your leisure, and place it on the cookie sheet with the other dough shapes.)

4. Preheat the oven to 400 degrees.

(CONTINUED)

TOTAL TIME

1 ¼ hours

YIELD

4 servings

NUTRITION

292 calories

3 g protein

12 g fat

7 g saturated fat

31 mg cholesterol

37 mg sodium

45 g carbohydrate

3 g dietary fiber

Apples are rich in fiber and contain plant polyphenols, which are powerful antioxidants.

CLAUDINE

What I like about the apple rounds is that you can build them at the last minute with friends: everybody can make their own, and then you pop them in the oven and let them cook while you're having dinner. I love having everybody help make dessert.

5. *For the Garnish:* Peel the apples, and core them whole with a sharp knife, apple corer, or vegetable peeler. Cut each apple crosswise into 12 thin slices. Place 6 slices of apple on each dough circle, arranging the larger slices on the bottom of the circles and the remaining ones in a circular overlapping manner on top, and finishing with the smallest slice in the center. Alternatively, peel, core, and cut the apples into thin wedges. Arrange the wedges, overlapping them slightly, in a concentric pattern on top of the dough circles. Sprinkle the apples with the sugar, dividing it among the four desserts.

6. Place the cookie sheet in the 400-degree oven, and bake for about 20 minutes for the leaves and 30 minutes for the stems, removing them carefully with a spatula as they finish cooking and arranging them on a rack to cool. Continue baking the apple tartlets for a total of 50 minutes, until the apples are nicely browned and the dough underneath them very crisp. Place them on a cooling rack until lukewarm, then arrange the tartlets on four individual dessert plates.

7. *For the Calvados Glaze:* Mix the preserves and Calvados together in a small bowl, and coat the top of each warm tartlet with the mixture, applying it carefully with a pastry brush or spoon.

8. Arrange the pastry leaves and stems alongside each tartlet to make it resemble an apple. Serve the desserts immediately.

Apple Rounds with Calvados Glaze (page 49)

Flavors of Italy

Cream of Tomato Soup with Basil Oil

Basil Oil

Fish, Spinach, and Pasta Gratin

Roasted Red Snapper

Stew of Spring Vegetables

Orange Cubes in Orange "Baskets"

———

This menu features some favorite dishes I've enjoyed with Italian friends and is a fond reminder of visits I've made to Italy. There are too many dishes here for this to constitute a real menu; I've included more than should be served at one sitting with the idea of demonstrating the use of leftovers to Claudine. ✲ We start with a creamy tomato soup. Served hot here with homemade basil oil on top, it is also excellent served cold with or without the basil oil. ✲ Our main dish, red snapper (or another whole fish – black bass, striped bass, or porgy, for example), is easy to prepare. The fish is seasoned with white wine, olive oil, oregano, and scallions, and very simply roasted in the oven. Cooked like this, the flesh of the fish extracts wonderful flavor from the bones. I suggest in the recipe that the carving be done at the table, but if you would feel more comfortable carving and plating the fish beforehand in the privacy of your kitchen, do so. ✲ The pasta gratin with fish and spinach is a dish we often make with leftovers we have after cooking a whole fish. Flesh is scraped from the bones and combined with spinach, leftover sauce, and pasta for a delicious gratin that makes a good main course at another meal. ✲ The spring vegetable stew which follows is done in the old style, with a little roux added to give a bit of viscosity to the base sauce in which the vegetables are cooked. Served with a salad and piece of cheese, this also can be the main course of a meal. Finally, this copious menu ends with a simple fruit dessert consisting of orange cubes served in orange "baskets."

White
PEPI RESERVE,
SAUVIGNON
BLANC

Red
SAN LORENZO,
ROSSO CONERO

Cream of Tomato Soup with Basil Oil

TOTAL TIME

About 30 minutes

YIELD

4 servings

NUTRITION

286 calories

3 g protein

23 g fat

5 g saturated fat

16 mg cholesterol

1094 mg sodium

19 g carbohydrate

3 g dietary fiber

Tomatoes are rich in vitamin C, providing more than 75% of the daily value in each serving of this recipe. They also contain the carotenoid lycopene, a powerful antioxidant.

To deepen the color of this soup and intensify the flavor of the fresh tomatoes, a little tomato paste and some sugar are added. Any leftover soup can be used as a sauce for pasta; in fact, the entire recipe (minus the basil oil) can be transformed into a tomato sauce by reducing the water addition at the beginning to ½ cup.

1 TABLESPOON VIRGIN OLIVE OIL

1 MEDIUM ONION (5 OUNCES), PEELED AND COARSELY CHOPPED (1 CUP)

2 LARGE CLOVES GARLIC, PEELED

2 SPRIGS FRESH THYME

1 SPRIG FRESH OREGANO

2 POUNDS RIPE TOMATOES, CUT INTO 2-INCH PIECES (ABOUT 5 CUPS)

2½ TABLESPOONS TOMATO PASTE

2 TEASPOONS SUGAR

1½ TEASPOONS SALT

½ TEASPOON FRESHLY GROUND BLACK PEPPER

1¼ CUPS WATER

2 TABLESPOONS UNSALTED BUTTER

ABOUT 4 TABLESPOONS BASIL OIL (SEE FOLLOWING RECIPE ON PAGE 56)

1. Heat the olive oil in a sturdy, non-reactive saucepan. Add the onion, garlic, thyme, and oregano, and cook over medium heat for 5 minutes. Then add the tomato pieces, tomato paste, sugar, salt, pepper, and water. Mix well, bring to a boil, cover, reduce the heat to low, and boil gently for 15 minutes.

2. Push the tomato mixture through a food mill fitted with a fine screen. (The soup can be made to this point up to 1 day ahead and refrigerated.)

3. At serving time, heat the soup, and add the butter a little at a time, stirring it in gently until incorporated. Then, if a smoother, creamier-textured soup is desired, emulsify the mixture with a handheld immersion blender for 15 to 20 seconds.

4. Divide the soup among four soup plates, and drizzle about 1 tablespoon of Basil Oil over the top of each serving (do not stir it in) to decorate as well as flavor the soup. Serve immediately.

Basil Oil

You will notice that after this flavored oil sits for a few days in the refrigerator, the solids sink to the bottom, and the green oil rises to the top. For the first week or so you can use the whole mixture, the basil paste as well as the oil, as a garnish for soup, pasta, poached fish, mashed potatoes, or grilled steak. After eight or ten days, however, it is best to filter out the oil and discard the solids, which have begun to discolor at this point, don't have any more flavor, and may begin to sour. Refrigerated, the strained oil will keep for several months.

TOTAL TIME
About 15 minutes

YIELD
2½ cups

NUTRITION
121 calories
.1 g protein
13 g fat
1 g saturated fat
0 mg cholesterol
58 mg sodium
0 g carbohydrate
0 g dietary fiber

CLAUDINE

This beautiful basil oil is something you can make and keep; it tastes marvelous and it's much less expensive than buying a similar oil in the store.

4 CUPS (LIGHTLY PACKED) BASIL LEAVES, RINSED AND THOROUGHLY DRIED (4 OUNCES)

1 TEASPOON SALT

2½ CUPS CANOLA OIL

1. Bring 6 cups of water to a boil in a large saucepan. Drop in the basil leaves, and stir. Cook the leaves for 45 seconds, just until the water returns to a boil. Drain the leaves in a colander, and rinse them under cold water until they are cool. Drain again, then press the leaves gently between your palms to remove excess water.

2. Place the leaves in a blender with the salt and ½ cup of the canola oil. Process the mixture for 1 minute (stopping the machine a few times and pushing any of the mixture collected on the sides of the blender bowl down into the mixture), until you have a smooth puree. Then add the remaining 2 cups of oil, and process for 5 seconds.

3. Transfer the basil oil to a jar or bottle, cover, and refrigerate. After two days, you will notice that the solids will sink to the bottom, and the green oil will rise to the top. Use as needed over the next eight to ten days, shaking the jar first to recombine the mixture. Alternatively, after at least two days (but no more than ten days), strain the mixture through a kitchen towel, pressing on it to extrude as much of the oil as possible. Discard the solids, place the oil in a clean jar or bottle, cover, and refrigerate until needed.

Fish, Spinach, and Pasta Gratin

I often prepare this dish — or a variation of it — when I have cooked fish left over. Here, I use fish and sauce from the Roasted Red Snapper (page 59), layering it on top of cooked spinach and farfalle in a gratin dish. A light béchamel sauce and a sprinkling of Parmesan cheese complete the dish, which is then crusted or gratinéed in a hot oven.

❦   ❦   ❦   ❦   ❦   ❦   ❦   ❦   ❦

LEFTOVER FISH AND SAUCE FROM ROASTED RED SNAPPER, PAGE 59 (8 TO 10 OUNCES)

2 TABLESPOONS VIRGIN OLIVE OIL

12 OUNCES SPINACH, STEMS AND ANY DAMAGED LEAVES REMOVED, REMAINING LEAVES WASHED AND DRAINED

¼ TEASPOON SALT

½ TEASPOON FRESHLY GROUND BLACK PEPPER

6 OUNCES FARFALLE (BOW-TIE PASTA)

1 TABLESPOON UNSALTED BUTTER

2 TABLESPOONS ALL-PURPOSE FLOUR

2 CUPS MILK

3 TABLESPOONS GRATED PARMESAN CHEESE

1. Preheat the oven to 400 degrees.

2. Pick the flesh from the fish bones, and combine the flesh with the leftover sauce from the Roasted Red Snapper (see page 59). (We had a total of about 10 ounces.) Set the mixture aside.

3. Heat 1 tablespoon of the oil in a skillet until it is hot but not smoking. Add the spinach, still wet from washing, and cook it, covered, over medium to high heat for about 4 minutes, until it is wilted and soft. Add ¼ teaspoon each of the salt and pepper, mix well, and spoon the spinach into the bottom of a 6-cup gratin dish.

4. Bring 3 quarts of water to a boil in a pot. Add the farfalle, and boil, uncovered, for about 10 minutes. Drain the pasta in a colander, then cool it by running cold water over it in the colander for 30 seconds. Drain the pasta well, toss it with the combined fish and sauce, and spread it on top of the spinach in the gratin dish.

5. Heat the remaining tablespoon of oil and the butter in a saucepan, add the flour, and mix well. Cook for 30 seconds, then add the milk, and bring the mixture to a boil while stirring it with whisk. Add the remaining ½ teaspoon of salt and ¼ teaspoon pepper, and mix well. Pour this sauce over the fish and pasta mixture in the gratin dish. Sprinkle the Parmesan cheese on top.

6. Place the gratin in the 400-degree oven, and bake for 25 to 30 minutes, until hot throughout and browned on top. Serve immediately.

About 1 hour

YIELD

4 servings

NUTRITION

453 calories

21 g protein

21 g fat

8 g saturated fat

51 mg cholesterol

762 mg sodium

44 g carbohydrate

3 g dietary fiber

Spinach is rich in vitamins A and C, folate, beta-carotene, and other carotenoids and phytochemicals.

Roasted Red Snapper

Red snapper was commonly prepared and served like this years ago, and, happily, roasting the whole fish and carving it in the dining room just before serving is becoming popular again. The advantages: it is an easy dish to prepare, fish cooked on the bone is more flavorful, the presentation of the whole fish at the table is impressive, and carving it in view of guests is a convivial activity that encourages everyone's participation in the dining experience.

TOTAL TIME
About 1 hour

YIELD
4 servings

NUTRITION
359 calories
46 g protein
13 g fat
3 g saturated fat
88 mg cholesterol
840 mg sodium
5 g carbohydrate
1 g dietary fiber

Snapper is a good source of omega-3 fatty acids.

1 LARGE RED SNAPPER (ABOUT 4 POUNDS) SCALED, GUTTED, AND HEAD AND TAIL REMOVED (ABOUT 2 ¼ POUNDS READY-TO-COOK WEIGHT)

1 SMALL ONION (3 OUNCES), PEELED AND FINELY CHOPPED (½ CUP)

4 SCALLIONS, CLEANED AND FINELY MINCED (⅓ CUP)

1 LARGE TOMATO (9 OUNCES), HALVED, SEEDED, AND CUT INTO ½-INCH PIECES (1¼ CUPS)

2 TABLESPOONS COARSELY CHOPPED FRESH OREGANO

1 TEASPOON SALT

½ TEASPOON FRESHLY GROUND BLACK PEPPER

¾ CUP DRY, FRUITY WHITE WINE

2 TABLESPOONS VIRGIN OLIVE OIL

1 TABLESPOON UNSALTED BUTTER

1. Preheat the oven to 400 degrees.

2. Cut 3 evenly-spaced slits, each about ¼ inch deep, across the surface of one side of the fish. Place the onion, scallions, tomato, oregano, salt, pepper, wine, oil, and butter in a saucepan, bring the mixture to a boil, and boil it for 30 seconds. Distribute half of the mixture in the bottom of a sturdy gratin dish, preferably enameled cast iron, large enough to accommodate the fish.

3. Place the fish, cut side up, on top of the vegetable mixture, and pour the remaining mixture on top of the fish.

4. Place the fish in the 400-degree oven, and cook it for 25 to 30 minutes, just until the fish is cooked through and the flesh separates from the center bone when lifted with a fork.

5. Carve the fish at the table, and serve it with some of the surrounding juices and vegetable garnish.

Stew of Spring Vegetables

TOTAL TIME

About 20 minutes

YIELD

4 to 6 servings

NUTRITION

331 calories

10 g protein

6 g fat

3 g saturated fat

16 mg cholesterol

704 mg sodium

60 g carbohydrate

10 g dietary fiber

This assortment of spring vegetables provides significant amounts of vitamins A and C, folate, and dietary fiber.

These spring vegetables are prepared in the "old" style: onion and garlic are sautéed first in a little butter, flour is added along with seasonings and water to create a slightly thickened base, and the vegetables are cooked in this base. The dish can be prepared ahead, but don't add the peas until the last minute as they tend to yellow if cooked ahead and rewarmed. Although delicious with this menu, the stew is also good with poultry, pork, or steak.

2 TABLESPOONS UNSALTED BUTTER

1 MEDIUM ONION (4 TO 5 OUNCES), PEELED AND COARSELY CHOPPED (1 CUP)

3 TO 4 LARGE CLOVES GARLIC, PEELED AND COARSELY CHOPPED (1 TABLESPOON)

1 TABLESPOON ALL-PURPOSE FLOUR

1 TEASPOON *HERBES DE PROVENCE*, OR A MIXTURE OF YOUR FAVORITE DRIED HERBS (LIKE THYME, OREGANO, SAVORY, AND MARJORAM)

1 TEASPOON SALT

½ TEASPOON FRESHLY GROUND BLACK PEPPER

1½ CUPS WATER

3 POTATOES, PREFERABLY NEW (YOUNG), PEELED AND CUT INTO 1-INCH PIECES (3 CUPS)

12 OUNCES CARROTS, PREFERABLY NEW (YOUNG), PEELED AND CUT INTO 1-INCH PIECES (2 CUPS)

2 POUNDS FRESH PEAS, SHELLED (ABOUT 1 POUND SHELLED) (2 CUPS) OR 2 CUPS FROZEN TINY PEAS, RINSED WELL UNDER WARM WATER IN A COLANDER

1 TABLESPOON CHOPPED FRESH PARSLEY (OPTIONAL)

1. Heat the butter until melted in a sturdy saucepan. Add the onion and garlic, and sauté over medium heat, stirring occasionally, for 1½ minutes. Add the flour, stir well, then mix in the *herbes de Provence*, salt, pepper, and water, and bring to a boil.

2. Add the potatoes and carrots, bring back to a boil, and cook, covered, for 10 minutes.

3. Add the peas, bring back to a boil, reduce the heat to low, and cook, covered, until the peas are just tender, 6 to 8 minutes if using fresh peas, or 1½ to 2 minutes if using tiny frozen peas that have been rinsed in warm water. Garnish with parsley, if desired, and serve.

Note: If preparing this dish ahead, complete through step 2, then set aside. At serving time, bring the mixture to a boil, add the peas, and cook as indicated above.

Orange Cubes in Orange "Baskets"

Since this is the simplest of fresh fruit desserts — half an orange, plain except for a mint sprig garnish — it is imperative that you use good quality seedless oranges. The unusual presentation makes it easy to extract and enjoy the orange cubes.

❧ ❧ ❧ ❧ ❧ ❧ ❧ ❧ ❧

2 SEEDLESS ORANGES, 6 TO 8 OUNCES

4 SPRIGS MINT

1. Cut a ½-inch slice from both the stem end and the flower end of each orange, and set these slices aside.

2. Place one of the oranges rounded side down on the table, and cut it in half horizontally. Repeat with the other orange. Using a paring knife, cut all around the flesh in each orange half, and remove it in one thick piece from the surrounding cottony pith. You will have 4 disks of orange flesh and 4 hollow orange halves or receptacles, which will be used as "baskets."

3. Gently press a reserved end slice flesh side up into each orange basket to create a lining. Quarter each of the orange flesh disks and place the orange cubes back in the orange baskets in their original form, arranging them to simulate the appearance of an uncut orange half.

4. Decorate each orange basket with a sprig of mint, and serve one basket per person with toothpicks for easy removal of the orange cubes.

TOTAL TIME

10 to 15 minutes

YIELD

4 servings

NUTRITION

26 calories

1 g protein

0 g fat

0 g saturated fat

0 mg cholesterol

0 mg sodium

6 g carbohydrate

1 g dietary fiber

Heartwarming Winter Meal

CREAM OF TURNIP AND SWEET POTATO SOUP
WITH LEEK JULIENNE

CAULIFLOWER *SALMIS*

CHICKEN WITH SAFFRON RICE

PINEAPPLE IN APRICOT SAUCE

———

This winter menu of comforting dishes starts with a soup made of turnips and sweet potato. Although I use purple-topped turnips, you could substitute yellow turnips, which will give the soup a slightly different taste. The soup's creaminess comes from regular potato and the sweet potato, the latter of which also gives it a beautiful yellow or orange color. A julienne-of-leek garnish lends an appealing taste contrast and adds a bit of sophistication to the otherwise earthy soup. This heartwarming starter could be used as a main course for a light dinner. ↡ Chicken with saffron rice is the hearty main dish of this menu. I use chicken legs in stews of this kind, much preferring them to breasts because the legs can withstand longer cooking without losing their moistness. Prior to cooking, I remove the tip of the drumsticks and the skin from the legs, which doesn't alter the flavor of the dish but reduces its calories. The rice, an imported Italian Arborio or another short-grain variety, is flavored with saffron, made from the pistils of a special, small purple crocus plant. An expensive spice, it's an essential ingredient in this particular dish. ↡ As a side dish, I serve a cauliflower *salmis*, a stew-like concoction that is almost a type of condiment. The cauliflower is chopped into small pieces for this dish and combined with a mixture of shallots, garlic, and Chinese hot sauce. Although this dish goes especially well with the chicken and saffron rice, it is also a good accompaniment to a roast. ↡

To finish this heartwarming winter meal, we fittingly serve a simple, light, flavorful fruit dessert. Thin slices of pine-apple flavored with apricot jam and kirschwasser provide the perfect ending to this menu.

White
CAMBRIA,
VIOGNIER

Red
LOUIS JADOT,
VOSNE-
ROMANÉE

Cream of Turnip and Sweet Potato Soup with Leek Julienne

TOTAL TIME

About 1 hour

YIELD

4 servings

(about 6 cups)

NUTRITION

259 calories

8 g protein

13 g fat

8 g saturated fat

41 mg cholesterol

1325 mg sodium

28 g carbohydrate

2 g dietary fiber

One sweet potato provides enough beta-carotene to supply the recommended daily amount of vitamin A.

While purple-topped turnips give this soup its distinctive taste, sweet potatoes are responsible for its beautiful orange color and creaminess. Earthy and elegant at the same time, it is the perfect beginning for almost any meal.

¾ POUND PURPLE-TOPPED TURNIPS, PEELED AND CUT INTO 1-INCH PIECES

1 SWEET POTATO (YELLOW OR ORANGE VARIETY), (ABOUT 8 OUNCES), PEELED AND CUT INTO 1-INCH PIECES

1 WHITE POTATO (6 OUNCES), PEELED AND CUT INTO 1-INCH PIECES

3½ CUPS LIGHT CHICKEN, BEEF, OR PORK STOCK, UNSALTED

1 TEASPOON SALT, PLUS ADDITIONAL TO TASTE, IF DESIRED

LEEK GARNISH

1 SMALL LEEK (ABOUT 4 OUNCES)

1 TABLESPOON UNSALTED BUTTER

½ CUP WATER

¼ TEASPOON FRESHLY GROUND BLACK PEPPER, PLUS ADDITIONAL TO TASTE, IF DESIRED

½ CUP LIGHT CREAM

1. Place the turnip, sweet potato, and white potato pieces in a pot with the stock and salt. Bring the mixture to a boil, then reduce the heat to low, cover, and cook gently for 45 minutes, or until the vegetables are very tender when pierced with a fork.

2. Meanwhile, prepare the leek garnish. Trim the leek to remove any damaged or fibrous outer leaves but retain most of the green top. Cut the leek crosswise into thirds, with each chunk about 4 inches long. Then, cut each segment in half lengthwise, and separate the layers. Stack the layers together so they are flat, and cut them into very thin lengthwise strips (a julienne). You should have about 1¾ cups. Wash and drain the leek in a colander.

3. Place the leek strips in a saucepan with the butter and water. Bring to a boil, reduce the heat to low, cover, and cook for 10 to 12 minutes, until the leek is tender. Set aside in any remaining cooking liquid.

4. When the vegetables in the soup are tender, process it in a food processor or with a handheld immersion blender until it is emulsified into a smooth-textured mixture. Add the pepper, cream, and the reserved leek julienne along with its liquid.

5. Bring the mixture back to a boil, adding additional salt and pepper to taste, if desired, and serve immediately.

Cauliflower Salmis

A *salmis* is, by definition, a kind of stew or ragout of different types of precooked meats. I use the word loosely here, applying it to a stew of small pieces of cooked cauliflower combined with shallots, scallions, garlic, ketchup, and some hot sauce. This makes a great side dish that is particularly complementary to poultry, meat, and fish.

TOTAL TIME
About 15 minutes

YIELD
4 servings

NUTRITION
107 calories
3 g protein
7 g fat
1 g saturated fat
0 mg cholesterol
407 mg sodium
9 g carbohydrate
3 g dietary fiber

Cauliflower is a good source of vitamin C and folate.

1 CUP WATER

1 HEAD CAULIFLOWER (ABOUT 2 POUNDS), LEAVES AND ROOT END REMOVED, AND REMAINDER (ABOUT 1¼ POUNDS) DIVIDED INTO FLOWERETS

2 TABLESPOONS VIRGIN OLIVE OIL

2 TO 3 SHALLOTS, PEELED AND FINELY CHOPPED (⅓ CUP)

2 TO 3 SCALLIONS, CLEANED AND MINCED (¼ CUP)

2 LARGE CLOVES GARLIC, PEELED, CRUSHED, AND CHOPPED (2 TEASPOONS)

2 TABLESPOONS KETCHUP

½ TEASPOON SALT

1 TEASPOON HOT SAUCE (LIKE SATÉ SAUCE, CHINESE HOT GARLIC SAUCE, OR ½ TEASPOON TABASCO HOT PEPPER SAUCE)

1 TABLESPOON MINCED FRESH PARSLEY

1. Bring the water to a boil in a large saucepan. Add the flowerets, bring the water back to a boil, cover, and cook over high heat for 7 to 8 minutes, until the cauliflower is tender. Drain (there should be very little water remaining), and cool to lukewarm.

2. Meanwhile, heat the oil in a large skillet. Add the shallots, scallions, and garlic, and cook for 1 minute over medium heat.

3. Cut the cooked cauliflower coarsely into 1-inch pieces (you should have about 4 cups), and add it to the mixture in the skillet along with the ketchup, salt, and hot sauce. Mix well.

4. Serve the cauliflower lukewarm with parsley sprinkled on top.

Chicken with Saffron Rice

This dish is always welcome at our house. Although the classical version of the recipe includes sausage, I omit it here and use chicken legs, which are more moist than chicken breasts. I remove the skin from the legs before cooking them; it tends to get gummy and adds a lot of fat without improving the taste much. The dish is made with short-grain or Arborio rice that I flavor with *alcaparrado*, a mixture of unpitted olives, capers, and red pepper that is available commercially in specialty food stores and some supermarkets.

TOTAL TIME

About 1 hour

YIELD

4 servings

NUTRITION

587 calories
38 g protein
15 g fat
3 g saturated fat
99 mg cholesterol
1745 mg sodium
73 g carbohydrate
5 g dietary fiber

This dish is high in fiber. Peppers contribute substantial vitamin C — each serving provides more than 50% of the daily value.

4 LARGE CHICKEN LEGS WITHOUT CARCASS BONES (ABOUT 3¼ POUNDS)

1 TABLESPOON VIRGIN OLIVE OIL

3 MEDIUM ONIONS (ABOUT 1 POUND), PEELED AND SLICED THIN (4 CUPS)

4 TO 6 CLOVES GARLIC, PEELED AND COARSELY CHOPPED (2 TABLESPOONS)

1½ CUPS ARBORIO OR SHORT-GRAIN RICE (10 OUNCES)

3 BAY LEAVES

1 CUP PEELED AND DICED TOMATO

1½ CUPS MIXTURE OF UNPITTED GREEN OLIVES, CAPERS, AND RED PEPPER (SOMETIMES CALLED *ALCAPARRADO*)

1½ TABLESPOONS CHOPPED JALAPEÑO HOT PEPPER (MORE OR LESS DEPENDING ON YOUR TOLERANCE FOR "HOTNESS")

1¼ TEASPOONS SALT

1 TEASPOON SAFFRON PISTILS

2½ CUPS WATER

TABASCO HOT PEPPER SAUCE TO TASTE (OPTIONAL)

1. Cut off the end of each drumstick, remove the skin from the chicken, and cut off and discard any visible fat from the flesh. Cut the legs in half at the joint so you have 4 thighs and 4 drumsticks.

2. Heat the oil until hot in a large skillet. Add the chicken pieces in one layer, and sauté them over medium to high heat, turning them occasionally, for 10 minutes, until they are browned on all sides. Transfer the chicken to a plate, and set it aside.

3. Add the onion and garlic to the drippings in the skillet, and cook them for 2 minutes. Add the rice, and mix well. Stir in the bay leaves, tomato, *alcaparrado*, jalapeño, salt, and saffron. Add the water, and mix well.

4. Return the browned chicken pieces to the skillet, pushing them down into the liquid and rice until they are imbedded in the mixture. Bring to a boil, reduce the heat to low, cover, and cook gently for 30 minutes without stirring.

5. To serve, place 2 pieces of chicken and some of the rice mixture on each of four dinner plates. If desired, add Tabasco to taste, and serve immediately.

Chicken with Saffron Rice (this page) and Cream of Turnip and Sweet Potato Soup (page 64)

Pineapple in Apricot Sauce

TOTAL TIME

20 minutes

YIELD

4 to 6 servings

NUTRITION

245 calories

1 g protein

.5 g fat

0 g saturated fat

0 mg cholesterol

34 mg sodium

61 g carbohydrate

2 g dietary fiber

Be sure to use a well-ripened pineapple for this delightful dessert. After the whole fruit is peeled and cut in an ornamental way, the bottom half is sliced horizontally and the slices are arranged on a platter around the uncut top half, which is then decorated with a collar of strawberries. Served with an apricot sauce made from apricot preserves, lime juice, kirschwasser, and mint, this dessert couldn't be more refreshing.

1 VERY RIPE PINEAPPLE (ABOUT 4 POUNDS)

6 STRAWBERRIES

APRICOT SAUCE

1 CUP APRICOT PRESERVES

2 TABLESPOONS LIME JUICE

2 TABLESPOONS KIRSCHWASSER (CHERRY BRANDY), OR WATER

2 TABLESPOONS SHREDDED MINT LEAVES

1. Using a sharp knife, remove a thin layer of skin from the surface of the pineapple to expose the flesh. (The eyes will still be visible.) Then, still using the sharp knife, cut "v" shaped diagonal furrows to remove the eyes of the pineapple and create a diagonal line design all around the fruit. Pull or cut off all the lower leaves from the stem of the pineapple, leaving only a few leaves at the top of the stem. (This is for decorative effect.)

2. Starting at the bottom, cut about half the pineapple into thin horizontal slices, and remove the core from the center of these slices. Place the top half of the pineapple, with stem and upper leaves intact, on a large attractive platter, and arrange the pineapple slices around it.

3. Using round toothpicks, attach the strawberries to the leafless base of the stem to create a decorative collar. Mix the sauce ingredients together in a small bowl.

4. Serve 2 slices of pineapple per person with a little sauce spooned over them. If additional pineapple slices are needed, slice them from the bottom of the remaining pineapple half.

The Inspired Chef

SPINACH AND MOZZARELLA SALAD
WITH CROUTONS

BROCCOLI VELVET PUREE

SEAFOOD COMBO SHORELINE

INDIVIDUAL CHOCOLATE NUT PIES

―――――

For this menu, I took Claudine to the market to show her how to plan a meal on the spur of the moment, which is usually what we do at home, where our menus are determined by what the market has to offer. I may go to the market with an idea of cooking zucchini, for example, but return home with spinach instead because it was so beautiful and well priced that day. ⩔ This is essentially what happened on the day Claudine and I went to the market together. With our unexpected "finds" that day, we made a salad of spinach with croutons and a bit of mozzarella cheese and created a quick, fresh-tasting main dish stew from a seafood mixture. We used scallops, shrimp, and monkfish in our seafood combo, but one could vary the fish, depending on what the market has to offer. This is true of the vegetable additions as well – ours ranged from broccoli to mushrooms to zucchini – which lend texture, taste, and color to the stew. ⩔ Our menu also yielded a broccoli puree, which can be served on its own or with any type of roast. For this dish, two stalks of broccoli are cooked with a little jalapeño pepper and a dash of garlic, and, ultimately, are pureed with a little unsalted butter and olive oil. ⩔ Claudine wanted to know how to make small chocolate nut pies that she had eaten once at home. For this menu, I first taught her how to make the graham cracker crust for the pies and then how to make the filling with pecans, almonds, and pignola nuts. Quite rich, these pies are great to do for a party, as they can be made ahead and brought back to room temperature at serving time. ⩔ My advice: go to the market and get inspired by the produce, then bring it home and cook it with inspiration.

SUGGESTED WINES

White
KENDALL-
JACKSON,
GRAND RESERVE,
CHARDONNAY

White dessert
MUSCAT DE
LUNEL

Spinach and Mozzarella Salad with Croutons

TOTAL TIME

About 30 minutes

YIELD

4 servings

NUTRITION

288 calories

16 g protein

15 g fat

5 g saturated fat

25 mg cholesterol

748 mg sodium

23 g carbohydrate

3 g dietary fiber

Spinach is rich in vitamins A, C, and folate.

Spinach tends to bruise easily, so handle the leaves gently, without pressing or squeezing, when washing them. Then dry them thoroughly so as not to dilute the dressing. Toss the salad at the last moment, and serve it topped with croutons made from a day-old baguette and thin slices of mozzarella cheese.

SOY-VINAIGRETTE DRESSING

1 TABLESPOON DIJON-STYLE MUSTARD

1 TABLESPOON RED WINE VINEGAR

1 TABLESPOON SOY SAUCE

2 TABLESPOONS VIRGIN OLIVE OIL

½ TEASPOON FRESHLY GROUND PEPPER

1 5-OUNCE PIECE OF DAY-OLD BAGUETTE, ABOUT 2 INCHES IN DIAMETER, CUT INTO 16 THIN (¼-INCH) SLICES

10 OUNCES SPINACH (SMALL, TENDER LEAVES), TRIMMED OF ANY TOUGH STEMS OR DAMAGED LEAVES (ABOUT 8 OUNCES TRIMMED)

6 OUNCES MOZZARELLA CHEESE, CUT INTO ¼-INCH SLICES (3 TO 4 SLICES PER PERSON)

1. Preheat the oven to 400 degrees.

2. In a bowl large enough to hold the spinach greens, combine the dressing ingredients. Set aside.

3. Arrange the baguette slices in a single layer on a cookie sheet. Place in the 400-degree oven for 10 minutes, or until the slices are nicely browned.

4. Wash the spinach by submerging it in a basin of cool water. Then, lift it gently from the water, and dry it thoroughly in a salad spinner. (You should have about 10 loosely packed cups of spinach.)

5. At serving time, toss the spinach with the dressing in the bowl. Divide the salad among four plates, and top each serving with croutons and mozzarella. Serve.

Broccoli Velvet Puree

This is an unusual but delicious way to serve broccoli. First, I cook the vegetable until it is tender with some garlic and jalapeño pepper. Then I emulsify the mixture with a little butter and a dash of olive oil in a food processor to create a smooth, creamy puree.

⌄   ⌄   ⌄   ⌄   ⌄   ⌄   ⌄   ⌄

2 LARGE STALKS BROCCOLI (ABOUT 1½ POUNDS)

1½ CUPS WATER

¾ TEASPOON SALT

1 CLOVE GARLIC, PEELED

1 TEASPOON COARSELY CHOPPED JALAPEÑO PEPPER

2 TABLESPOONS UNSALTED BUTTER

1 TABLESPOON VIRGIN OLIVE OIL

1. Cut the broccoli heads from the stalks, then cut the heads into 2-inch pieces. Peel the stalks with a vegetable peeler, and cut them into 2-inch pieces.

2. Bring the water to a boil in a medium-size saucepan. Add the broccoli, salt, garlic, and jalapeño pepper, and bring the mixture back to a boil over high heat. As soon as it boils, cover the pan, and cook it over high heat for 10 minutes, until the broccoli is very tender and there is no more than ⅔ cup of liquid left in the pan.

3. Transfer the broccoli mixture and the liquid to the bowl of a food processor. Add the butter and oil, and process for about 1 minute, until the mixture is very smooth. Serve immediately.

TOTAL TIME

20 to 30 minutes

YIELD

4 servings

NUTRITION

124 calories

4 g protein

10 g fat

4 g saturated fat

16 mg cholesterol

488 mg sodium

8 g carbohydrate

4 g dietary fiber

Broccoli is rich in vitamins A and C, folate, and calcium. It also contains protective phyto-chemicals.

Seafood Combo Shoreline

TOTAL TIME
About 45 minutes

YIELD
4 servings

NUTRITION
299 calories
33 g protein
12 g fat
4 g saturated fat
137 mg cholesterol
946 mg sodium
10 g carbohydrate
2 g dietary fiber

*Broccoli is a good
source of vitamins A
and C, folate, and
calcium. Shellfish
is a terrific source
of protein without
much fat.*

This is one of those excellent seafood dishes that includes a colorful assortment of vegetables along with the fish and shellfish — in this instance, scallops, shrimp, and monkfish, although another firm-textured fish can be substituted if monkfish is not available. It takes a while to cut up all the vegetables and fish, but the dish takes only 5 to 6 minutes to cook, from beginning to end.

½ CUP DRY, FRUITY WHITE WINE

1½ TABLESPOONS VIRGIN OLIVE OIL

1½ TABLESPOONS UNSALTED BUTTER

1 TEASPOON SALT

1 TEASPOON FRESHLY GROUND BLACK PEPPER

4 OUNCES MUSHROOMS, WASHED AND CUT INTO ½-INCH SLICES

1 LARGE TOMATO (10 OUNCES), HALVED, SEEDED, AND CUT INTO 1-INCH PIECES (ABOUT 1 CUP)

1 SMALL STALK BROCCOLI (6 OUNCES), STEM PEELED AND CUT INTO 1½-INCH PIECES (ABOUT 1½ CUPS)

1 ZUCCHINI (6 OUNCES), WASHED AND CUT INTO STICKS 2 INCHES LONG AND ½ INCH THICK (ABOUT 1 CUP)

¼ CUP CHOPPED ONION

2 TEASPOONS FINELY CHOPPED GARLIC

10 OUNCES SCALLOPS, WASHED AND CUT INTO 1-INCH PIECES (1¼ CUPS)

8 OUNCES MEDIUM SHRIMP (31-35 PER POUND), SHELLED AND EACH CUT INTO 3 PIECES (¾ CUP)

1 PIECE MONKFISH (9 OUNCES), WITH BLACK SKIN REMOVED (ABOUT 8 OUNCES TRIMMED) AND CUT INTO 1-INCH PIECES (1 CUP)

1. Place the wine, oil, butter, salt, pepper, mushrooms, tomato, broccoli, zucchini, onion, and garlic in a stainless-steel saucepan. Bring the mixture to a strong boil, and cook it for 30 seconds.

2. Add the scallops, shrimp, and monkfish to the mixture in the pan, cover, and cook over high heat for 4 to 5 minutes, stirring once or twice. Set the pan aside, covered, off the heat for 5 minutes before ladling it into soup plates. Serve immediately.

*Seafood Combo
Shoreline
(this page) and
Spinach and
Mozzarella
Salad (page 72)*

Individual Chocolate Nut Pies

TOTAL TIME
About 1 hour

YIELD
4 servings

NUTRITION
556 calories
8 g protein
33 g fat
11 g saturated fat
71 mg cholesterol
289 mg sodium
64 g carbohydrate
4 g dietary fiber

The filling for this rich dessert is primarily a mixture of bittersweet chocolate, corn syrup, eggs, and mixed nuts. Baked in a classic graham cracker crust that has been molded into individual ramekins, it is easy to serve and quite delicious. The dessert can be made up to a day ahead and refrigerated, but should be rewarmed in a low-temperature oven to bring it back to room temperature for serving.

CRUST

5 GRAHAM CRACKERS (3½ OUNCES)

1½ TABLESPOONS UNSALTED BUTTER

1 TABLESPOON CANOLA OIL

2 TABLESPOONS SUGAR

FILLING

⅔ CUP MIXED NUTS (PECANS, ALMONDS, AND PIGNOLA NUTS, WITH THE PIGNOLA NUTS RESERVED IN A SEPARATE BOWL)

3½ OUNCES BITTERSWEET CHOCOLATE, BROKEN INTO PIECES

2 TEASPOONS UNSALTED BUTTER

1 TEASPOON CORNSTARCH

⅓ CUP LIGHT CORN SYRUP

1 LARGE EGG, LIGHTLY BEATEN WITH A FORK

1 TEASPOON PURE VANILLA EXTRACT

1. *For the Crust:* Place the graham crackers, 1½ tablespoons butter, canola oil, and sugar in the bowl of a food processor, and process for 1 minute, until the mixture is finely chopped, mealy, and starting to come together.

2. Divide the graham cracker mixture among four ramekins, each with a capacity of 1 cup, and press the mixture evenly into the bottom and around the sides of each cup to create a shell. Note: Although these desserts usually slide easily from their molds when cooled briefly after baking, lining your ramekins first with aluminum foil will eliminate any concerns about the crusts breaking when the desserts are unmolded.

3. Preheat the oven to 350 degrees.

4. *For the Filling:* Place the pecans and almonds in the bowl of a food processor, and process them for a few seconds to chop them coarsely. Stir in the pignola nuts, and divide the nuts among the graham cracker-lined ramekins.

5. Melt the chocolate and the 2 teaspoons butter in a microwave oven or in the top of double boiler set over hot water. Add the cornstarch, mix well, then add the corn syrup, and mix it in well. Add the egg and vanilla, and mix well. Divide the mixture among the four ramekins.

6. Arrange the ramekins on a tray, and bake the pies in the middle of the preheated 350-degree oven for about 25 minutes, until the filling is set but still somewhat soft in the middle. Cool the ramekins to lukewarm or room temperature on a rack.

7. At serving time, invert each of the ramekins onto a dessert plate, and, if using aluminum foil, gently peel it off the crusts. Carefully turn the ramekins right side up, and return them to the plates. Serve at room temperature.

Everyday Cooking

STUFFED TOMATOES EMILIA

PITA PIZZAS

STEW OF EGGPLANT AND CHINESE SAUSAGE

CANDIED GRAPEFRUIT, ORANGE,
AND LEMON CHIPS

What to make for dinner or for lunch often leads to heated discussion and sometimes generates more fuss than is necessary. Most people do not realize that the ordinary ingredients they have in their pantry or refrigerator can be transformed into delicious dishes. ↯ In this menu, I teach Claudine what to do with leftover meat from a roast of pork, veal, beef, or even a ham, and some leftover bread. We make a stuffed tomato dish that would be a great main course for an everyday meal. ↯ Claudine loves pizza, so we make easy pizzas from ingredients we have on hand. As our "dough" base, we use pita bread, splitting and separating it into thin disks of dough weighing about 1½ ounces each. Spared the hassle of making and cooking conventional pizza dough, Claudine and I have fun devising different toppings. We make six different pizzas: one with a tomato and dried herb topping; one with salad greens and tomatoes; one with Gruyère cheese, yellow pepper, and nuts; one with leftover chicken; one with shrimp; and one with canned anchovies, which I always have available in my cupboard. These very colorful pizzas are favorites with everyone. ↯ I also show Claudine how to make a stew of eggplant containing Chinese sausage and a hot ginger sauce. This dish could be served as the first course of a more elaborate meal with a roasted poultry entree. ↯ Finally, we make an unusual fruit dessert consisting of slices of grapefruit, orange, and lemon that are dried out slowly in the oven into chewy, almost candylike chips. A favorite with family and friends, these citrus chips keep for weeks and make a terrific holiday gift. ↯ Although this everyday menu encompasses more food than you would serve at a single meal, it provides many good lessons for the everyday cook.

SUGGESTED WINES

White
CHATEAU DE JAU, LA JA JA GRENACHE BLANC/ VERMENTINO

Red
VINA CALINA, CABERNET FRANC

Stuffed Tomatoes Emilia

This is in the spirit of dishes my mother used to make when she had a little stale bread on hand and some leftover meat from a roast or stew. Most any meat — beef, veal, pork, or ham — will work here, adding a little richness to a stuffing for large tomatoes and transforming leftovers into a fresh, new dish. The tomato insides make a delicious sauce for the stuffed tomatoes, which can be served, as they are here, as a first course, or as a main course, preceded by a soup and followed by fresh fruit for dessert.

TOTAL TIME

1½ hours

YIELD

4 servings

NUTRITION

243 calories

17 g protein

6 g fat

2 g saturated fat

139 mg cholesterol

841 mg sodium

31 g carbohydrate

4 g dietary fiber

Tomatoes are rich in vitamin C and lycopene, a powerful antioxidant.

4 OUNCES LEFTOVER BREAD, CUT INTO ½-INCH PIECES (2 CUPS)

¾ CUP WATER AT ROOM TEMPERATURE

6 OUNCES COOKED MEAT FROM A ROAST (PORK, VEAL, OR BEEF), COARSELY CHOPPED (2 CUPS)

¼ CUP CHOPPED ONION

4 SCALLIONS, CLEANED AND COARSELY CHOPPED (½ CUP)

2 MUSHROOMS (ABOUT 3 OUNCES), WASHED AND COARSELY CHOPPED (1 CUP)

2 CLOVES GARLIC, PEELED, CRUSHED, AND CHOPPED (2 TEASPOONS)

1 TEASPOON SALT

½ TEASPOON FRESHLY GROUND PEPPER

1 LARGE EGG

4 LARGE TOMATOES (ABOUT 2½ POUNDS)

1. Preheat the oven to 400 degrees.

2. Place the bread pieces in a bowl, and sprinkle them with the water. Using your hands, squeeze the bread gently until it absorbs the water and becomes soft. Add the cooked meat, onion, scallions, mushrooms, garlic, ½ teaspoon of the salt, ¼ teaspoon of the pepper, and the egg. Mix well. The mixture should hold together but not be pasty.

3. Using a sharp knife, remove the top ½ inch from the stem end of each tomato, and reserve these "caps." Scoop out the insides of each tomato with a measuring spoon, leaving only the fleshy shell of the tomato.

4. Chop the tomato insides coarsely. The combined juices and seeds should measure about 2 cups. Sprinkle with the remaining ½ teaspoon salt, and set aside.

5. Stand the tomato shells upright in a gratin dish and fill them with the stuffing. Place the reserved tomato caps on top, and pour the reserved tomato mixture around the tomatoes in the dish.

6. Place the dish in the 400-degree oven, and bake for 50 to 60 minutes, until the tomatoes are nicely browned and the stuffing mixture cooked and hot through-out. Serve with the surrounding juices.

Pita Pizzas

I don't think that Claudine had ever made pizza before preparing these. Like many people, she was put off by the difficulty of making the dough — obviously the hardest part of the process. Here, instead of conventional pizza dough, we use commercial pita bread rounds, splitting them in half to have six very thin "crusts." Fun, colorful, and delicious, these pizzas couldn't be easier to prepare.

❧   ❧   ❧   ❧   ❧   ❧   ❧   ❧

3 LARGE PITA BREAD DISKS (7 TO 8 INCHES IN DIAMETER), EACH CUT ALONG THE SEAM AND SEPARATED INTO HALVES

1. To begin, arrange all the pita bread halves crust side down in one layer on a large cookie sheet.

2. Preheat the oven to 400 degrees.

ANCHOVY PIZZA

1 PITA BREAD HALF (SEE ABOVE)

2 SCALLIONS, CLEANED AND CUT INTO THIN SLICES (⅓ CUP)

1 LARGE CLOVE GARLIC, PEELED AND THINLY SLICED (1 TEASPOON)

1 DOZEN PITTED KALAMATA OLIVES, CUT INTO ½-INCH PIECES (¼ CUP)

4 ANCHOVY FILLETS, HALVED

1 TEASPOON EXTRA VIRGIN OLIVE OIL

¼ CUP SHREDDED MOZZARELLA CHEESE

1. Arrange the scallions and garlic on a pita bread half.

2. Top with the olives, anchovy fillets, oil, and mozzarella.

SHRIMP-CILANTRO PIZZA

1 PITA BREAD HALF (SEE ABOVE)

2½ OUNCES SMALL SHELLED RAW SHRIMP

2 TABLESPOONS FRESH CILANTRO LEAVES

¼ CUP COARSELY CHOPPED MUSHROOMS

1 TABLESPOON COMBINED SESAME OIL AND CANOLA OIL (1½ TEASPOONS OF EACH)

1 TEASPOON SOY SAUCE

1 DOZEN DROPS TABASCO HOT PEPPER SAUCE

1 TABLESPOON PARMESAN CHEESE

1. Arrange the shrimp and cilantro leaves on a pita bread half.

2. Sprinkle on the mushrooms, oils, soy sauce, Tabasco, and cheese.

(CONTINUED)

TOTAL TIME

45 minutes

YIELD

4 to 6 servings

NUTRITION

ANCHOVY PIZZA

313 calories

16 g protein

15 g fat

1 g saturated fat

24 mg cholesterol

1316 mg sodium

22 g carbohydrate

.9 g dietary fiber

SHRIMP-CILANTRO PIZZA

248 calories

20 g protein

10 g fat

2 g saturated fat

111 mg cholesterol

714 mg sodium

19 g carbohydrate

.7 g dietary fiber

84

NUTRITION

TOMATO PIZZA

246 calories

4 g protein

14 g fat

1 g saturated fat

0 mg cholesterol

463 mg sodium

25 g carbohydrate

2 g dietary fiber

GREEN PIZZA

269 calories

8 g protein

16 g fat

3 g saturated fat

6 mg cholesterol

764 mg sodium

23 g carbohydrate

3 g dietary fiber

TOMATO AND *HERBES DE PROVENCE* PIZZA

1 PITA BREAD HALF (SEE ABOVE)

2 THIN SLICES RED ONION (1 OUNCE)

1 PLUM TOMATO (4 OUNCES), CUT INTO 6 SLICES

½ TEASPOON *HERBES DE PROVENCE*

DASH OF SALT

DASH OF FRESHLY GROUND BLACK PEPPER

1 TABLESPOON MINCED FRESH CHIVES

⅓ CUP GRATED MOZZARELLA CHEESE

1 TABLESPOON EXTRA VIRGIN OLIVE OIL

1. Arrange the onion slices on a pita bread half, and cover them with the tomato slices.

2. Top with the *herbes de Provence*, salt, pepper, chives, and cheese. Sprinkle on the oil.

GREEN PIZZA

1 PITA BREAD HALF (SEE ABOVE)

1 CUP LOOSELY PACKED MESCLUN SALAD GREENS

⅓ CUP DICED (½-INCH) TOMATO

2 TABLESPOONS COARSELY CHOPPED MILD ONION (PREFERABLY VIDALIA)

DASH OF SALT

DASH OF FRESHLY GROUND BLACK PEPPER

1 TABLESPOON VIRGIN OLIVE OIL

1½ TABLESPOONS GRATED PARMESAN CHEESE

1. Spread the salad greens on a pita bread half, and arrange the tomatoes on top.

2. Add the onion, salt, pepper, olive oil, and cheese.

YELLOW PEPPER, GRUYÈRE, AND PINE NUTS PIZZA

1 PITA BREAD HALF (SEE ABOVE)

3 TABLESPOONS DICED (½-INCH) YELLOW BELL PEPPER

2 TABLESPOONS PINE NUTS

10 OIL-CURED BLACK OLIVES, PITTED AND COARSELY CHOPPED

2 SCALLIONS, CLEANED AND COARSELY CHOPPED

1 TABLESPOON EXTRA VIRGIN OLIVE OIL

DASH OF FRESHLY GROUND BLACK PEPPER

⅓ CUP GRATED GRUYÈRE CHEESE

1. Arrange the diced yellow pepper on a pita bread half, and add the nuts.

2. Sprinkle the olives and scallions over the peppers, and top with the oil, pepper, and cheese.

CHICKEN PIZZA

1 PITA BREAD HALF (SEE ABOVE)

2 OUNCES THINLY SLICED COOKED CHICKEN PIECES

⅓ CUP THINLY SLICED MUSHROOMS

1 PIECE (2 OUNCES) ZUCCHINI, CUT INTO JULIENNE STRIPS

1 CLOVE GARLIC, PEELED AND THINLY SLICED (1 TEASPOON)

2 TABLESPOONS SOFT GOAT CHEESE

1 TABLESPOON EXTRA VIRGIN OLIVE OIL

DASH OF SALT

DASH OF FRESHLY GROUND BLACK PEPPER

1. Arrange the sliced chicken on top of a pita bread half, and cover it with the mushrooms and zucchini.

2. Top with the garlic, goat cheese, oil, salt, and pepper.

3. *To cook the pizzas:* Place the cookie sheet containing the pizzas in the 400-degree oven, and bake the pizzas for 13 to 15 minutes, until they are bubbly, brown, and cooked through.

4. Transfer the pizzas to a plate, cut each of them into four wedges, and serve them immediately.

NUTRITION

YELLOW PEPPER PIZZA

557 calories

19 g protein

42 g fat

10 g saturated fat

41 mg cholesterol

739 mg sodium

27 g carbohydrate

1 g dietary fiber

CHICKEN PIZZA

390 calories

27 g protein

22 g fat

6 g saturated fat

61 mg cholesterol

600 mg sodium

21 g carbohydrate

1 g dietary fiber

CLAUDINE

Pita pizzas are a good thing, because you don't have to follow the specific recipes we've given. You can make them with anything that you happen to have around the house.

Stew of Eggplant and Chinese Sausage

TOTAL TIME
About 30 minutes

YIELD
4 servings

NUTRITION
149 calories
7 g protein
8 g fat
2 g saturated fat
16 mg cholesterol
722 mg sodium
15 g carbohydrate
4 g dietary fiber

Like Japanese eggplants, Chinese eggplants are long and narrow — 2½ to 3 inches in diameter — but whereas the Japanese variety is the same dark purple color as the large, pear-shaped eggplants more familiar in the United States, Chinese eggplants are a beautiful purple-red color. I like these narrow eggplants, which are available now in most markets, because they have fewer seeds and are sweet. ↓ We combine the eggplants here with Chinese sausage, obtainable in most Asian markets and also in the ethnic section of many supermarkets. Usually about 6 inches long, these narrow (about 1 inch in diameter), slightly sweet sausages go particularly well with the eggplant, although another sausage variety can be used instead. The sausage and eggplant are combined with ginger and jalapeño pepper to give it some "hotness." A good companion dish to our Pita Pizzas (page 83) it also goes well as a garnish with meat and poultry.

3 SMALL, FIRM CHINESE EGGPLANTS (ABOUT 1½ POUNDS), CUT INTO 1½-INCH CHUNKS

2 CHINESE SAUSAGES (4 OUNCES), CUT INTO ¼-INCH SLICES

2 TEASPOONS CANOLA OIL

½ CUP WATER

3 CLOVES GARLIC, PEELED

1 PIECE GINGER ABOUT THE SIZE OF A LARGE OLIVE, PEELED

1 PIECE JALAPEÑO PEPPER, SIZE DEPENDING ON THE HOTNESS OF THE PEPPER AND YOUR TOLERANCE FOR "HOTNESS"

2 TABLESPOONS SOY SAUCE

2 TEASPOONS SUGAR

1. Place the eggplant pieces, sausages, oil, and water in a saucepan, and bring the mixture to a boil. Cover, and boil over medium to high heat for 15 minutes, until most of the moisture has evaporated. Remove the lid, and continue cooking over medium heat for a few additional minutes, if needed, until all the moisture is gone and the eggplant is lightly glazed with the oil.

2. Place the garlic, ginger, jalapeño, soy, and sugar in a mini-chopper or blender, and process the mixture until it is pureed. Add the sauce to the eggplant mixture, mix well, and cook for 1 minute. Remove the saucepan from the heat, cool to luke-warm, and serve.

Candied Grapefruit, Orange, and Lemon Chips

This is a great Christmas holiday recipe, yielding delicacies that are quite inexpensive to make but quite expensive if store-bought. Slices of Ruby Red grapefruit, seedless orange (or thinner skinned Florida orange, if you prefer), and lemon and /or lime are arranged on baking trays, sprinkled with sugar, and dried in a low-temperature oven. Hardening slightly but remaining somewhat chewy, the slices will keep almost indefinitely if stored in an airtight container.

TOTAL TIME
About 5 hours

YIELD
About 30 slices

NUTRITION
85 calories
1 g protein
.2 g fat
0 g saturated fat
0 mg cholesterol
1 mg sodium
24 g carbohydrate
1 g dietary fiber

Citrus fruits are an excellent source of vitamin C.

1 RUBY RED GRAPEFRUIT (ABOUT 1 POUND)
1 LARGE SEEDLESS ORANGE (ABOUT 12 OUNCES)
1 LARGE LEMON (ABOUT 9 OUNCES)
5 TABLESPOONS SUGAR

1. Preheat one or two ovens to 200 degrees. (See step 4, below.)

2. Cut the grapefruit into 10 slices, each ¼ inch thick, and discard the end pieces.

3. Line a jelly roll pan with aluminum foil, and arrange the grapefruit slices in one layer in the pan. Sprinkle the slices with 2 tablespoons of the sugar. Repeat with the orange and lemon slices, cutting each into about 10 slices and arranging the slices in a single layer on a foil-lined jelly roll pan. Sprinkle the orange and lemon slices with the remaining 3 tablespoons of sugar.

4. Place the pans on different racks in the 200-degree oven (or use two ovens, if available) for 3½ to 4 hours, until the slices are dried and candied but not browned. Remove them immediately from the pan, and cool them to room temperature on a rack.

5. Store the citrus chips in a plastic container, tightly covered. Serve as a garnish or snack.

Cuisine Bon Marché

CRANBERRY BEAN AND TUNA SALAD

BAKED MACKEREL MARIE-LOUISE

GLAZED CARROTS WITH OLIVES

APRICOT COMPOTE

———

We begin this tasty, inexpensive meal with a tuna salad made with cranberry beans. The fresh beans are especially flavorful, but if they aren't available, reconstituted dried cranberry beans work equally well in this recipe. ⅄ For our main course, mackerel is baked in the oven on a bed of sliced potatoes flavored with *herbes de Provence* and a bit of white wine. I selected mackerel because it was of good quality and quite inexpensive at my market, but other well-priced fish – porgy or whiting, for example – could be substituted for the mackerel. ⅄ While this sturdy, filling baked-fish main dish could stand alone as a one-dish meal, we extend our menu with a side dish featuring glazed carrots and olives. Also an excellent companion to roasted poultry or veal, this dish has beautiful color, and the texture and taste of the olives and capers contrast

White
KENDALL-
JACKSON,
GRAND RESERVE,
SAUVIGNON
BLANC

Red
ROSEMOUNT,
GSM

well with the carrots. Be sure to wait until serving time to add the olives, however, as they tend to muddy the color of the carrots if mixed into the dish too early. ⅄ The dessert is a compote made with both fresh and dried apricots. The mixture is concentrated and rich and, although it can be served on its own, it goes well with a bit of yogurt or sour cream.

Cranberry Bean and Tuna Salad

I especially like to prepare this recipe when fresh cranberry beans are in season, but you can use reconstituted dried cranberry beans with good results. Combined with tuna that's been seasoned with garlic, parsley, pepper, oil, and mustard, the beans are served on salad greens.

TOTAL TIME
50 minutes

YIELD
4 servings

NUTRITION
368 calories
33 g protein
11 g fat
1 g saturated fat
26 mg cholesterol
898 mg sodium
33 g carbohydrate
1 g dietary fiber

CLAUDINE

The first time I saw this menu, I didn't think I'd like the fresh cranberry bean and tuna salad. But when I tasted it, I decided it was the greatest thing. You can make it a day ahead and bring it to work for lunch — very practical.

2 POUNDS FRESH CRANBERRY BEANS, SHELLED (ABOUT 1 POUND WHEN SHELLED, OR 2½ CUPS)

1 BAY LEAF

1 MEDIUM ONION (5 OUNCES), PEELED AND CUT INTO 1-INCH PIECES (1 CUP)

1 TEASPOON SALT

1 TEASPOON *HERBES DE PROVENCE*

1½ CUPS COOL WATER

2 CANS (6 OUNCES EACH) TUNA IN WATER

2 LARGE CLOVES GARLIC, PEELED, CRUSHED, AND CHOPPED (2 TEASPOONS)

¼ CUP MINCED FRESH PARSLEY

¾ TEASPOON FRESHLY GROUND BLACK PEPPER

3 TABLESPOONS VIRGIN OLIVE OIL

1 TABLESPOON DIJON-STYLE MUSTARD

8 TO 10 LETTUCE LEAVES, PREFERABLY FROM BOSTON LETTUCE

1. Place the beans, bay leaf, onion, salt, *herbes de Provence*, and water in a saucepan. Bring to a boil, cover, reduce the heat to very low, and cook gently for 35 to 40 minutes, until the beans are tender. (If using dried beans, you may have to cook them for 10 to 15 minutes longer.) Cool the mixture to lukewarm. At this point most of the liquid will have been absorbed by the beans.

2. Place the tuna including its water in a salad bowl. Add the garlic, parsley, pepper, oil, and mustard, and mix well, breaking the tuna into small pieces. Add the beans, discarding some of the liquid if it is excessive, and toss gently to mix all the ingredients together. (The mixture should be moist but not liquid.)

3. Divide the lettuce leaves among four plates, and spoon the bean mixture onto the leaves. Serve at room temperature as a first course.

Baked Mackerel Marie-Louise

This recipe involves layering and baking sliced potatoes, onions, and tomatoes in a gratin dish until they are tender, then arranging fish on top and finishing the dish under the broiler. If fresh mackerel is not available, substitute another fish of about the same weight — whiting, small sea bass, small red snapper, or cod, for example.

❧ ❧ ❧ ❧ ❧ ❧ ❧ ❧

1¼ POUNDS RED BLISS OR YUKON GOLD POTATOES, PEELED AND SLICED THIN (ABOUT 3 CUPS)

2 MEDIUM ONIONS (8 OUNCES TOTAL), PEELED AND THINLY SLICED

1 TABLESPOON CHOPPED FRESH SAVORY

1½ TABLESPOONS VIRGIN OLIVE OIL

¼ TEASPOON FRESHLY GROUND BLACK PEPPER

¾ TEASPOON SALT

⅓ CUP CHICKEN STOCK, PREFERABLY HOMEMADE UNSALTED

⅓ CUP DRY WHITE WINE

2 LARGE RIPE TOMATOES (1 POUND), CUT INTO ½-INCH SLICES

4 MACKEREL, EVISCERATED (12 TO 15 OUNCES EACH), WITH HEADS AND TAILS REMOVED (ABOUT 8 OUNCES EACH READY-TO-COOK WEIGHT)

½ TEASPOON *HERBES DE PROVENCE*

2 TABLESPOONS CHOPPED FRESH PARSLEY

1. Preheat the oven to 400 degrees.

2. Rinse the potato slices well in cool water, then drain them thoroughly in a colander. Place the drained potato slices in a bowl with the onion slices, savory, oil, pepper, and ½ teaspoon of the salt. Mix well and transfer to a gratin dish. Add the stock, and arrange the sliced tomatoes over the potato and onion mixture.

3. Place the gratin dish in the 400-degree oven for 60 to 75 minutes, until the potatoes are tender. Remove, and add the wine. Preheat the broiler.

(CONTINUED)

About 1 ½ hours

YIELD

4 servings

NUTRITION

530 calories

28 g protein

21 g fat

4 g saturated fat

66 mg cholesterol

602 mg sodium

54 g carbohydrate

6 g dietary fiber

*Tomatoes and
potatoes both
provide substantial
vitamin C.
Mackerel is a very
good source of
protective omega-3
fatty acids.*

4. Meanwhile, make three horizontal slits, each about ¼ inch deep, through the skin on both sides of each mackerel. Sprinkle the fish with the remaining salt and the *herbes de Provence*, and arrange them in one layer on top of the tomatoes in the gratin dish.

5. Place the dish under the broiler so it is about 10 inches from the heat, and broil for 10 minutes.

6. Sprinkle with the parsley, and serve as soon as possible.

Note: The potato-onion-tomato mixture can be prepared up to 1 hour ahead. Bake for 60 to 75 minutes, as indicated in the recipe, then set aside until about 10 minutes before serving time. Arrange the mackerel on top, and finish under the broiler according to the recipe instructions.

*Baked Mackerel
Marie-Louise
(page 91) and
Glazed Carrots
with Olives
(page 94)*

Glazed Carrots with Olives

TOTAL TIME

About 15 minutes

YIELD

4 servings

NUTRITION

131 calories

1 g protein

9 g fat

2 g saturated fat

8 mg cholesterol

898 mg sodium

12 g carbohydrate

0 g dietary fiber

Carrots get their color from beta-carotene. Each serving contains enough beta-carotene to supply 25% of the daily value for vitamin A.

For this unconventional dish, baby carrots are combined with salt, a bit of sugar, butter, and water and cooked until the moisture has evaporated and the carrots are beginning to glaze. Then they are finished with olives and capers. The result is colorful and quite flavorful.

1 POUND SMALL BABY CARROTS, PEELED

1 TEASPOON SUGAR

¼ TEASPOON SALT

1 TABLESPOON UNSALTED BUTTER

⅔ CUP WATER

½ CUP OIL-CURED OLIVES, EITHER PITTED OR UNPITTED

2 TABLESPOONS CAPERS

2 TEASPOONS MINCED FRESH CHIVES

1. Place the carrots, sugar, salt, butter, and water in a sturdy saucepan. Cook the mixture, covered, over high heat for about 8 minutes, until all the water is gone and the carrots are tender and starting to glaze. (If some moisture remains in the pan with the carrots, cook them, uncovered, for 2 to 3 minutes to evaporate the water so they will glaze lightly on all sides.)

2. Add the olives and capers to the saucepan, and cook for 1 minute, just long enough to heat the olives through. Sprinkle with the chives, and serve.

Apricot Compote

I love apricots in any form. For this recipe, I mix fresh apricots, which I've processed with orange juice into a puree, with dried apricot slices. Then I cook them together with a little honey and some pignola nuts. The dessert is best served at room temperature with a garnish of sour cream or yogurt.

❧   ❧   ❧   ❧   ❧   ❧   ❧   ❧

¾ POUND RIPE FRESH APRICOTS (ABOUT 5)

1 CUP ORANGE JUICE

5 OUNCES DRIED APRICOT HALVES, CUT INTO
  ½-INCH SLICES (1¼ CUPS)

¼ CUP PIGNOLA NUTS

2 TABLESPOONS HONEY

½ CUP SOUR CREAM OR PLAIN YOGURT

1. Pit the fresh apricots, and place the fruit in the bowl of a food processor with the orange juice. Process the apricot mixture until it is pureed, then transfer it to a saucepan.

2. Add the dried apricots, nuts, and honey to the saucepan, and bring the mixture to a boil over high heat. Reduce the heat to low, cover, and cook for 10 minutes, scraping the bottom of the pan with a spoon a few times to assure that the mixture is not sticking.

3. Cool the compote to room temperature, and divide it among four dessert bowls. Top each serving with a spoonful of sour cream or yogurt.

TOTAL TIME

About 20 minutes, plus cooling time

YIELD

4 servings (2 cups)

NUTRITION

252 calories

7 g protein

5 g fat

.9 g saturated fat

1 mg cholesterol

28 mg sodium

50 g carbohydrate

5 g dietary fiber

Apricots are loaded with beta-carotene; they are also good sources of vitamin C.

A Kosher Menu for Friends

ARTICHOKE HYMN TO SPRING

SALMON *GRENOBLOISE*

ORZO WITH ARUGULA SAUCE

CHERRY COMPOTE

———

In this menu, we salute our many Jewish friends. Since most of them are not Orthodox Jews and follow a less rigid diet than the orthodox would, our menu is relaxed, following basic guidelines of the kosher diet: meals may not mix meat and dairy products, and some of the prohibited foods are shellfish, pork, and fish without scales. ↓ We start our meal with a hymn to spring vegetables. We use peas, asparagus, Boston lettuce, and artichokes in this recipe, cooking them together in a fresh and flavorful stew. ↓ The main course features salmon prepared in the classic style of Grenoble, a French town at the foot of the Alps. Cooked skin side down in a skillet, boneless salmon fillet steaks are served with garnishes of capers, croutons, diced lemon, and chives. A little red wine vinegar, mixed with the salmon pan juices and poured over the fish at serving time, lends acidity that contrasts well with the richness of the salmon. ↓ As an accompaniment to the salmon, I cook orzo, a type of pasta that looks like rice, with spicy arugula, a green that is plentiful in my garden each summer. The combination of the orzo and arugula is surprisingly flavorful and attractive. ↓ This menu ends with a cherry compote made with large Bing cherries. First the cherries are pitted for this recipe, then the pits are cracked, tied in cheesecloth, and cooked along with the mixture to intensify the taste of the cherries. Flavored with kirschwasser, a cherry brandy, this compote is best when garnished with sour cream and served with cookies.

White
CHATEAU DE LA
GENAISERIE,
COTEAUX DU
LAYON,
ST. AUBIN

Red
CAMELOT,
PINOT NOIR

Artichoke Hymn to Spring

TOTAL TIME

About 1 hour

YIELD

4 servings

NUTRITION

194 calories

7 g protein

10 g fat

2 g saturated fat

8 mg cholesterol

660 mg sodium

22 g carbohydrate

9 g dietary fiber

Artichokes, snow-peas, and asparagus are all good sources of vitamin C and folate.

An explosion of spring vegetables, this recipe features artichokes, which are cooked first in water until tender. The flesh is then scraped from the leaves and cooked again, along with the hearts and stems, a little onion and sugar. At the last moment, fresh snow peas, asparagus spears, and Boston lettuce are added to the pan. A wonderful stew of vegetables, it makes an excellent side dish as well as a great first course.

4 ARTICHOKES (ABOUT 10 OUNCES EACH)

1 WHITE ONION (4 OUNCES), PEELED AND CUT INTO 1-INCH PIECES (¾ CUP)

2 TABLESPOONS VIRGIN OLIVE OIL

¾ TEASPOON SALT

1 TEASPOON SUGAR

1 TABLESPOON UNSALTED BUTTER

½ CUP WATER

6 OUNCES SNOW PEAS, STRINGS REMOVED FROM SEAMS ON BOTH SIDES

6 OUNCES LARGE ASPARAGUS SPEARS, PEELED AND CUT INTO 1-INCH PIECES (1¼ CUPS)

1 SMALL HEAD BOSTON LETTUCE (ABOUT 6 OUNCES), WASHED AND CUT INTO 2-INCH PIECES (2½ TO 3 CUPS)

1. Bring 2 quarts of water to a boil in a stainless-steel or other nonreactive pot. Remove the stems from the artichokes, and peel off the fibrous outside membrane of each stem with a paring knife. Cut the trimmed stems into 1-inch pieces, and set them aside.

2. Carefully drop the artichokes into the boiling water, and place an ovenproof plate on top of them to hold them under the water. Bring the water back to a boil, cover the pot partially with a lid, and boil the artichokes over high heat for 25 to 30 minutes, until a leaf pulled from the base of the artichokes is very tender. Discard the hot water in the pot, and run cold water over the artichokes in the pan until they are cold.

3. Meanwhile, place the reserved artichoke stem pieces, onion, oil, salt, sugar, butter, and water in a stainless-steel saucepan, and bring the mixture to a boil. Reduce the heat to low, cover, and boil gently for 5 minutes. Remove from the heat, and set aside in the pan.

4. When the artichokes are cold, squeeze them gently to press out the water. Remove and reserve the leaves to expose the heart, keeping the center clump of leaves that cover each of the chokes together for use later as a decoration along with 6 large leaves from each artichoke.

5. Using a small spoon, scrape the end of each of the remaining leaves to remove any edible flesh from them (about ⅓ cup of flesh per artichoke), and add the flesh to the artichoke stem mixture in the pan. Remove and discard the chokes from the artichoke hearts, and cut each heart into 4 pieces. (Note: The recipe can be prepared a few hours ahead to this point.)

6. No more than 15 minutes before serving, bring the artichoke stem and onion mixture to a boil in the pan. Add the snow peas and asparagus to the pan, and bring the mixture back to a boil over high heat. Boil, covered, for 2 minutes, then add the lettuce pieces. Boil, covered, for an additional 2 minutes. Place the artichoke heart pieces on top of the vegetable stew mixture in the pan, and heat the mixture for 1 or 2 minutes longer.

7. To serve, spoon some of the vegetable stew into the center of four plates, and arrange the artichoke heart pieces on top. Decorate the edges of each plate with the reserved artichoke leaves, and place a clump of the reserved center artichoke leaves in the middle of each serving. Serve immediately.

A friend of mine, Mark, eats kosherly — I guess that's the right word for it. I appreciate this menu because it lets me put something together that I know I can make that he'll really like too. Kosher or not, this is a terrific menu — very healthy and springlike.

Salmon Grenobloise

TOTAL TIME

10 to 15 minutes

YIELD

4 servings

NUTRITION

379 calories

35 g protein

22 g fat

6 g saturated fat

110 mg cholesterol

589 mg sodium

8 g carbohydrate

.9 g dietary fiber

*Salmon is
a good source of
protective omega-3
fatty acids.*

This classic salmon dish is prepared with unskinned salmon fillet steaks. Cooked in a skillet on the skin side only – first uncovered, then covered – they cook all the way through, with the flesh remaining slightly rare. The fat that melts out of the salmon in the cooking process is discarded from the skillet, and a little butter and vinegar are added. This flavorful blend is poured over the fillets, and they are served with a garnish of croutons, lemon flesh, capers, and chives.

1½ TABLESPOONS CANOLA OIL

2 SLICES BREAD, CUT INTO ½-INCH CROUTONS (1 CUP)

4 SALMON FILLET STEAKS WITH SKIN ON (6 TO 7 OUNCES EACH)

½ TEASPOON SALT

¼ TEASPOON FRESHLY GROUND BLACK PEPPER

4 TABLESPOONS ¼-INCH PIECES OF LEMON FLESH

2 TABLESPOONS DRAINED CAPERS

2 TEASPOONS MINCED FRESH CHIVES

2 TABLESPOONS UNSALTED BUTTER

1 TABLESPOON RED WINE VINEGAR

1. Heat the oil until it is hot but not smoking in a nonstick skillet. Add the croutons, and cook them for about 2 minutes, stirring them occasionally until they are nicely browned on all sides. Transfer the croutons to a bowl, and set them aside.

2. Sprinkle the fish steaks on both sides with the salt and pepper, and place them skin side down in the hot skillet you used to sauté the croutons. (No additional fat is required.) Cook the fish, uncovered, for 3 minutes over medium to high heat, then cover, and cook it for another 2 minutes. Place the steaks skin side up on a warm platter, and sprinkle them with the croutons, lemon flesh pieces, capers, and chives.

3. Discard any fat that has accumulated in the skillet. (I had 2 tablespoons of melted fat from the fish in my skillet.) Add the butter to the skillet, and cook it over medium heat until it is lightly browned. Add the vinegar, shake the pan to mix it in, then pour the mixture over the fish steaks on the platter. Serve immediately.

*Salmon
Grenobloise
(this page) and
Orzo with
Arugula Sauce
(page 102)*

Orzo with Arugula Sauce

TOTAL TIME

About 30 minutes

YIELD

4 servings

NUTRITION

685 calories

29 g protein

22 g fat

4 g saturated fat

16 mg cholesterol

1475 mg sodium

96 g carbohydrate

5 g dietary fiber

This dish is high in fiber. Anchovies are rich in protective omega-3 fatty acids. Tomatoes and arugula contribute more than 35% of the daily value for vitamin C.

Orzo, sometimes called *risole*, is a pasta shaped like kernels of rice. Since each small kernel releases starch as it cooks, orzo should be cooked in a lot of water — otherwise, it tends to stick together or doesn't cook sufficiently throughout. Although I like my pasta cooked slightly al dente, I prefer orzo cooked at least 8 minutes to develop its full volume and texture.

2 TABLESPOONS VIRGIN OLIVE OIL

½ CUP PIGNOLA NUTS

1 SMALL ONION (ABOUT 3 OUNCES), PEELED AND FINELY CHOPPED (½ CUP)

5 TO 6 SCALLIONS, TRIMMED, CLEANED, AND COARSELY MINCED (½ CUP)

1 CAN (2 OUNCES) ANCHOVY FILLETS IN OIL, CUT INTO ½-INCH PIECES

8 CUPS (LOOSELY PACKED) ARUGULA (8 TO 10 OUNCES), WASHED AND CUT INTO 2-INCH PIECES

1 TEASPOON SALT

½ TEASPOON FRESHLY GROUND BLACK PEPPER

2 LARGE TOMATOES (ABOUT 1 POUND TOTAL), PEELED, HALVED, SEEDED, AND CUT INTO 1-INCH PIECES (ABOUT 2 CUPS)

1 POUND ORZO (TINY RICE-SHAPED PASTA)

¼ CUP SHAVED OR GRATED PARMESAN CHEESE (OPTIONAL)

1. Heat the olive oil in a saucepan. When it is hot, add the pignola nuts and chopped onion. Cook over medium heat for 5 minutes, until the nuts are nicely browned and the onion is soft and translucent.

2. Add the scallions, anchovies (along with the oil from the can), and the arugula. Mix well, and cook for 5 minutes, uncovered, until the arugula is wilted and soft. Add ½ teaspoon of the salt, the pepper, and the tomatoes, and cook for 1 minute. (The recipe can be made to this point up to 1 hour ahead.)

3. Near serving time, bring 8 cups of water to a boil, and add the remaining ½ teaspoon of salt. Add the orzo, bring the water back to a boil, and boil, uncovered, mixing occasionally, for 7 to 8 minutes, or until cooked to your liking (about 7 minutes if you like it al dente, 8 minutes or longer if you like it soft).

4. Meanwhile, reheat the sauce mixture if necessary. Drain the pasta in a colander. (You will have about 5 cups, although some brands swell up more, and the yield could be as much as 6 cups.) Add the orzo to the sauce, and mix well.

5. Divide the mixture among four plates, and sprinkle each serving with 1 tablespoon of the Parmesan, if desired. Serve immediately.

Cherry Compote

I like to make this dessert in summer, when large Bing cherries are available and of excellent quality. I first pit the cherries and then, to concentrate their flavor, cook them along with the cracked pits in a sturdy white wine flavored with cherry jam. The pits give the fruit a slightly bitter, almondlike taste that I find particularly appealing.

TOTAL TIME
About 15 minutes, plus cooling time

YIELD
4 servings

NUTRITION
240 calories
2 g protein
.7 g fat
1 g saturated fat
6 mg cholesterol
19 mg sodium
43 g carbohydrate
3 g dietary fiber

Cherries are a good source of vitamin C.

1¼ POUNDS LARGE BING CHERRIES, STEMS REMOVED

¾ CUP STURDY WHITE WINE (LIKE A CHARDONNAY)

3 TABLESPOONS SUGAR

¼ CUP CHERRY JAM

1 TEASPOON CORNSTARCH DISSOLVED IN 1 TABLESPOON WATER

1 TABLESPOON KIRSCHWASSER (OPTIONAL)

4 TABLESPOONS SOUR CREAM

COOKIES (OPTIONAL)

1. Pit the cherries, and reserve the pits. Place the pitted cherries, wine, sugar, and jam in a stainless-steel saucepan.

2. Arrange the reserved cherry pits on a piece of plastic wrap set on a cutting board, and cover them with another piece of plastic wrap. Using a meat pounder or the base of a small, heavy saucepan, pound the pits to crack them. Place the cracked pits in a piece of cheesecloth, and tie them into a compact package. Add this package to the cherry mixture in the saucepan.

3. Bring the cherry mixture to a boil, cover, reduce the heat to low, and boil the mixture gently for 5 minutes. Add the dissolved cornstarch, and mix well. Cool. Stir in the kirshwasser, if desired.

4. Serve the compote in glass goblets with 1 tablespoon of sour cream on top of each serving and, if desired, a few cookies.

Modern American Cuisine

Broiled Striped Bass
with Broccoli Rabe and Anchovies

Spicy Chicken Breasts

Cucumber-Yogurt Relish

Celeriac Puree

Cantaloupe Sherbet

————

This menu reflects the cooking of today: different and interesting combinations, free-spirited ideas, and a certain amount of casualness. ❡ We begin with a broiled striped bass. A white-fleshed, flaky, soft-textured fish with a mild, nutty taste, striped bass is now farmed and available in most reliable fish markets. We serve the bass with a broccoli rabe and anchovy mixture, an unconventional garnish that goes well with it, but it could be grilled and served plain. ❡ The fish is followed by boldly flavored chicken breasts, and the taste of this dish can be varied a great deal depending on the rub used on the chicken. I use juniper berries, coriander, peppercorns, and mustard seeds in my rub, but you can create a rub mixture of your own with spices you like, and give your own imprimatur to the dish. The skinless breasts of chicken are sautéed very briefly in a skillet on top of the stove, then placed in a low-temperature oven to finish cooking and rest. ❡ The spicy chicken is complemented by a refreshing cucumber and yogurt relish that is similar to relishes served with hot dishes in Indian cooking. A mixture of diced cucumber, fresh mint, Tabasco sauce, and yogurt, it contrasts the hotness of the Tabasco with the coolness of the yogurt and mint. ❡ We also serve a celeriac puree. Celeriac, a very large, beige, knobby root, is peeled, cubed, and cooked until tender. Thickened with a small amount of Cream of Wheat, the mixture is then processed until creamy. ❡ The dessert for this Modern American Cuisine menu is a cantaloupe sherbet. In this recipe, some of the cantaloupe is turned into a puree and frozen, and the remainder is cut into slices and served with the sherbet.

White
STONESTREET,
GEWURZTRA-
MINER

Red
BOISSET, CÔTES
DU RHÔNE

Port
KWV, FULL
RUBY PORT

Broiled Striped Bass
with Broccoli Rabe and Anchovies

TOTAL TIME
About 1 hour

YIELD
4 servings

NUTRITION
327 calories
43 g protein
8 g fat
1 g saturated fat
171 mg cholesterol
1296 mg sodium
20 g carbohydrate
3 g dietary fiber

Although I serve this dish as a first course here, it also would make an excellent main course. Since the bass takes only about 5 minutes to cook under a hot broiler, it should be broiled at the last minute. The fish is served on a bed of broccoli rabe that has been sautéed with sliced garlic and potatoes.

8 OUNCES SMALL YUKON GOLD OR RED POTATOES, WASHED

10 OUNCES BROCCOLI RABE, TRIMMED AND CLEANED (8 OUNCES TRIMMED AND CLEANED)

1 JAR OR CAN (2 OUNCES) ANCHOVY FILLETS IN OIL

4 BLACK OLIVES

4 SMALL CHERRY TOMATOES

4 FILLETS OF STRIPED BASS, SCALED BUT WITH SKIN LEFT ON (7 OUNCES EACH), EACH FILLET ABOUT ¾ INCH THICK

1 TEASPOON SALT

2 TABLESPOONS VIRGIN OLIVE OIL

2 TABLESPOONS SLICED GARLIC (ABOUT 5 LARGE CLOVES)

⅓ CUP WATER

½ TEASPOON FRESHLY GROUND BLACK PEPPER

1. Place the potatoes in a medium saucepan, add water to cover, and bring the water to a boil. Then reduce the heat to low, cover, and boil gently for 20 to 25 minutes, until the potatoes are tender. Drain, and when the potatoes are cool enough to handle, peel and cut them into ½-inch slices, and set them aside in a bowl.

2. Prepare the broccoli rabe: Cut off the stems and, using a small sharp knife, peel them to remove their fibrous outer skin. (This skin will peel off easily.) Cut the peeled stems into 2-inch pieces, and cut the leaves into 1-inch pieces. Wash the leaves in cold water, and drain them in a colander. Combine the leaves and the stems in a bowl, and set them aside until ready to cook.

3. Pour the oil surrounding the anchovies into a small bowl, and reserve it for later use. Wrap an anchovy fillet around each of the black olives and cherry tomatoes. Set these aside for use as a decoration.

4. Score the striped bass fillets by cutting four crosswise bias slits, each about ¼ inch deep, through the skin on each fillet. Using about ¼ teaspoon of the salt, sprinkle the fillets on both sides, then coat them, again on both sides, with the reserved anchovy oil. Place the fillets skin side up on a cookie sheet lined with aluminum foil, and set them aside until ready to cook. (The recipe can be prepared to this point a few hours ahead.)

5. When ready to finish the dish, preheat the broiler.

6. Meanwhile, heat the olive oil in a large sturdy skillet, and sauté the sliced garlic for about 1 minute, until it is blond in color. Add the broccoli rabe stems and leaves, the water, the remaining salt, and the pepper. Mix thoroughly, cover, and cook over high heat for 3 to 5 minutes, until the broccoli

rabe is tender and the water in the pan has evaporated. Add the reserved cooked potato slices, cover, and set the pan aside while you cook the fish. (The heat in the pan will warm the potatoes.)

7. Place the cookie sheet containing the fish fillets under the broiler so the fish are about 4 inches from the heat. Broil for about 5 minutes. (The heat will penetrate and lightly cook the fish through the slits in the skin, and the skin will get brown and crunchy.)

8. Divide the broccoli rabe and potatoes among four plates, and place a fillet of fish on top of the vegetables on each plate. Arrange an anchovy-wrapped olive and tomato on top of the fish on each plate, and serve immediately.

Striped bass and anchovies contribute protective omega-3 fatty acids. Broccoli, tomatoes, and potatoes provide more than 100% of the daily value for vitamin C.

Spicy Chicken Breasts

TOTAL TIME

30 minutes

YIELD

4 servings

NUTRITION

279 calories

44 g protein

10 g fat

2 g saturated fat

119 mg cholesterol

394 mg sodium

0 g carbohydrate

.1 g dietary fiber

CLAUDINE

With these menus, as with all foods, you should feel free to improvise. I think it is really fun to just kind of improvise and have fun when you're cooking.

This is a good make-ahead dish that is easy to prepare, nutritionally sound, and very tasty. The recipe is special because of the rub, the composition of which can be changed based on your taste preferences. Toasting the berries and seeds used in the rub intensifies their flavor.

SPICE RUB

½ TEASPOON TOASTED JUNIPER BERRIES

½ TEASPOON TOASTED CORIANDER SEEDS

½ TEASPOON BLACK PEPPERCORNS

½ TEASPOON TOASTED MUSTARD SEEDS

½ TEASPOON SALT

4 SKINLESS, FATLESS CHICKEN BREAST HALVES (ABOUT 6 OUNCES EACH)

1½ TABLESPOONS VIRGIN OLIVE OIL

1. Place all the rub ingredients except the peppercorns and salt in a skillet, and cook them over a medium to high heat for 2 minutes, until lightly toasted.

2. Place all the rub ingredients in a spice grinder or coffee grinder, and process them for 20 to 30 seconds, until ground.

3. Sprinkle both sides of the chicken breasts with the ground spice mixture, and rub it gently into the breasts. Brush the breasts on both sides with the 1½ tablespoons olive oil, then wrap them in plastic wrap and refrigerate until ready to cook. (The recipe can be prepared to this point up to 12 hours ahead.)

4. When ready to cook the chicken, preheat the oven to 200 degrees.

5. Heat a very large nonstick skillet. When it is hot, add the chicken breasts. Cook them over medium to high heat for 3 minutes on one side. Then, turn the breasts over, and cook them for 3 minutes on the other side.

6. Arrange the breasts on an ovenproof platter, and place them in the 200-degree oven to keep warm and continue cooking while you complete your meal preparations. (The chicken should remain in the oven for at least 10 to 15 minutes so it is cooked through and rested, but it can remain in the oven for up to 45 minutes without becoming too dry.)

7. Serve one chicken breast half on each of four dinner plates.

Spicy Chicken Breasts (this page), Cucumber-Yogurt Relish (page 110), and Celeriac Puree (page 111)

Cucumber-Yogurt Relish

TOTAL TIME

10 minutes, plus
macerating time

YIELD

4½ cups

NUTRITION

56 calories
1 g protein
0 g fat
0 g saturated fat
0 mg cholesterol
141 mg sodium
13 g carbohydrate
.4 g dietary fiber

Nutritional
analysis is based on
¼ cup serving.

This is the type of palate cleanser that appears often as an accompaniment to hot dishes in Indian cooking. I think it goes particularly well with almost any highly seasoned food, like the Spicy Chicken Breasts (page 108) in this menu. Always welcome at my table, the relish will keep, refrigerated, for a couple of days.

2 CUCUMBERS (1½ POUNDS TOTAL), PEELED, SEEDED, AND CUT INTO ½-INCH DICE (3½ CUPS)

1 CUP NONFAT YOGURT

¼ CUP CHIFFONADE OF FRESH MINT LEAVES

1 TEASPOON SALT

1 TEASPOON SUGAR

¾ TEASPOON TABASCO HOT PEPPER SAUCE

1 TABLESPOON WHITE WINE VINEGAR

1 SMALL CLOVE GARLIC, PEELED, CRUSHED, AND FINELY CHOPPED (½ TEASPOON)

¼ TEASPOON CURRY POWDER

1. Mix all the ingredients together in a bowl. Let macerate for at least 1 hour at room temperature, or cover and refrigerate overnight.

2. Serve as a garnish for the Spicy Chicken Breasts (page 108) or for roasted or stewed chicken.

Celeriac Puree

In this recipe, celeriac — the homely, knobby root of a special celery cultivated for its root — is cooked until tender in water seasoned with a little salt and sugar. The small amount of liquid remaining in the pan is then thickened and blended with the cooked celeriac into a smooth puree with a wonderfully intense celery flavor.

TOTAL TIME

35 to 40 minutes

YIELD

4 servings

NUTRITION

154 calories

3 g protein

6 g fat

3 g saturated fat

16 mg cholesterol

864 mg sodium

22 g carbohydrate

2 g dietary fiber

1 LARGE CELERIAC (CELERY ROOT), ABOUT 1½ POUNDS

¾ TEASPOON SALT

1 TEASPOON SUGAR

2¼ CUPS WATER

⅓ CUP CREAM OF WHEAT

2 TABLESPOONS UNSALTED BUTTER

1. Using a sharp paring knife, remove the skin and any damaged areas from the celeriac, and cut it into 2-inch pieces.

2. Place the celeriac pieces in a large saucepan with the salt, sugar, and water. Bring to a boil, reduce the heat to low, cover, and boil gently for 20 minutes, until the celeriac is very tender.

3. Using a skimmer, remove some of the celeriac pieces, and place them in a bowl so the liquid in the pan is more visible. Gradually add the Cream of Wheat to the liquid in the pan, whisking it in as you add it so that it doesn't lump. Return the celeriac pieces to the saucepan, and bring the mixture back to a boil, stirring occasionally. Reduce the heat to low, cover, and boil gently for 5 minutes.

4. Place the contents of the saucepan in the bowl of a food processor, and add the butter. Process for 20 to 30 seconds, until the mixture is smooth and creamy. (Yield: 3½ cups.) Serve.

Cantaloupe Sherbet

Peel a well-ripened, fragrant cantaloupe for this recipe and retain four crosswise slices for serving. The remainder is processed with sugar and lime juice and, eventually, transformed into sherbet in an ice-cream maker. I serve the sherbet on top of the melon slices, which have been flavored with a little port wine and grenadine.

TOTAL TIME
About 20 minutes,
plus churning time

YIELD
4 servings

NUTRITION
261 calories
2 g protein
.7 g fat
0 g saturated fat
0 mg cholesterol
32 mg sodium
63 g carbohydrate
2 g dietary fiber

1 RIPE CANTALOUPE (ABOUT 3 POUNDS)

¼ CUP PORT WINE

4 TABLESPOONS GRENADINE

2 LIMES

½ CUP SUGAR

EDIBLE FLOWERS OR HERBS FOR DECORATION
  (OPTIONAL)

1. Using a sharp paring knife, peel the cantaloupe, removing the outer skin and green covering underneath so that the orange flesh is visible. Cut the melon in half crosswise, and, using a spoon, remove and discard the seeds. Cut 4 thin (¼-inch) crosswise slices from one of the melon halves to create 4 "wheels" or "rings," (about 6 ounces total). Place these rings in a gratin dish with the wine and 2 table-spoons of the grenadine, cover, and set aside. Cut the rest of the melon into 1-inch pieces. (You should have about 5 cups.)

2. Using a lemon zester, remove enough thin strips of rind from one of the limes to measure 1 teaspoon. Set the strips aside. Halve and squeeze the limes to obtain 3 tablespoons of lime juice.

3. Place the melon pieces in the bowl of a food processor with the lime juice, sugar, and remaining 2 tablespoons of grenadine, and process until smooth. (You will have about 4 cups.)

4. Transfer the pureed melon to an ice-cream maker, and process according to the manufacturer's instructions, churning the mixture for 25 to 30 minutes, until it is solid. Serve immediately, or transfer the sherbet to cold containers, and store it in the freezer.

5. If freezing the sherbet for later use, move it from the freezer to the refrigerator about 1½ hours before serving time to soften.

6. At serving time, arrange a ring of melon (whole or in pieces) on each of four plates, and pour the accumulated juice in the gratin dish on top and around the rings. Place a scoop of the sherbet in the center of each ring and sprinkle a few of the reserved strips of lime rind on top. Decorate the sherbet with an edible flower or herb, if desired, and serve immediately.

Cantaloupe Sherbet (this page) and Vincent's Almond Short-bread Cookies (page 139)

A Bon Vivant Feast

TOMATO, BASIL, AND CHEESE SOUFFLÉ

VEAL SHANK *PRINTANIÈRE*

CALIFORNIA ARBORIO RICE AND PECANS

BREAD PUDDING SOUFFLÉS
WITH CHOCOLATE-BOURBON SAUCE

———

This classic, elegant, and savory menu is a sure winner that I would be happy to serve to any of my bon vivant friends. ↯ We begin with a soufflé made with tomato, basil, and cheese. For this recipe, tomato insides are cooked, thickened, and combined with basil and cheese. This mixture then is lightened with egg white and baked in the tomato shells until puffed and nicely browned on top. A delicate dish, this must be cooked at the last moment. ↯ The main course is a veal shank *printanière*, a French version of the Italian osso buco. For this colorful and flavorful dish, boneless veal is braised slowly with white wine, onion, carrots, and shallots, then finished with snap peas and shelled peas. ↯ The veal shank is best served with rice. I use an Arborio short-grain rice from California, a similar but less expensive version of the original Arborio from Italy, and flavor it with pecans and onions. ↯ For dessert, we serve soufflés of another type than the one served as our first course. Our bread pudding soufflés are made with bread that is soaked in milk, flavored with raisins and maple syrup, then lightened with beaten egg whites. Baked in individual molds until firm, the soufflés are served warm with a simple sauce made of chocolate and milk flavored with bourbon.

White
VINA CALINA,
CHARDONNAY

Red
KENDALL-
JACKSON,
GRAND RESERVE,
MERLOT

Tomato, Basil, and Cheese Soufflé

TOTAL TIME

About 1 hour

YIELD

4 servings

NUTRITION

237 calories

11 g protein

13 g fat

3 g saturated fat

168 mg cholesterol

542 mg sodium

29 g carbohydrate

3 g dietary fiber

This dish is a good source of fiber. Tomatoes are rich in vitamin C — each serving provides more than 90% of the daily value.

A soufflé always makes an elegant first course. For this particularly appealing one, tomato tops and insides are processed into a puree, which is first thickened, then lightened with egg whites, and, finally, spooned into tomato cavities and baked. A summery delight, this soufflé has a somewhat soft center because of the juice rendered by the tomatoes as they cook.

4 LARGE, RIPE (BUT FIRM) TOMATOES (ABOUT 2½ POUNDS)

¾ TEASPOON SALT

2 TABLESPOONS VIRGIN OLIVE OIL

4 TABLESPOONS ALL-PURPOSE FLOUR

¼ TEASPOON FRESHLY GROUND BLACK PEPPER

3 EGGS

3 TABLESPOONS CHIFFONADE OF BASIL

4 TABLESPOONS GRATED SWISS CHEESE

1 TABLESPOON GRATED PARMESAN CHEESE

1. Preheat the oven to 375 degrees.

2. Using a sharp knife, remove the top ½ inch from the smooth end of each tomato, and reserve these "caps." Scoop out the insides of each tomato with a measuring spoon, removing and reserving the center and ribs in a bowl, and leaving tomato shells that are about ½ inch thick.

3. Sprinkle the shells with ¼ teaspoon of the salt, and place them, hollow side down, in a gratin dish. Bake the shells in the 375-degree oven for 8 to 10 minutes to soften them.

4. Meanwhile, place the reserved tomato caps and tomato insides in the bowl of a food processor, and process the mixture for 15 seconds. (Yield: About 2 cups.)

5. Heat the oil in a medium saucepan. Add the flour, mix it in with a whisk, and cook the mixture over medium to high heat for 30 seconds. Add the processed tomato insides, the remaining ½ teaspoon of salt, and the pepper, and bring the mixture to a boil, stirring it continuously with a whisk. Boil for about 30 seconds.

6. Meanwhile, separate the eggs, placing the yolks in a small bowl and the whites in a larger mixing bowl. Whisk the yolks, basil, and Swiss cheese into the tomato mixture in the saucepan. Beat the egg whites until they form soft peaks (they should not be too firm), then combine them well with the tomato mixture.

7. Turn the tomato shells over so they are hollow side up in the gratin dish, and fill the shells with the tomato soufflé mixture. Spoon any remaining soufflé mixture around the tomatoes, and sprinkle them with the Parmesan cheese. Place the tomatoes in the 375-degree oven, and bake for 25 minutes, until the soufflé mixture puffs up and browns nicely on top.

8. Serve one tomato per person with some of the extra soufflé mixture alongside.

Veal Shank Printanière

The shank is a sinewy muscle from the leg of a calf. Although this muscle can be removed from the attached bone by sliding a sharp knife along the bone, the shank is most often found at supermarkets already sliced crosswise with the round bone in the center for use in osso buco, the classic Italian dish. Here, however, the shank is cut lengthwise into elongated pieces, which are sautéed, flavored with wine, then finished with an abundance of vegetables, including carrots, onions, sugar snap peas, and fresh shelled peas.

TOTAL TIME
About 2¼ hours

YIELD
6 servings

NUTRITION
427 calories
49 g protein
12 g fat
5 g saturated fat
114 mg cholesterol
517 mg sodium
24 g carbohydrate
4 g dietary fiber

The combination of these spring vegetables provides the following daily values: 275% vitamin A, 40% vitamin C, and 25% folate.

2¼ POUNDS BONELESS VEAL SHANK

2 TABLESPOONS UNSALTED BUTTER

¾ POUND SHALLOTS, PEELED

½ POUND SMALL, PEELED CARROTS

2 CUPS WATER

½ CUP CHOPPED ONION

2 TEASPOONS PEELED, CRUSHED, AND CHOPPED GARLIC

1 TABLESPOON ALL-PURPOSE FLOUR

1 TEASPOON *HERBES DE PROVENCE*

½ CUP DRY WHITE WINE

1 TEASPOON SALT

½ TEASPOON FRESHLY GROUND BLACK PEPPER

4 OUNCES SUGAR SNAP PEAS, ANY STRINGS REMOVED (1 CUP)

4 OUNCES FRESH SHELLED PEAS (8 OUNCES UNSHELLED) OR EQUIVALENT FROZEN PEAS (1 CUP)

1. Cut the shank meat lengthwise into about 12 pieces, each 5 inches long and 1½ inches thick. (Note: Do not remove the silver skin visible in the pieces; it is not fat and becomes moist, chewy, and delicate in texture as it cooks.)

2. Melt the butter over medium heat in a large saucepan. When it begins to brown, add the meat strips in one layer, and cook them over medium to high heat for about 20 minutes, turning them occasionally, until they are nicely browned on all sides.

3. Meanwhile, place the peeled shallots and carrots in a medium saucepan with the 2 cups of water. Bring the water to a boil, reduce the heat to low, cover, and boil the vegetables gently for about 8 minutes, until they are tender but still firm. Drain, reserving the cooking liquid. (You should have about 1 cup; adjust yield accordingly, adding water, if necessary, to bring to 1 cup.) Set the shallots and carrots aside in a small bowl.

4. When the veal is nicely browned, transfer it to a plate. Add the chopped onion and garlic to the meat drippings in the pan, and cook them for 1 minute. Add the flour and *herbes de Provence*, mix well, and cook for 10 to 20 seconds longer.

(CONTINUED)

118

5. Add the cup of reserved cooking liquid from the carrots and shallots to the pan along with the wine, salt, and pepper, and bring the mixture to a boil. Return the meat to the pan, bring back to a boil, reduce the heat to very low, cover, and cook gently for 1½ hours, until the meat is tender. (The recipe can be made to this point a few hours ahead.)

6. At serving time, add the reserved shallots and carrots to the stew along with the sugar snap and shelled peas. Bring the stew back to a boil, reduce the heat to low, cover, and boil gently for 10 minutes. Serve.

California Arborio Rice and Pecans

TOTAL TIME
About 30 minutes

YIELD
4 servings

NUTRITION
*290 calories
6 g protein
10 g fat
1 g saturated fat
5 mg cholesterol
309 mg sodium
44 g carbohydrate
2 g dietary fiber*

Although Arborio rice used to be grown exclusively in Italy, this high-starch grain with shorter, fatter kernels than other short-grain rice is now being grown in California, too. I cook Arborio rice from California with pecans in this recipe that goes especially well with stews, braised meat, or fish.

1 TABLESPOON VIRGIN OLIVE OIL

⅓ CUP CHOPPED ONION

⅓ CUP ½-INCH PIECES PECAN NUTS

1 CUP ARBORIO RICE

1¾ CUPS LIGHT CHICKEN STOCK

½ TEASPOON SALT

¼ TEASPOON FRESHLY GROUND BLACK PEPPER

1. Heat the oil in a medium saucepan. Add the onion and pecans, and cook over medium to high heat for 1 minute, stirring constantly. Add the rice, and mix well.

2. Stir in the stock, salt, and pepper, and bring the mixture to a boil. Cover, reduce the heat to low, and cook for 18 to 20 minutes. Serve immediately.

*Veal Shank
Printanière
(page 117) and
California Arborio
Rice and Pecans
(this page)*

Bread Pudding Soufflés with Chocolate-Bourbon Sauce

This dessert can be made ahead and refrigerated, then reheated at serving time until lukewarm in a regular oven, a microwave oven, or on top of the stove in a skillet, with the molds surrounded by water.

❧ ❧ ❧ ❧ ❧ ❧ ❧ ❧

CHOCOLATE SAUCE

1 CUP MILK, WITH 1 TABLESPOON RESERVED (SEE BELOW)

2 TABLESPOONS SUGAR

1 TEASPOON CORNSTARCH DISSOLVED IN THE RESERVED 1 TABLESPOON MILK (SEE ABOVE)

3 OUNCES BITTERSWEET CHOCOLATE, CUT INTO 1-INCH PIECES

1 TABLESPOON BOURBON OR 1 TEASPOON PURE VANILLA EXTRACT

SOUFFLÉS

½ CUP MILK

3 THIN SLICES BREAD (2 OUNCES)

2 TABLESPOONS GOLDEN RAISINS

2 TABLESPOONS MAPLE SYRUP

2 EGGS, SEPARATED

1½ TEASPOONS UNSALTED BUTTER (FOR BUTTERING THE MOLDS)

4 TABLESPOONS SEEDLESS RASPBERRY JAM

1. *For the Chocolate Sauce:* Place the cup of milk (minus 1 tablespoon) and the sugar in a saucepan, and bring the mixture to a boil. Immediately remove the pan from the heat, and stir in the dissolved cornstarch. Add the chocolate pieces, and stir the mixture occasionally until the chocolate is dissolved. Cool to room temperature, and stir in the bourbon or vanilla. (If making the sauce ahead, refrigerate it, covered, and reheat to room temperature in a microwave oven at serving time.)

2. *For the Soufflés:* Preheat the oven to 350 degrees.

3. Place the ½ cup of milk in a bowl, add the bread pieces, and let the bread soak in the milk until it is well saturated, soft, and mushy. Add the raisins, maple syrup, and egg yolks, and stir until the mixture is well homogenized but the bread pieces are still visible.

4. Beat the egg whites in a bowl until they form soft peaks. (They should not be too firm.) Mix the whites into the bread mixture.

5. Butter four individual 1-cup molds. Place 1 tablespoon of the jam in the bottom of each mold, and divide the bread mixture among the molds. Arrange the molds on a tray, and cook them in the 350-degree oven for about 20 minutes, until they are set but not completely firm. Remove from the molds and serve lukewarm with the chocolate sauce.

TOTAL TIME

About 45 minutes

YIELD

4 servings

NUTRITION

392 calories

10 g protein

15 g fat

8 g saturated fat

123 mg cholesterol

202 mg sodium

57 g carbohydrate

2 g dietary fiber

CLAUDINE

Chocolate is man's greatest invention, and together with the bread soufflé and the jam it's a real treat. I hope to be able to make this one for a lot of friends.

Old Favorites Revisited

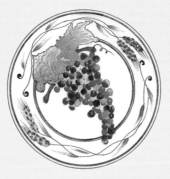

GRATIN OF ASPARAGUS AND HAM

PENNE AU GRATIN

ENDIVE, RADICCHIO, AND WALNUT SALAD

GRAPES AND RAISINS IN CITRUS JUICE

———

Although most of the menus I create for dinner guests are composed of new recipes that I am trying out, sometimes I feel like going back in time and rediscovering the tastes of old favorite dishes. ✢ Claudine had the occasion of eating a classic gratin of asparagus and ham in France. It was made in the conventional way, with a cream sauce poured over packages of ham-wrapped asparagus that are then sprinkled with cheese and baked in the oven. In this menu, I wanted to show her a different interpretation of the same dish. Done in a lighter way, the asparagus is still rolled up in small slices of ham, but the packages are finished simply in the oven with only a little Parmesan cheese and olive oil on top. ✢ The main course is a gratin of pasta. Just like a macaroni au gratin except that it is made with penne, it is a dish that Claudine remembers from her youth and wanted to know how to make. I show her how to prepare a classic light béchamel sauce, add cheddar cheese and tomato to it, then combine it with cooked pasta and bake it into a delightful gratin. ✢ To counterbalance that rich gratin, we serve a bitter salad consisting of radicchio, endive, and walnuts in an  invigorating Dijon mustard-flavored dressing. ✢ A simple fruit dessert, a plain mixture of grapes and raisins, concludes our menu. The chewiness of the raisins contrasts well with the softness of the grapes and finishes our menu nicely.

Red
GRAN
COLEGIATA,
CRIANZA

PEPI, COLLINE
DI SASSI,
SANGIOVESE

Gratin of Asparagus and Ham

TOTAL TIME
About 30 minutes

YIELD
4 servings

NUTRITION
133 calories
12 g protein
8 g fat
2 g saturated fat
21 mg cholesterol
505 mg sodium
3 g carbohydrate
1 g dietary fiber

Asparagus is rich in vitamin C and folate, a B vitamin.

This dish, consisting of asparagus spears wrapped in ham slices, is an old standard. Classically the asparagus packages are served in a rich cream sauce; however, I lighten the dish considerably by simply sprinkling them with a little cheese before finishing them in the oven.

1½ POUNDS LARGE ASPARAGUS (ABOUT 16 SPEARS)

1 CUP WATER

1 TABLESPOON VIRGIN OLIVE OIL

1½ TEASPOONS UNSALTED BUTTER

⅛ TEASPOON SALT

⅛ TEASPOON FRESHLY GROUND BLACK PEPPER

4 SLICES BOILED OR BAKED HAM, BEST POSSIBLE QUALITY (4 OUNCES)

1⅛ TABLESPOONS GRATED PARMESAN CHEESE

1. Preheat the oven to 400 degrees.

2. Using a vegetable peeler, peel the lower third of the asparagus spears, and wash them well in cool water.

3. Bring the water to a boil in a large skillet. Add the asparagus, arranging them in one layer. Bring the water back to a boil, cover, and cook over high heat for about 4 minutes, until the asparagus are tender but still firm. Lift the asparagus spears from the cooking liquid (retaining the liquid in the skillet), and place them on a plate. (You should have ⅓ cup of cooking liquid. If you have less, add additional water to make ⅓ cup; if you have more, boil the liquid until it is reduced to ⅓ cup.)

4. Add the oil, butter, salt, and pepper to the cooking liquid, and set this mixture aside in the skillet.

5. Place 4 asparagus spears together on 1 slice of the ham, and roll the ham tightly around the asparagus. Repeat with the remaining ham and asparagus to make 4 bundles. Place the bundles seam side down and side by side in an attractive gratin dish. Sprinkle with the cheese.

6. Bake the ham and asparagus bundles in the 400-degree oven for 5 to 6 minutes to warm them through, then finish under a hot broiler, placing the dish so the bundles are 3 to 4 inches from the heat. Broil for about 4 minutes, until lightly browned. Meanwhile, reheat the reserved sauce in the skillet.

7. Serve one bundle per person with the sauce spooned over the bundles.

Penne au Gratin

This satisfying dish is a variation of the old favorite, macaroni and cheese. Although the cream sauce is traditionally made with milk and cream, I use only whole milk in this recipe, and the result is quite velvety and rich. To reduce the calorie count even further, use skim milk instead of whole milk.

❦ ❦ ❦ ❦ ❦ ❦ ❦ ❦ ❦

6 OUNCES PENNE PASTA (2¼ CUPS)

1½ TEASPOONS UNSALTED BUTTER

1 TABLESPOON VIRGIN OLIVE OIL

2 TABLESPOONS ALL-PURPOSE FLOUR

2½ CUPS MILK

4½ OUNCES CHEDDAR CHEESE, CUT INTO ½-INCH
   DICE (1 CUP)

¾ TEASPOON SALT

¾ TEASPOON FRESHLY GROUND BLACK PEPPER

1 LARGE TOMATO (8 OUNCES), HALVED, SEEDED,
   AND THE FLESH CUT INTO ½-INCH DICE (1¼ CUPS)

1½ TABLESPOONS GRATED PARMESAN CHEESE

½ TEASPOON PAPRIKA

1. Bring 2½ quarts of water to a boil in a pot. Add the penne, bring the water back to a boil, and boil the pasta over medium heat, uncovered, for about 8 minutes. (The pasta should be al dente, firm to the bite.) Drain the penne in a colander, rinse it under cold tap water until cool, and set it aside.

2. Heat the butter and oil in a saucepan, and add the flour. Cook the mixture over medium heat for about 10 seconds, then add the milk, and stir it in quickly with a whisk so the mixture doesn't scorch. Bring the mixture to a boil, and boil it for 10 seconds. Add the cheddar cheese, salt, and pepper, mix well, then cook over low heat for 3 to 4 minutes. Set aside.

3. When ready to finish the gratin, preheat the oven to 400 degrees.

4. Mix the pasta with the cheddar sauce, and transfer the mixture to a 6-cup gratin dish. Sprinkle the tomato on top of the pasta and sauce. Combine the Parmesan and paprika in a small bowl, and sprinkle the mixture on the pasta. Bake in the 400-degree oven for 30 minutes, until the gratin is bubbly and nicely browned on top. Serve immediately.

Note: If making the gratin at the last moment, and assembling it while the sauce and pasta are both hot, do not bake the gratin. Instead, place it under a hot broiler until golden brown on top.

TOTAL TIME

About 1 hour

YIELD

4 servings

NUTRITION

463 calories

21 g protein

22 g fat

11 g saturated fat

60 mg cholesterol

906 mg sodium

46 g carbohydrate

2 g dietary fiber

CLAUDINE

This penne au gratin is my family's version of macaroni and cheese. It's much healthier and it's fun for everyone to make.

Endive, Radicchio, and Walnut Salad

Made with two bitter greens, endive and radicchio, this salad awakens the taste buds. Carrots and walnuts provide a nice contrast in terms of both taste and texture, and the mustard-flavored vinaigrette is a complementary addition.

TOTAL TIME

15 minutes

YIELD

4 servings

NUTRITION

238 calories

5 g protein

20 g fat

2 g saturated fat

1 mg cholesterol

363 mg sodium

13 g carbohydrate

6 g dietary fiber

Walnuts are a good plant source of omega-3 fatty acids. Endive is a good source of vitamin C and folate.

2 BELGIAN ENDIVES (10 OUNCES), WASHED

1 SMALL HEAD RADICCHIO (5 OUNCES), WASHED

2 CARROTS (6 OUNCES), PEELED AND SHREDDED (1½ CUPS)

½ CUP WALNUT PIECES

DRESSING

1 TABLESPOON DIJON MUSTARD

½ TEASPOON SALT

½ TEASPOON FRESHLY GROUND BLACK PEPPER

1½ TABLESPOONS RED WINE VINEGAR

3 TABLESPOONS VIRGIN OLIVE OIL

1. Cut 1½ inches from the root end of the 2 endives and the radicchio head, and cut these root end pieces into ½-inch chunks. (You should have about 3 cups.) Reserve the pointed endive leaf tips and the radicchio leaves for use later in the recipe. Combine the root end chunks with the shredded carrot and nuts in a bowl.

2. Combine the dressing ingredients in a small bowl, then add the dressing to the endive and radicchio pieces, carrots, and nuts. Toss well.

3. Arrange the radicchio leaves attractively on four plates, and spoon the dressed mixture into the center of the leaves. Arrange the endive leaf tips so they stand, pointed tips up, next to one another all around the dressed salad. Serve immediately.

Grapes and Raisins in Citrus Juice

A simple dessert of grapes and raisins marinated in sweetened citrus juice completes this menu. I love the combination of two contrasting textures in this refreshing dish: the seedless grapes provide crispness, the raisins chewiness.

2 TABLESPOONS LEMON JUICE

⅓ CUP SUGAR

2½ CUPS WHITE SEEDLESS GRAPES

1 CUP DARK RAISINS

1. Mix the lemon juice and sugar together in a bowl large enough to hold the fruit.

2. Wash the grapes, and pat them dry with paper towels. Add the grapes and the raisins to the mixture in the bowl. Mix well, and serve immediately, or refrigerate for up to 4 hours.

3. Serve cold in wine glasses.

TOTAL TIME
10 minutes

YIELD
4 servings

NUTRITION
211 calories
2 g protein
.4 g fat
.1 g saturated fat
0 mg cholesterol
6 mg sodium
56 g carbohydrate
2 g dietary fiber

Puttin' on the Ritz

SCALLOP AND POTATO NAPOLEONS
WITH CHIVE SAUCE

GRILLED STEAK WITH LEMON-THYME BUTTER

STUFFED BUTTERNUT SQUASH

FRENCH VANILLA ICE CREAM

VINCENT'S ALMOND SHORTBREAD COOKIES

———

This menu starts with a dish made of large scallops, which are sliced and cooked, then presented in tiers between layers of crisp potato slices. The most complex part of the recipe is assembling and baking the potato slices; cut so thinly that they are almost transparent, the slices are "sandwiched" around herbs, weighted so they lay flat on a cookie sheet, and baked. The layering of the potato and scallop slices for serving imitates the look of a napoleon, the classic dessert made with puff pastry. This modern, nouvelle cuisine dish is served with a chive sauce. ↓ The main course is a small grilled steak. We use good quality New York strip steaks weighing approximately 7 ounces each for this recipe. After grilling, the steaks are served with pats of butter flavored with thyme and lemon juice. Accompanying the steaks is a stuffed butternut squash, appealingly seasoned with ginger and garlic. ↓ This elegant weekend meal finishes with a simple vanilla ice cream made in the classic French way from a custard cream flavored with flecks of vanilla bean. Almond-flavored cookies are the perfect accompaniment. ↓ Since this menu requires a fair amount of last minute work, it is best prepared during a weekend when you have extra time to devote to it and your invited guests.

White
CAMBRIA,
KATHERINE'S VD,
CHARDONNAY

DOMAINE JEAN-
MAX ROGER,
SANCERRE

Red
DOMAINE DE
CASSAN,
GIGONDAS

Scallop and Potato Napoleons with Chive Sauce

This is an elegant, modern cuisine dish that you might prepare for good friends joining you for a weekend dinner. Thin potato slice "sandwiches" with an herb leaf "filling" are cooked in the oven until tender, then layered with cooked scallop slices. The visual effect is reminiscent of the classic napoleon dessert made with layers of puff pastry. An appealing chive sauce is the perfect accompaniment.

1 LARGE IDAHO POTATO (ABOUT 10 OUNCES)

1 TABLESPOON VIRGIN OLIVE OIL

¼ TEASPOON SALT

1 TABLESPOON FRESH HERB LEAVES (TARRAGON, PARSLEY, OREGANO, AND BASIL)

12 VERY LARGE SCALLOPS (14 OUNCES TO 1 POUND)

½ CUP DRY, FRUITY WHITE WINE

¼ TEASPOON SALT

¼ TEASPOON FRESHLY GROUND BLACK PEPPER

⅓ CUP COARSELY CHOPPED FRESH CHIVES

1½ TABLESPOONS UNSALTED BUTTER

1½ TABLESPOONS EXTRA VIRGIN OLIVE OIL

1. Preheat the oven to 350 degrees.

2. Peel, wash, and trim the potato to make it uniformly oval. Using a potato slicer, cut the potato lengthwise into very thin slices. (You should have 36 to 40 slices.) Do not wash the potato slices.

3. Brush a nonstick cookie sheet lightly with a little of the tablespoon of olive oil, and sprinkle the ¼ teaspoon of salt on top. Place 16 of the potato disks side by side in a single layer on the oiled tray, and place a leaf of one herb in the center of each potato slice.

4. Place another slice of potato on top of each herb leaf to create a sandwich consisting of 2 potato slices with an herb leaf in the middle. Brush the potatoes with the remainder of the tablespoon of oil. Cover the potatoes with a piece of parchment paper, and place a cookie sheet or tray on top to weigh down the potatoes and make them lay flat. Place in the 350-degree oven, and bake for about 20 minutes.

(CONTINUED)

About 1 ½ hours

YIELD

4 servings

NUTRITION

273 calories

17 g protein

13 g fat

4 g saturated fat

42 mg cholesterol

443 mg sodium

16 g carbohydrate

1 g dietary fiber

Potatoes are rich in vitamin C (each serving provides 33% of the daily value). Scallops are a relatively fat-free protein source.

CLAUDINE

*Not only are these
scallop and potato
napoleons elegant,
they also teach
some good tech-
nique. You could
prepare these
potatoes on their
own with just
a dash of sea salt;
they'd go great
with any fish.*

5. Remove the upper tray and parchment paper from the potato slices, and, using a large, flat spatula, remove any potato sandwiches that are nicely browned. Continue cooking the remaining potatoes for another 5 to 8 minutes, removing them with a spatula as they brown. (Note: The potatoes closest to the edges of the cookie sheet brown faster.) When all the potatoes have browned, set them aside until serving time. Reduce the oven temperature to 170 degrees.

6. At serving time, cut each scallop into ½-inch crosswise slices, and place the scallops, wine, and ¼ teaspoon each salt and pepper in a stainless-steel saucepan. Bring the mixture to a boil, and boil the scallops for 10 seconds. Drain, reserving the liquid in the saucepan you just used, and transfer the scallops to an ovenproof dish.

7. Place the scallops and the browned potato slices in the 170-degree oven to keep them warm while you make the chive sauce. Place the chives in the reserved scallop cooking liquid, and bring the liquid to a boil. Transfer the contents of the saucepan to the bowl of a blender, and add the butter and the 1½ tablespoons of olive oil. Blend until smooth and creamy.

8. Divide the sauce among four plates, and place 1 slice of potato on top of the sauce on each plate. Cover the potato slice with 2 slices of scallop, then add more potato, more scallops, etc., until you create a "napoleon," or layered dish of about three or four tiers. Serve immediately.

Stuffed Butternut Squash

TOTAL TIME

About 1 ½ hours

YIELD

4 servings

NUTRITION

272 calories

5 g protein

13 g fat

1 g saturated fat

0 mg cholesterol

531 mg sodium

35 g carbohydrate

1 g dietary fiber

The very simple stuffing for this butternut squash is made primarily of the flesh of the squash itself. Garlic, a bit of ginger, and chopped scallions are added for flavor. If you are not fond of ginger, which gives this combination its unusual taste, you may want to use less of it, or eliminate it altogether. Bread crumbs, tossed with a little oil and sprinkled on top of the filling, become brown and crisp in the oven, and their crunchy texture contrasts nicely with the creaminess of the filling.

1 LARGE BUTTERNUT SQUASH, ABOUT 2¼ POUNDS

3½ TABLESPOONS CANOLA OIL

ABOUT 8 SCALLIONS, MINCED (1 CUP)

3 CLOVES GARLIC, PEELED, CRUSHED, AND
   FINELY CHOPPED (2 TEASPOONS)

½ TABLESPOON CHOPPED FRESH GINGER

½ TEASPOON SALT

¼ TEASPOON FRESHLY GROUND BLACK PEPPER

2 SMALL SLICES BREAD, PROCESSED IN A FOOD
   PROCESSOR TO MAKE 1 CUP FRESH BREAD CRUMBS

1. Preheat the oven to 400 degrees.

2. Split the squash in half lengthwise, and remove the seeds. Score the flesh of the squash, making ½-inch deep cuts through it one way and then the other (in a checkerboard pattern). Arrange the squash halves cut side up on a cookie sheet, and place them in the 400-degree oven for about 60 minutes, until the flesh is tender when pierced with a fork.

3. Meanwhile, heat 2 tablespoons of the canola oil in a large skillet. When the oil is hot, add the scallions, and sauté them for 1½ minutes. Mix in the garlic and ginger, and set the pan aside off the heat.

4. When the squash is cool enough to handle, use a spoon to gently scoop the flesh from the shells (reserving the shells), and add it to the scallions along with the salt and pepper. Mix well, stirring until the squash flesh and scallions are well combined but the mixture is still chunky. Fill the reserved shells with the mixture.

5. In a small bowl, lightly mix the bread crumbs with the remaining 1½ tablespoons of oil, and sprinkle the mixture over the stuffed squash. Arrange the squash halves on a cookie sheet, and place them in the 400-degree oven for about 20 minutes (a little longer if the stuffing is cool). The crumb mixture on top should be nicely browned; if it is not, place the squash under a hot broiler for a few minutes.

6. Cut each of the squash halves in half again, and serve one piece per person.

Note: The skin or shell of the squash is edible.

Butternut squash provides enough beta-carotene in a 3-ounce serving to supply 100% of the daily value for vitamin A.

Grilled Steak with Lemon-Thyme Butter

For this recipe, use good quality strip steaks, prime if you can afford it. Grilled so that the grids of the grill rack form a lattice design on one side, the steaks are served lattice side up with a little butter scented with lemon juice and fresh thyme.

LEMON-THYME BUTTER

2 TABLESPOONS UNSALTED BUTTER

1 TABLESPOON LEMON JUICE

¼ TEASPOON SALT

¼ TEASPOON FRESHLY GROUND BLACK PEPPER

1 TABLESPOON FRESH THYME LEAVES

4 WELL-TRIMMED NEW YORK STRIP STEAKS
(7 OUNCES EACH, TRIMMED WEIGHT)

1 TEASPOON VIRGIN OLIVE OIL

½ TEASPOON SALT

½ TEASPOON FRESHLY GROUND BLACK PEPPER

1. *For the Lemon-Thyme Butter:* Place all the lemon-thyme butter ingredients in the bowl of a blender or spice grinder, and process them into a smooth paste. Set the mixture aside.

2. At cooking time, heat a grill until very hot.

3. Meanwhile, rub the steaks with the teaspoon of olive oil, and sprinkle them on both sides with the ½ teaspoon each salt and pepper. Place the steaks on the rack of the very hot grill, and cook them for about 1 minute on one side, then turn them over, and cook them for 1½ minutes on the other side.

4. Turn the steaks over again, and place them back on the rack at a 90-degree angle from their original grilling position to create a lattice marking from the grids of the grill rack. Cook the steaks for 1 minute longer on the hot grill, for a total of about 3½ minutes for a medium-rare result. (Note: My steaks were approximately ¾-inch thick; increase or reduce the cooking time if your steaks are thinner or thicker, or if you like your meat more well done.) Serve immediately with the lemon-thyme butter.

TOTAL TIME

About 20 minutes

YIELD

4 servings

NUTRITION

383 calories

44 g protein

21 g fat

9 g saturated fat

109 mg cholesterol

525 mg sodium

1 g carbohydrate

.1 g dietary fiber

CLAUDINE

If I have anything to say about it, steak IS what's for dinner — I love it. What I like about this preparation is that it gives you steak in the right proportions.

Grilled Steak with Lemon-Thyme Butter (this page) and Stuffed Butternut Squash (page 135)

French Vanilla Ice Cream

TOTAL TIME
*About 1 hour, plus
churning time*

YIELD
4 servings

NUTRITION
*371 calories
9 g protein
22 g fat
11 g saturated fat
377 mg cholesterol
82 mg sodium
33 g carbohydrate
0 g dietary fiber*

Real French vanilla ice cream is a custard cream, made mostly of milk and egg yolks, that is frozen. In this variation, I combine milk, egg yolks, sugar, and vanilla to make a classic *crème anglaise*. This mixture then is processed in an ice-cream maker, which inflates air into it and lightens it. In addition to vanilla extract, I use vanilla beans in this ice cream; they lend additional flavor and color, producing the black flecks characteristic of this ice cream.

1 VANILLA BEAN, CUT INTO ½-INCH PIECES
⅓ CUP SUGAR
⅓ CUP HEAVY CREAM
6 EGG YOLKS
1 TABLESPOON PURE VANILLA EXTRACT
2 CUPS MILK

1. Place the vanilla pieces and 3 tablespoons of the sugar in a mini-chop or blender bowl, and process them until the vanilla appears as small black dots in the mixture. Transfer the vanilla sugar to a large bowl. Bring the cream to a boil in a small saucepan, and add it to the bowl containing the vanilla sugar. Cool the mixture to room temperature.

2. In another bowl, whisk together the egg yolks, the rest of the sugar, and the vanilla extract. Bring the milk to a boil in a saucepan, and add it slowly to the yolk mixture, stirring constantly as you do so, until the milk is incorporated.

3. Return the milk and egg yolk mixture to the saucepan, and cook it over medium heat, stirring constantly with a flat wooden spatula, until the mixture reaches 170 to

175 degrees. (Take care to stir the mixture as it thickens, or it will curdle on the bottom and stick to the pan.)

4. As soon as the egg yolk mixture reaches 170 to 175 degrees, pour it through a fine strainer into the reserved vanilla and cold cream mixture. Mix well to combine the ingredients and lower the temperature of the mixture. Cool it to room temperature.

5. Place the cooled mixture in an ice-cream maker, and process it according to the manufacturer's instructions for 30 to 45 minutes, until it is thick and creamy. If serving the ice cream within 1 hour, spoon it directly from the ice-cream maker's canister (left suspended in the ice). If serving later, transfer the ice cream to cold containers, and store it in the freezer. Transfer ice cream stored 12 hours or more in the freezer to the refrigerator to soften for at least 45 minutes before serving.

6. To serve, divide the ice cream among four goblets or decorative dishes, and serve, if desired, with a cookie.

Vincent's Almond Shortbread Cookies

Vincent Nattress, who worked tirelessly behind the scenes as chef and manager of our kitchen staff during the taping of *Encore with Claudine*, served up a batch of these delicious almond-flavored cookies as a special treat for all of us on the set. I decided they were just too good not to share with you.

1½ STICKS (6 OUNCES) UNSALTED BUTTER, SOFTENED

½ CUP SUGAR

2 CUPS ALL-PURPOSE FLOUR

½ CUP BLANCHED ALMONDS, GROUND TO A FINE POWDER IN A FOOD PROCESSOR

¼ TEASPOON SALT

1½ TEASPOONS ALMOND EXTRACT

1 EGG YOLK

1 TO 2 TABLESPOONS CREAM (OPTIONAL)

⅓ CUP WHOLE BLANCHED ALMONDS

1. Mix the butter and sugar together in a mixing bowl until smooth and creamy. In a separate bowl, combine the flour, ground almonds, and salt. Add the flour mixture to the butter mixture, and mix well. Add the almond extract and egg yolk, and knead until well combined. Note: If the dough seems dry and doesn't come together well, mix in enough of the cream to enable you to form it into a ball. Refrigerate the dough for at least 1 hour.

2. When ready to bake the cookies, preheat the oven to 375 degrees.

3. Roll out the dough on a lightly floured surface until it about ¼ inch thick throughout. Cut into desired shapes, and arrange on a cookie sheet. Press a whole almond into the center of each of the cookies. Bake for 14 to 18 minutes, then cool on a rack.

TOTAL TIME

30 to 40 minutes

YIELD

About 4 dozen medium-sized cookies; serving size 2 cookies

NUTRITION

202 calories

3 g protein

13 g fat

5 g saturated fat

36 mg cholesterol

125 mg sodium

17 g carbohydrate

1 g dietary fiber

Casual Corner Café

TUNA STEAKS WITH *TAPENADE* COATING

BRAISED DUCK WITH FENNEL AND OLIVES

NOODLES AND PEAS

RHUBARB WITH BERRY NECTAR AND MINT

———

This menu features dishes that you might enjoy in the relaxed atmosphere of a small restaurant or bistro. This is a satisfying style of cooking with assertive tastes and, in this case, a lot of olives. ✷ Our menu begins with a small steak of tuna covered on one side with a mixture of olives and capers known as *tapenade*, which comes from the Provençal for caper, *tapeno*. The fish is sautéed briefly in a skillet *tapenade* side down and served surrounded by arugula leaves. ✷ The main dish is a braised skinless duck, which has about the same calorie and cholesterol count as skinless chicken. Cooked in a cast-iron *cocotte,* the duck is finished with fennel and green olives. ✷ We serve the duck with a dish of noodles and peas. If good quality fresh

White
STONESTREET,
SAUVIGNON
BLANC

Red
KENDALL
JACKSON,
BUCKEYE,
CABERNET
SAUVIGNON

peas are available, use them; if not, the frozen petite peas called for in the recipe are quite acceptable. The dessert is a rhubarb and berry mixture containing mint and red wine. For this delightful summer dish, the rhubarb is cooked first with the wine and mint, and the berries — blueberries, strawberries, and blackberries — are stirred in later and cooked very briefly.

Tuna Steaks with Tapenade Coating

This recipe is excellent when prepared with tuna, but it's good, too, made with other fish that will hold their shape when sautéed in a skillet. I use small but fairly thick steaks, covering each with *tapenade*, a mixture of different types of olives, capers, anchovy fillets, and garlic. For maximum flavor transfer, I cook the steaks *tapenade* side down over high heat to start.

TOTAL TIME
About 30 minutes

YIELD
4 servings

NUTRITION
201 calories
28 g protein
9 g fat
1 g saturated fat
53 mg cholesterol
1099 mg sodium
1 g carbohydrate
.4 g dietary fiber

Tuna and anchovies are good sources of omega-3 fatty acids. The fat in olives is predominantly monounsaturated, the type that helps lower "bad" cholesterol and increase "good" cholesterol in the body. Arugula lends vitamin C, folate, and carotenoids.

TAPENADE

¼ CUP PITTED KALAMATA OLIVES

¼ CUP OIL-CURED OLIVES

2 TABLESPOONS DRAINED CAPERS

3 ANCHOVY FILLETS (PACKED IN OIL)

1 LARGE CLOVE GARLIC, PEELED

1 POUND YELLOWFIN TUNA (CENTER CUT), COMPLETELY CLEANED OF ALL SINEW (ABOUT 5 INCHES LONG AND 2½ TO 3 INCHES IN DIAMETER)

1 TABLESPOON CANOLA OIL

½ TEASPOON SALT

1 CUP ARUGULA LEAVES, CLEANED

1. Place all the *tapenade* ingredients in the bowl of a small food processor, and process until finely chopped but not pureed. (Yield: About ½ cup.)

2. Cut the tuna into 4 equal-size pieces, each about 1 inch thick and 2½ to 3 inches in diameter. Cover the top of each steak with 2 tablespoons of the *tapenade* mixture, patting it firmly over the surface of the steak.

3. At serving time, preheat the oven to 180 degrees.

4. Heat the tablespoon of oil until hot in a large skillet. Place the steaks *tapenade* side down in the hot skillet, and sprinkle them with the salt. Cover, and cook the steaks over high heat for about 1½ minutes. Turn them over, *tapenade* side up, cover, and cook for another 1½ minutes over medium to high heat.

5. Transfer the steaks to an ovenproof platter, and warm them in the 180-degree oven for at least 5 to 10 minutes but up to 30 minutes. Serve the steaks whole or sliced, surrounded by the arugula leaves.

Braised Duck with Fennel and Olives

TOTAL TIME

About 1 ½ hours

YIELD

4 servings

NUTRITION

264 calories

14 g protein

16 g fat

4 g saturated fat

47 mg cholesterol

1744 mg sodium

12 g carbohydrate

2 g dietary fiber

Without the skin, breast of duck can contain as little as 1.2 grams of fat per cooked ounce.

Many people do not realize that duck has no more calories than chicken, and the calorie count for both is considerably lower when the skin is removed, as it is from the duck in this recipe. ↴   I use a little of the duck fat in place of olive oil or butter to brown the duck pieces. Then, in the pan drippings, I cook fennel, flavoring it with red wine, wine vinegar, and a dash of sugar to caramelize it a little. I finish cooking the duck in the same mixture, at the end adding the olives and duck liver. This is a delicious stew, and one duck is plenty for four people.

1 LONG ISLAND DUCK (ABOUT 5¼ POUNDS)

½ TEASPOON SALT

½ TEASPOON FRESHLY GROUND BLACK PEPPER

1 BULB FENNEL (1 POUND)

1 CUP WATER

¼ CUP RED WINE

¼ CUP RED WINE VINEGAR

1 TABLESPOON SUGAR

20 LARGE BLACK OR GREEN OLIVES, OR A MIXTURE OF BOTH, WITH OR WITHOUT PITS (8 OUNCES), RINSED UNDER COLD WATER

1 TABLESPOON MINCED FRESH PARSLEY (OPTIONAL)

1. Cut the duck into 4 pieces, 2 legs and 2 breasts. Using a towel, grab hold of the skin, and peel it off. (The skin is not used in this recipe. It can be kept to make crackling or discarded.) Remove the breast from the carcass, and cut each wing into 2 segments. Cut off the tips of each drumstick. Use of the gizzard is optional but, if using it, cut off and discard the silver skin surrounding it. (The 2 legs and 2 breast pieces should weigh about 1½ pounds; the 4 wing pieces, gizzard, liver, and heart should weigh about 12 ounces.) Cut enough duck fat into ¼-inch pieces so that you have 1 tablespoon of duck fat pieces.

2. Heat the tablespoon of duck fat until melted and hot in a large, sturdy saucepan. Add the wings and gizzard, and cook them over medium heat for 15 minutes, turning the duck pieces occasionally. Add the breasts and legs, and sprinkle the duck pieces with ¼ teaspoon each of the salt and pepper. Brown the duck pieces on all sides over medium heat for 15 minutes. Transfer the duck to a plate.

3. Meanwhile, slice the fennel bulb in half and cut each half, into ¼-inch slices. Place the fennel in the same saucepan you used to cook the duck, and add 1 cup water. Bring the water to a boil over high heat, then reduce the heat to low, cover, and cook gently for 6 to 8 minutes, until all the water has evaporated and the fennel is starting to brown.

4. Add the duck heart to the pan along with the remaining ¼ teaspoon each salt and pepper, wine, vinegar, and sugar. Cook over medium heat for 10 minutes.

5. Return the duck pieces to the pan, arranging them on top of the fennel. Bring to a boil, reduce the heat to very low, cover, and cook for 30 minutes. (The recipe can be prepared to this point up to 4 hours ahead.)

6. At serving time, add the olives and duck liver, and bring the mixture to a boil. Reduce the heat to low, cover, and warm over low heat for 15 minutes. Serve, sprinkled with the parsley, if desired.

I don't use fennel that much, but I really love it. It's very easy to use: you can just sauté the fennel by itself and serve it up.

Braised Duck with Fennel and Olives (these pages) and Noodles and Peas (page 146)

Noodles and Peas

TOTAL TIME

25 minutes

YIELD

4 servings

NUTRITION

448 calories

16 g protein

13 g fat

2 g saturated fat

84 mg cholesterol

413 mg sodium

66 g carbohydrate

4 g dietary fiber

Peas are a good source of vitamin C and folate, a B vitamin.

Use imported fettucine or tagliatelle for this dish, cooking it at the last moment and combining it with the petite peas, Parmesan cheese, salt, pepper, and some of the cooking water from the pasta.

¾ POUND PASTA, EITHER EGG NOODLES OR FETTUCINE (INCLUDING THE LARGE FETTUCINE, CALLED TAGLIATELLE), PREFERABLY IMPORTED

1 CUP FROZEN PETITE PEAS, DEFROSTED

3 TABLESPOONS GRATED PARMESAN CHEESE

2½ TABLESPOONS VIRGIN OLIVE OIL

½ TEASPOON SALT

½ TEASPOON FRESHLY GROUND BLACK PEPPER

⅔ CUP COOKING WATER FROM THE PASTA

1. Bring 3 to 4 quarts of water to a boil in a large pot. Add the pasta, and boil it until tender (about 10 minutes for imported pasta). Note: I prefer my pasta slightly al dente, a little firm to the bite, but tender.

2. Place the frozen peas in a strainer, then run them under hot tap water until all the ice particles have melted and the peas are defrosted. Place the peas in a large serving bowl with the cheese, oil, salt, and pepper.

3. When the pasta is cooked, remove ⅔ cup of its cooking liquid, and add it to the bowl with the peas. Drain the pasta, and add it to the bowl. Toss well, and serve immediately.

Rhubarb and Berry Nectar with Mint

This is one of my favorite desserts in full summer, when rhubarb is available and mint abounds in my garden. I like a deep, berry-flavored red wine in this preparation. I add cranberry juice along with the wine, but feel free to substitute another type of juice. Likewise, instead of adding strawberry jam, take this perfect opportunity to use all the little dabs of leftover jams taking up space in the refrigerator.

½ BUNCH FRESH PEPPERMINT (ABOUT 1 CUP LOOSELY PACKED LEAVES)

1 POUND RHUBARB STALKS (ALL LEAVES REMOVED AND DISCARDED), CUT INTO 2-INCH PIECES

½ CUP RED WINE (BEAUJOLAIS OR SYRAH ARE GOOD CHOICES)

½ CUP CRANBERRY JUICE

6 OUNCES STRAWBERRY JAM

2 TABLESPOONS SUGAR

6 OUNCES BLACKBERRIES, BLUEBERRIES, OR STRAWBERRIES, WASHED AND HULLED

½ CUP SOUR CREAM

4 TO 6 SLICES BRIOCHE OR POUND CAKE, OR 8 TO 12 COOKIES

1. Remove the stem tips with a few leaves attached from 4 to 6 of the mint sprigs, and set them aside for use as a decoration. Gather the remaining sprigs of mint into a bundle, and tie them together with kitchen twine. Place in a saucepan (preferably stainless steel), and add all the remaining ingredients except the berries, sour cream, and pound cake.

2. Bring the mixture to a boil, cover, reduce the heat to low, and cook for about 8 minutes. Add the berries, bring back to a boil, and cook, covered, for 2 minutes. The mixture should be somewhat soupy. Cool, cover, and refrigerate until serving time.

3. For each serving, arrange about 1 cup of the rhubarb and berry mixture in a deep plate. Place 1 rounded tablespoon of sour cream in the middle. Top with one of the reserved mint sprig tips. Serve with a slice of brioche or pound cake or a few cookies.

TOTAL TIME
About 20 minutes, plus cooling time

YIELD
4 to 6 servings

NUTRITION
425 calories
4 g protein
8 g fat
4 g saturated fat
38 mg cholesterol
124 mg sodium
81 g carbohydrate
6 g dietary fiber

When combined in this dish, blackberries and rhubarb provide almost 70% of the daily value for vitamin C.

Comfort Food

Lentil and Barley Soup

Bean Sprout Salad

Catfish with Fresh Peas in Zucchini "Boats"

Apples Grandma

———

This menu starts with a robust and filling lentil and barley soup. Usually, when I make this type of soup, I prepare more than I need for one meal and freeze the leftovers to enjoy on a day when I am pressed for time. In this recipe, I use one pound of lentils, which serves eight people easily. The soup is flavored with a little hot Italian sausage and contains a large assortment of vegetables – from leeks to onions to carrots. Pearl barley thickens the mixture and makes it creamy. An easy soup to make, it is always a satisfying crowd-pleaser. ✦ The main course is catfish, now widely available, well-priced, and quite delicious. The fish is combined with fresh peas and mushrooms and, for an attractive and different presentation, is served in little containers made of zucchini. ✦ A refreshing bean sprout salad affords us an unusual way of using bean sprouts. An excellent addition to sandwiches, the salad will keep for several days in the refrigerator. ✦ We finish with a homey apple dessert. To flavor this classic recipe featuring whole apples, we add some grenadine syrup, sugar, and pignola nuts. The apples are cooked on slices of bread, which soak up their juices and are great eaten with them. This dish is best served at room temperature.

White
STONESTREET,
CHARDONNAY

Red
KENDALL
JACKSON,
GRAND
RESERVE,
ZINFANDEL

Dessert White
MUSCAT
DE ST. JEAN
DE MINERVOIS

Lentil and Barley Soup

TOTAL TIME

About 2 hours

YIELD

8 servings

NUTRITION

423 calories

30 g protein

10 g fat

3 g saturated fat

43 mg cholesterol

1149 mg sodium

55 g carbohydrate

21 g dietary fiber

Lentils and barley are high in fiber. Lentils are very high in folate, a B vitamin.

This heavy, comforting, winter soup is one of my favorites and could be a meal in itself when served with a beautiful, crusty bread, a glass of wine, and a piece of cheese. This recipe serves more than four, but it is more economical to make it in larger batches and freeze what is not needed. When you are ready to eat the soup again, defrost it, heat it through, and enjoy it a second time.

1 POUND LENTILS, WASHED AND DRAINED

½ CUP (4 OUNCES) PEARL BARLEY

4 QUARTS LIGHT CHICKEN OR BEEF STOCK

2 HOT ITALIAN SAUSAGES (ABOUT 5 OUNCES TOTAL), CUT INTO ½-INCH PIECES

1 TABLESPOON *HERBES DE PROVENCE*

1 TABLESPOON SALT

1 LEEK (8 OUNCES), CUT INTO ½-INCH PIECES AND WASHED (ABOUT 3 CUPS)

1 LARGE ONION (8 OUNCES), PEELED AND CUT INTO ½-INCH PIECES (ABOUT 2 CUPS)

2 CARROTS (6 OUNCES), PEELED AND CUT INTO ½-INCH PIECES (ABOUT ¾ CUP)

5 LARGE CLOVES GARLIC, PEELED, CRUSHED, AND COARSELY CHOPPED (2 TABLESPOONS)

½ TEASPOON TABASCO HOT PEPPER SAUCE (OPTIONAL)

½ CUP GRATED SWISS CHEESE (OPTIONAL)

1. Place all the ingredients except the Tabasco and cheese (optional) in a large kettle, and bring the mixture to a boil. Reduce the heat to very low, cover, and cook gently for 1½ hours. (Yield: 16 cups)

2. Emulsify the cooked soup with a handheld immersion blender for 8 to 10 seconds to make the mixture somewhat creamy. (Alternatively, place 2 cups of the soup in the bowl of a food processor, and process for 20 seconds. Combine the puree with the remaining soup.)

3. Add the Tabasco to the soup. Serve in bowls, garnished, if desired, with the grated Swiss cheese.

Note: This soup tends to thicken as it cools. When reheating leftover soup, thin it, if necessary, by adding a little water.

Bean Sprout Salad

I often sauté bean sprouts for dishes I prepare at home, and sometimes have extra raw sprouts. This versatile salad quickly and easily solves the problem of what to do with those leftover sprouts. It's become a family favorite.

2 TEASPOONS BLACK SESAME SEEDS

2 TEASPOONS WHITE SESAME SEEDS

1 POUND BEAN SPROUTS

6 SCALLIONS, CLEANED AND CUT INTO
   ½-INCH PIECES (¾ CUP)

2 TABLESPOONS RED WINE VINEGAR

1½ TEASPOONS SUGAR

½ TEASPOON SALT

1 TABLESPOON SESAME SEED OIL

1 TABLESPOON CANOLA OIL

⅛ TEASPOON TABASCO HOT PEPPER SAUCE

1. Preheat the oven to 375 degrees.

2. Distribute the black and white sesame seeds on a cookie sheet. Bake them in the 375-degree oven for 6 to 8 minutes, until they are lightly toasted. Set the seeds aside.

3. Bring 4 cups of water to a boil in a large saucepan. Add the bean sprouts, and bring the water back to a boil, which will take 3 to 4 minutes. Boil the sprouts for 10 seconds, then drain them.

4. In a bowl large enough to hold the finished salad, mix together the remaining ingredients. Add the sprouts and toasted sesame seeds, and mix well. Serve at room temperature, or refrigerate and serve cold. (This dish will keep, refrigerated, for 3 to 4 days.)

TOTAL TIME

About 20 minutes

YIELD

4 servings

NUTRITION

120 calories

4 g protein

8 g fat

.9 g saturated fat

0 mg cholesterol

300 mg sodium

9 g carbohydrate

2 g dietary fiber

Bean sprouts are rich in vitamin C and folate. They also contain phytoestrogens that may protect against cancer.

Catfish with Fresh Peas in Zucchini "Boats"

Farmed catfish are now available all over the country, and the quality is much better than what I remember in my youth, when they came from muddy ponds. Today, catfish have a nice nutty taste, especially if you remove any black flesh from the surface of the fillets (which tends to be a bit stronger in taste). In this fast, easy recipe, the fish are prepared with zucchini, shelled peas, and mushrooms.

1½ TABLESPOONS VIRGIN OLIVE OIL

1 TABLESPOON UNSALTED BUTTER

1 ZUCCHINI (ABOUT 6 OUNCES), QUARTERED LENGTHWISE

1 POUND FRESH PEAS, SHELLED (8 OUNCES SHELLED), ABOUT 1⅓ CUPS

5 OUNCES MUSHROOMS, WASHED AND CUT INTO ½-INCH DICE (ABOUT 1¾ CUPS)

1 TEASPOON SALT

½ TEASPOON FRESHLY GROUND BLACK PEPPER

4 FILLETS CATFISH (ABOUT 6 OUNCES EACH, 1½ POUNDS TOTAL), CLEANED OF ALL FAT, SKIN, AND SINEWS

4 SLICES LEMON

PARSLEY SPRIGS, FOR GARNISH

1. Heat the oil and butter in a large skillet. Add the zucchini strips, peas, mushrooms, ¾ teaspoon of the salt, and ¼ teaspoon of the pepper. Cover, and cook over high heat for 4 minutes. Using a slotted spoon, remove the zucchini, peas, and mushrooms from the skillet, and place them on a plate.

2. Sprinkle the remaining ¼ teaspoon each of salt and pepper on the catfish fillets, and place them in a single layer in the hot drippings in the skillet. Cook them over high heat for 2½ minutes, then turn them over, reduce the heat to medium, and cook them for 2½ minutes on the second side.

3. Meanwhile, make a slit down the fleshy center of each zucchini strip (without cutting through the surrounding skin at the edges) to create small receptacles or "boats." Arrange one zucchini boat on each of four dinner plates, and fill the center cavity of the boats with the mushroom and pea mixture.

4. Place a fish fillet alongside the zucchini boat on each plate. Garnish the fillets with the lemon slices and parsley.

TOTAL TIME

20 to 30 minutes

YIELD

4 servings

NUTRITION

365 calories

31 g protein

21 g fat

5 g saturated fat

88 mg cholesterol

676 mg sodium

12 g carbohydrate

4 g dietary fiber

This dish is a good source of fiber. Peas and zucchini are rich in vitamin C. Peas are also a good source of folate. Wild catfish (not grain fed) is rich in protective omega-3 fatty acids.

Catfish with Fresh Peas in Zucchini "Boats" (this page) and Bean Sprout Salad (page 151)

Apples Grandma

TOTAL TIME

About 1 ½ hours

YIELD

4 servings

NUTRITION

337 calories

4 g protein

9 g fat

3 g saturated fat

12 mg cholesterol

90 mg sodium

65 g carbohydrate

6 g dietary fiber

*Although not
notably high in
vitamins, apples
contain polyphe-
nols, natural plant
chemicals that
are powerful
antioxidants.*

This classic French-style apple dessert is made with whole, cored apples. In this recipe, I place slices of bread underneath the apples. These slices soak up the juice of the apples, the apricot preserves, and the grenadine to produce a very flavorful dessert, especially when it is served lukewarm.

4 GOLDEN DELICIOUS APPLES (ABOUT 2 POUNDS)

4 THIN SLICES BREAD (2 OUNCES)

5 SPRIGS FRESH MINT

1½ TABLESPOONS UNSALTED BUTTER

¼ CUP APRICOT PRESERVES

2 TABLESPOONS GRENADINE SYRUP

½ CUP WATER

2 TABLESPOONS SUGAR

3 TABLESPOONS PIGNOLA NUTS

1. Preheat the oven to 400 degrees.

2. Core the apples, and peel the skin from the top third of each apple.

3. Arrange the 4 slices of bread in a single layer in a gratin dish, and place an apple, peeled side up, in the center of each slice. Place a sprig of mint in the hole in the center of each apple, then divide the butter among the apples, placing it on top of the mint in each hole.

4. In a small bowl, mix together the apricot preserves, grenadine, and water. Pour the mixture over the apples, and sprinkle them with the sugar and nuts.

5. Bake the apples in the 400-degree oven for 60 to 75 minutes, or until the apples are very tender and nicely browned on top. Cool, garnish with the remaining mint sprig, and serve lukewarm or at room temperature with the nuts and surrounding juices.

Fall Colors Feast

Broccoli Cream with Tapioca

Wild Rice with Pignola Nuts and Peas

Monkfish *Américaine*

Roast Caramelized Pears

———

This fall meal starts with a cream of broccoli soup. Readily available and good this time of year, broccoli is pureed for this recipe into a smooth, velvety mixture. The soup is thickened with pearl tapioca. The tiny, perfectly round pellets of this starchy substance triple in size and become transparent when cooked. ⅄ We follow the soup with a sturdy stew made with monkfish, because it holds its shape well, and including tomato, leek, white wine, and Armagnac, with a garnish of fresh tarragon.

White
LE BONHEUR,
CHARDONNAY

Red
CAMBRIA, SYRAH

Dessert
MALMSEY
10 YEAR
MADEIRA

This monkfish *Américaine* is served with wild rice flavored with pignola nuts and peas. The rice makes a very nice accompaniment that also works well with roasts or sautéed meats. ⅄ Our delightful autumn menu finishes with roasted pears. When cooking pears whole, as they are in this recipe, ripe Anjou or Bartlett varieties are the best choice.

Broccoli Cream with Tapioca

TOTAL TIME

About 45 minutes

YIELD

4 servings

NUTRITION

181 calories

7 g protein

8 g fat

4 g saturated fat

36 mg cholesterol

654 mg sodium

21 g carbohydrate

4 g dietary fiber

*Broccoli is rich in
vitamins A and C,
folate, carotenoids,
calcium, and fiber.*

This cream of broccoli soup is made with the heads, or crowns, of broccoli; the stems are cut into a julienne and served as a garnish. The soup is thickened with pearl tapioca – tiny, glistening jewel-like balls – which are cooked on their own first in a lot of water. The cooked tapioca tends to thicken and stick together after sitting awhile, but its pellets can be loosened again by adding a little water. The tapioca makes a great addition to the soup, enhancing its taste as well as its appearance.

¼ CUP PEARL TAPIOCA

2 STALKS BROCCOLI, ABOUT 1¼ POUNDS

3½ CUPS GOOD QUALITY CHICKEN STOCK

1 MEDIUM ONION (6 OUNCES), PEELED AND CUT INTO 1-INCH PIECES

1 TEASPOON SALT

¼ TEASPOON FRESHLY GROUND BLACK PEPPER

⅓ CUP HEAVY CREAM

1. Bring 4 cups of water to a boil in a medium saucepan. Add the tapioca, bring the mixture to a boil, cover, reduce the heat to low, and boil gently for 20 minutes. Drain the tapioca in a colander, then rinse it for 15 to 20 seconds under cold water to stop the cooking. Set the tapioca aside. You should have about ¾ cup.

2. Cut off the heads of the broccoli stalks. (The heads should weigh about 12 ounces.) Cut the heads into chunks, and set them aside. Peel the broccoli stems to remove the fibrous outer skin, and cut the stalks into 2- to 3-inch chunks. Cut these chunks into ⅜-inch-thick slices, then stack the slices, and cut them into ⅜-inch sticks. (You should have about 1¼ cups of broccoli sticks.)

3. Bring the stock to a boil in a large saucepan, and add the broccoli sticks. Bring the stock back to a boil, and boil the sticks for about 1½ minutes. Remove the sticks with a skimmer, and set them aside. Add the broccoli head pieces and onion to the stock, return the mixture to a boil, and cook, covered, over high heat for 10 minutes.

4. Transfer the contents of the saucepan to the bowl of a blender along with the salt and pepper, and blend the mixture for 45 seconds to 1 minute, until smooth. You should have about 4 cups of soup at this point.

5. At serving time, place the broccoli soup in a saucepan. If the reserved cooked tapioca pellets are sticking together (as they tend to do after sitting awhile), add 2 to 3 tablespoons of cold water to them, and mix it in until they separate. Add the tapioca to the soup along with the broccoli sticks. Stir in the cream, and bring the mixture to a simmer. Serve immediately.

Wild Rice with Pignola Nuts and Peas

Not really rice at all but a long-grain marsh grass, wild rice always enhances a meal and makes it a little more elegant. While it used to be very expensive, it is affordable nowadays. I flavor the rice with grated lemon rind and jalapeño pepper for this recipe, and garnish it with baby peas and pignola nuts.

¾ CUP WILD RICE

1 TABLESPOON UNSALTED BUTTER

1 TABLESPOON VIRGIN OLIVE OIL

½ CUP CHOPPED ONION

¼ CUP PIGNOLA NUTS

1 TEASPOON GRATED LEMON RIND

1 TEASPOON CHOPPED JALAPEÑO PEPPER (OR LESS
  IF YOU DO NOT TOLERATE "HOTNESS" WELL)

½ TEASPOON SALT

1¼ CUPS CHICKEN STOCK

½ CUP FROZEN BABY PEAS

1. Place the rice and 3 cups cold water in a medium saucepan, and bring the mixture to a boil. Cover, reduce the heat to low, and boil gently for 40 minutes. Drain. You will have about 2 cups of rice, some of which will have "blossomed" or "bloomed."

2. Heat the butter and oil in a large saucepan, and add the onion and nuts. Cook over medium to high heat for about 5 minutes, stirring occasionally, until the nuts are nicely browned.

3. Add the rice, lemon rind, jalapeño, salt, and chicken stock. Cook, covered, over low heat for 20 to 30 minutes, until most of the chicken stock is absorbed. Add the peas, and cook for 2 minutes longer. Serve.

TOTAL TIME

About 1 ½ hours

YIELD

4 servings

NUTRITION

249 calories

9 g protein

12 g fat

3 g saturated fat

12 mg cholesterol

316 mg sodium

28 g carbohydrate

3 g dietary fiber

This side dish
is a good source
of fiber.

Monkfish Américaine

This is a classic way to cook monkfish, and one that I am familiar with from childhood. The fish is made into a stew with onions, carrots, leeks, celery, tomatoes, and garlic. Seasoned with *herbes de Provence*, cayenne, and fennel seeds, it is flavored with white wine, Cognac, and tarragon, and is served with rice. The stew can be made ahead and reheated as needed.

❧   ❧   ❧   ❧   ❧   ❧   ❧   ❧   ❧

2¼ POUNDS MONKFISH, PREFERABLY LARGE FILLETS, WITH MOST OF THE BLACK FLESH REMOVED FROM THE SURFACE

2 TABLESPOONS VIRGIN OLIVE OIL

1 ONION (4 OUNCES), PEELED AND CUT INTO ½-INCH PIECES (1 CUP)

1 CARROT (2½ OUNCES), PEELED AND CUT INTO ½-INCH PIECES (½ CUP)

1 SMALL LEEK (3 OUNCES), PEELED, WASHED, AND CUT INTO ½-INCH PIECES (1 CUP)

1 RIB CELERY (2 OUNCES), CUT INTO ½-INCH PIECES (⅓ CUP)

1 LARGE TOMATO (8 OUNCES), CUT INTO ½-INCH PIECES (1¼ CUPS)

2 TABLESPOONS TOMATO PASTE

3 CLOVES GARLIC, PEELED

1 TEASPOON *HERBES DE PROVENCE*

1½ TEASPOONS SALT

⅛ TEASPOON CAYENNE PEPPER

½ TEASPOON FENNEL SEEDS

1 TABLESPOON ARMAGNAC OR COGNAC

½ CUP DRY, FRUITY WHITE WINE

1 CUP WATER

1 TABLESPOON UNSALTED BUTTER

1 TABLESPOON CHOPPED FRESH TARRAGON

1. Cut the monkfish fillets into 12 large (2- to 3-inch) pieces weighing a total of about 2 pounds.

2. Heat the oil in a large, sturdy saucepan until it is hot but not smoking. Add the onion, carrot, leek, and celery, and cook over low to medium heat for 5 minutes. Add the tomato, tomato paste, garlic, *herbes de Provence,* salt, cayenne, fennel seeds, Armagnac, wine, and water. Bring the mixture to a boil, and cook it over medium heat for 5 minutes.

3. Add the fish to the mixture in the saucepan, cover, and simmer gently over low heat for 15 minutes. Remove the pieces of fish from the saucepan, and set them aside on a platter. Add the tablespoon of butter to the mixture in the pan.

4. Using a handheld immersion blender, emulsify the vegetables in the saucepan into a fine puree or sauce. (Alternatively, transfer the mixture to the bowl of a conventional blender, process, then return the mixture to the pan.) Place the fish in the sauce, sprinkle with the tarragon, and bring to a boil. Serve immediately.

TOTAL TIME

30 to 40 minutes

YIELD

4 servings

NUTRITION

350 calories

35 g protein

14 g fat

3 g saturated fat

65 mg cholesterol

1175 mg sodium

13 g carbohydrate

2 g dietary fiber

CLAUDINE

The monkfish is a wonderful, dense fish; it used to be considered a garbage fish, but people are using it more and more, which I think it deserves.

Monkfish Américaine (this page) and Wild Rice with Pignola Nuts and Peas (page 159)

Roast Caramelized Pears

The success of desserts with pears depends largely on their quality and ripeness. For this recipe, Anjou or Bartlett pears are roasted at a high temperature for more than 1 hour, until their juices caramelize and turn a rich mahogany color. The juices are then diluted with a little Madeira wine, and the pears are served at room temperature with the Madeira juices.

TOTAL TIME

About 1 ½ hours

YIELD

4 servings

NUTRITION

216 calories

1 g protein

5 g fat

2 g saturated fat

12 mg cholesterol

1 mg sodium

43 g carbohydrate

4 g dietary fiber

Pears are high in fiber.

4 ANJOU OR BARTLETT PEARS WITH STEMS
(ABOUT 2 POUNDS), ALL OF EQUAL RIPENESS

2 TEASPOONS UNSALTED BUTTER

1 TABLESPOON LEMON JUICE

¼ CUP SUGAR

3 TABLESPOONS MADEIRA WINE

MINT LEAVES, FOR DECORATION

1. Preheat the oven to 425 degrees.

2. Do not remove the stems from the pears, but peel them with a vegetable peeler. Then, using a melon baller, citrus spoon, or half-teaspoon measuring spoon, remove the seeds from each pear by digging them out from the base.

3. Melt the butter in a small gratin dish. Stir the lemon juice into the butter. Roll the pears in this mixture and sprinkle them with the sugar.

4. Stand the pears upright in the gratin dish, and place them in the preheated 425-degree oven. Cook the pears for about 1¼ hours, basting them with their own cooking juices every 15 or 20 minutes, until they are nicely browned and tender when pierced with the point of a knife. The juices should be caramelized and a rich brown color at the end of the cooking; if they should begin to burn, prevent this by immediately adding 3 to 4 tablespoons of water to the gratin dish.

5. When the pears are tender, remove them from the oven. Add the Madeira to the dish, and stir well to combine it with the juices.

6. Cool the pears to room temperature. Serve them with the accumulated juices spooned over and around them. Decorate with mint leaves.

Relaxing Summer Supper

PÂTÉS OF MUSHROOM WITH TOMATILLO SAUCE OR
TOMATO DRESSING

GRILLED MARINATED PORK FILLET

EGGPLANT RAGOUT

CORN PANBREAD

BAKED PEACHES WITH ALMONDS

———

This summer menu begins with small pâtés of mushroom, which I particularly like when made with wild mushrooms I collect during the summer. Served cold,
these can be made ahead and are ideal as the first course of a hot summer evening dinner.
We prepare two sauces to serve with the pâtés: one is made with the fruit called
tomatillos, which resemble green tomatoes and are widely used in Mexican cooking;
and one is a standard tomato dressing. Either of these sauces are excellent with the
pâtés and can also be served with poached or steamed fish.   ✣   The main course is
a grilled pork tenderloin. We often grill during the summer, and the lean, tender pork
lends itself well to grilling, especially when it is marinated in a Asian-inspired sauce
made with Vietnamese fish sauce and jalapeño pepper.   ✣   We continue this eclectic
menu with an eggplant ragout. A type of ratatouille made here only with eggplant,
onion, and seasonings, it should be served cool or at room temperature. On its own,
it makes a good first course, or it can be served as an accompaniment for a roast, as it
is here, or a stew.   ✣   As a bonus, I wanted to show Claudine how to make a fast
panbread for days when she has no bread in the house and is
pressed for time. The one we make here, with cornmeal
and fresh corn kernels, is very quick and easy.   ✣   For our
dessert, unpeeled peaches are halved, pitted, and baked with
a little maple syrup and brown sugar. For optimum flavor,
serve this dish lukewarm or at room temperature.

SUGGESTED WINES

White
PEPI, MALVASIA
BIANCA

Red
LANGLOIS-
CHATEAU,
CHINON

Pâtés of Mushroom with Tomatillo Sauce or Tomato Dressing

TOTAL TIME

30 minutes, plus
cooling time

YIELD

4 servings

NUTRITION

279 calories

4 g protein

25 g fat

3 g saturated fat

0 mg cholesterol

867 mg sodium

12 g carbohydrate

3 g dietary fiber

I love to do this dish in summer with wild mushrooms that I pick up in the woods, but it can be prepared with any type of mushrooms, wild or domestic. The mushrooms are cooked for a fair amount of time, then the reduced liquid surrounding them is thickened lightly with gelatin. The mixture is molded into small containers, like individual pâtés. Because of the gelatin, the pâtés hold their shape when unmolded for serving with one of the two sauces below. One sauce, made with tomatillos, a member of the gooseberry family that is conventionally used in Mexican cooking, is acidic; the other is a traditional tomato dressing.

PÂTÉS

1 POUND MUSHROOMS (REGULAR CULTIVATED, CREMINI, PORTOBELLO, SHIITAKE, OR OYSTER, OR A MIXTURE OF SOME OR ALL OF THESE VARIETIES), WASHED AND CUT INTO ½-INCH PIECES (6½ CUPS)

½ ENVELOPE UNFLAVORED GELATIN (1 TEASPOON)

2 TABLESPOONS VIRGIN OLIVE OIL

3 LARGE SHALLOTS, PEELED AND CHOPPED FINE (⅓ CUP)

4 SCALLIONS, CLEANED AND FINELY MINCED (⅓ CUP)

1 LARGE CLOVE GARLIC, PEELED, CRUSHED, AND FINELY CHOPPED (1 TEASPOON)

¾ TEASPOON SALT

½ TEASPOON FRESHLY GROUND BLACK PEPPER

¼ TEASPOON TABASCO HOT PEPPER SAUCE

TOMATILLO SAUCE

4 TOMATILLOS (10 OUNCES), OUTSIDE HUSKS REMOVED AND CUT INTO 1-INCH PIECES (2 CUPS)

1 SMALL ANAHEIM CHILI PEPPER (ALSO CALLED CALIFORNIA PEPPER), SEEDS AND RIBS REMOVED AND DISCARDED, AND FLESH CUT INTO 1-INCH PIECES

1 SMALL ONION (2 OUNCES), PEELED AND CUT INTO 1-INCH PIECES

2 CLOVES GARLIC

2 TABLESPOONS VIRGIN OLIVE OIL

½ TEASPOON SALT

½ TEASPOON SUGAR

2 TABLESPOONS WATER

1 TABLESPOON FINELY CHOPPED FRESH CILANTRO LEAVES

TOMATO DRESSING

1 MEDIUM TOMATO (ABOUT 6 OUNCES), CUT INTO 1-INCH PIECES (¾ CUP)

2 TEASPOONS DIJON-STYLE MUSTARD

¼ TEASPOON SALT

¼ TEASPOON FRESHLY GROUND BLACK PEPPER

¼ CUP VIRGIN OLIVE OIL

1. *For the Pâtés:* Place the mushrooms in a saucepan, cover, and cook over high heat for 1 minute. Reduce the heat to low, and continue to cook, covered, for 15 minutes. Drain, reserving the liquid. (You should have about ½ cup of liquid. If you have more, reduce to this amount by boiling the liquid; if you have less, add water to bring the liquid to ½ cup.) Sprinkle the gelatin on the hot liquid. Let stand without stirring for 5 minutes.

2. After 5 minutes, stir the gelatin into the liquid, and pour the mixture into the bowl of a food processor. Add ½ cup of the mushrooms, and process the mixture until it is pureed. Transfer the puree to a mixing bowl. Stir in the remainder of the mushrooms.

3. Meanwhile, heat the 2 tablespoons olive oil in a skillet. Add the shallots, scallions, and garlic to the oil, and cook over medium heat for 2 to 3 minutes, taking care not to brown the mixture. Add it to the mushroom mixture, mix well, then stir in the salt, pepper, and Tabasco.

4. Fill four ½-cup ramekins or soufflé molds with the mushroom mixture, packing it tightly into the molds. Cover and refrigerate for at least 2 hours, or make the day before serving and refrigerate overnight.

5. *For the Tomatillo Sauce:* Place all the sauce ingredients except the cilantro in the bowl of a food processor, and process for 20 to 30 seconds. Transfer the sauce to a bowl. (For a smoother-textured sauce, emulsify the mixture with a handheld immersion blender at this point.) Add the cilantro, and mix well. (Yield: 1¾ cups.)

6. *For the Tomato Dressing:* Place all the dressing ingredients in the bowl of a food processor and process until smooth. Strain the mixture, if desired.

7. At serving time, place about ¼ cup of the tomatillo sauce on each of four plates. Unmold the pâtés, and place one pâté in the center of the sauce on each plate. Alternatively, unmold a pâté on each of four plates, and spoon 2 to 3 tablespoons of the tomato dressing around each pâté.

The tomatillo sauce and the dressing are both emulsified, which gives them a beautiful color and a smooth consistency. This mushroom pâté is a very elegant dish. And you can make it ahead.

Grilled Marinated Pork Fillet

TOTAL TIME

2½ hours, including

marinating time

YIELD

4 servings

NUTRITION

203 calories

29 g protein

6 g fat

1 g saturated fat

67 mg cholesterol

569 mg sodium

6 g carbohydrate

.1 g dietary fiber

Cooked fillet of pork

can be as low in fat as

1 gram per ounce —

comparable to skin-

less chicken breast.

Pork fillet, or tenderloin, contains about as little fat and cholesterol as chicken. Available now in most supermarkets, it is tender and moist. In this recipe, the pork is marinated in honey, jalapeño peppers, and *nuoc mam*, the fish sauce of the Vietnamese, then grilled.

MARINADE

1 SMALL PIECE GINGER, PEELED AND CUT INTO ½-INCH PIECES (1½ TEASPOONS)

1 CLOVE GARLIC, PEELED

1 TABLESPOON HONEY

1 PIECE JALAPEÑO PEPPER, SIZE DEPENDING ON YOUR TOLERANCE FOR HOTNESS (FROM 1 TABLESPOON TO ¼ CUP)

2 TABLESPOONS *NUOC MAM*, OR FISH SAUCE

3 TABLESPOONS WATER

1 LARGE PORK FILLET (ABOUT 1½ POUNDS), TRIMMED OF ALL FAT AND SILVER SKIN (1 POUND, 2 OUNCES TRIMMED WEIGHT)

1 TEASPOON CANOLA OIL

1. Place all the marinade ingredients in the bowl of a food processor and process until pureed. Pour the marinade into a plastic food bag, and add the trimmed pork fillet. Seal the bag tightly, and shake it until the meat is well coated with the marinade. Refrigerate for at least 2 and up to 8 hours.

2. About 30 minutes before cooking time, heat a grill until it is hot. Preheat the oven to 200 degrees.

3. Remove the pork fillet from the marinade, and reserve the marinade in an ovenproof skillet or metal gratin dish. Sprinkle the fillet with the oil, and place it on the hot grill. Cook, covered, about 6 minutes, then turn the fillet over. Cook, covered, for 6 minutes on the second side, until the meat is nicely grilled on all sides.

4. Bring the reserved marinade to a boil on top of the stove. Return the meat to the marinade and place it in the 200-degree oven for at least 10 minutes but as long as 40 minutes to rest. Slice the fillet, and serve it with some of the juices.

Grilled Mari-
nated Pork Fillet
(this page) and
Corn Panbread
(page 171)

Eggplant Ragout

TOTAL TIME

About 1 hour

YIELD

4 servings

NUTRITION

112 calories

3 g protein

3 g fat

.5 g saturated fat

0 mg cholesterol

590 mg sodium

16 g carbohydrate

5 g dietary fiber

Rather than fry pieces of raw eggplant, I bake whole eggplants in the oven until they are tender, then cut them into pieces for use in this ragout or stew. The advantage to baking the eggplants is that much less oil is used than would be required to fry the eggplants.

2 EGGPLANTS (1½ POUNDS TOTAL)

1 TABLESPOON VIRGIN OLIVE OIL

1 LARGE ONION (ABOUT 7 OUNCES), PEELED AND CUT INTO 1-INCH PIECES (1¾ CUPS)

4 TO 5 LARGE CLOVES GARLIC, PEELED AND SLICED THIN (3 TABLESPOONS)

1 TEASPOON *HERBES DE PROVENCE*

⅓ CUP DRY WHITE WINE

1 TEASPOON SALT

½ TEASPOON FRESHLY GROUND BLACK PEPPER

2 TABLESPOONS CHOPPED FRESH PARSLEY

1. Preheat the oven to 400 degrees.

2. Wash each eggplant under cool, running water, then wrap it in aluminum foil. Place the eggplants on a cookie tray, and bake them in the 400-degree oven for 1 hour, until they are very soft throughout.

3. Meanwhile, heat the olive oil in a large saucepan. When it is hot, add the onion pieces and sauté them, covered, over low heat for about 4 minutes, until they are tender. Add the garlic and *herbes de Provence* and cook 1 minute over medium heat. Stir in the wine, salt, and pepper.

4. Cut the eggplant flesh into 1½-inch pieces and add the pieces to the saucepan, mixing them in well. Bring the mixture to a boil, cover, and boil gently over low heat for 5 minutes. Sprinkle with the parsley, and serve immediately, or cool, refrigerate, and serve cold.

Corn Panbread

When in a bind, panbread is quick and easy to make. This one, containing cornmeal, flour, baking powder, eggs, milk, and fresh corn kernels, can be prepared from start to finish in a half hour or so.

1 CUP COARSE YELLOW CORNMEAL

1 CUP ALL-PURPOSE FLOUR

1 TABLESPOON BAKING POWDER

½ TEASPOON SALT

1 TEASPOON SUGAR

1 EGG

1 CUP MILK

1 CUP CORN KERNELS (CUT FROM ONE LARGE EAR OF CORN)

2 TABLESPOONS CANOLA OIL

1. Preheat the oven to 400 degrees.

2. Combine the cornmeal, flour, baking powder, salt, and sugar in a mixing bowl. Add the egg and milk and mix well. Stir in the corn kernels.

3. Heat 1 tablespoon of the oil in an 8- to 10-inch ovenproof skillet until it is hot but not smoking, and pour the panbread batter into the skillet. Sprinkle the remaining tablespoon of oil on top of the batter. Cook the panbread for about 2 minutes over medium to high heat, until the bread batter is sizzling at the edges.

4. Place the skillet in the 400-degree oven and bake it for 25 minutes, until the panbread is browned on top and cooked through. Remove the panbread from the skillet, and cool it on a wire rack for 15 to 30 minutes before cutting it into wedges and serving.

TOTAL TIME

30 to 40 minutes

YIELD

4 to 6 servings

NUTRITION

265 calories

7 g protein

7 g fat

1 g saturated fat

41 mg cholesterol

229 mg sodium

43 g carbohydrate

2 g dietary fiber

CLAUDINE

What I like about this bread is that when you have your guests over, and they start asking, "Can I help you in the kitchen?", you get them to make it. It's very easy.

171

Relaxing Summer Supper

Baked Peaches with Almonds

TOTAL TIME

About 1 hour

YIELD

4 servings

NUTRITION

199 calories

3 g protein

9 g fat

2 g saturated fat

8 mg cholesterol

127 mg sodium

30 g carbohydrate

2 g dietary fiber

This is an easy dish to prepare. Peach halves are baked with a little maple syrup, brown sugar, butter, and almonds in a gratin dish. Excellent served at room temperature with some of the natural juices, the dessert is also good – if you want to splurge – garnished with sour cream.

4 RIPE, FIRM PEACHES (1½ POUNDS)

2 CUPS WATER

¼ CUP MAPLE SYRUP

1½ TABLESPOONS LIGHT BROWN SUGAR

1 TABLESPOON UNSALTED BUTTER, BROKEN INTO PIECES

⅓ CUP WHOLE UNBLANCHED ALMONDS

SOUR CREAM (OPTIONAL)

1. Preheat the oven to 350 degrees.

2. Using a sharp paring knife, cut the unpeeled peaches in half, and remove the pits. Arrange the peaches cut side down in one layer in a gratin dish. Add the water, maple syrup, brown sugar, butter, and almonds.

3. Place the gratin dish on a cookie tray, and place the tray in the 350-degree oven for 40 minutes. Turn the peach halves so they are skin side down and cook them for another 15 minutes. (At this point, the juice around the peaches should be syrupy.)

4. Turn the peaches carefully in the syrup so they are skin side up again, and cool them to room temperature. Serve two peach halves per person with some of the syrup.

The Making of a Cook

Sautéed Shrimp, Potato, and Escarole Salad

Carrots with Orange and Dill

Petits Filets Mignons of Pork in Port Wine

Phyllo Tart with Fruit *Salpicon*

———

In this menu, Claudine learns how to create dishes from slightly different combinations of ingredients. ❧ The first course, for example, is a salad consisting of sautéed shrimp served on top of potatoes and escarole in a garlic and mustard vinaigrette. Claudine, who loves shrimp and often orders shrimp cocktail as a first course, was delighted with this salad, which would also make a good main course for a light lunch. ❧ The salad is followed by pork *filets mignons*, tiny steaks cut from totally trimmed pork fillet. Weighing only about 3 ounces each, the fillets are sautéed and served with a port wine sauce, the sweetness of which goes particularly well with pork. As an accompaniment, carrots are cooked in orange juice and served with a sprinkling of dill. ❧ The dessert finale is a phyllo tart with a *salpicon*, or mixture of fruit. For this recipe, phyllo dough is shredded, moistened with butter, oil, and sugar, and baked in a tart pan until crisp and brown. Topped with flavored, diced fruit at the last moment, it is served with a garnish of mint.

White
VINA CALINA,
CHARDONNAY

Red
BOISSET,
CLASSIC
BEAUJOLAIS

Sautéed Shrimp, Potato, and Escarole Salad

TOTAL TIME

About 45 minutes

YIELD

4 servings

NUTRITION

318 calories

21 g protein

16 g fat

4 g saturated fat

141 mg cholesterol

472 mg sodium

22 g carbohydrate

3 g dietary fiber

CLAUDINE

Everybody makes potato salad for a picnic: I think you should make the sautéed shrimp and potato salad with escarole and bring that — it would be a real hit.

This salad is best eaten at room temperature. One of my favorites, it combines potatoes and escarole in a garlicky dressing and freshly sautéed shrimp. There is a bonus to this recipe: the shells from the shrimp can be frozen for later use in soup or stock. (My wife makes a delightful Thai soup with a stock made from shrimp shells and flavored with lime juice and lemongrass.)

¾ POUND POTATOES, PREFERABLY A FIRM RED VARIETY

¾ POUND LARGE SHRIMP (21 TO 30 PER POUND), SHELLED AND CUT INTO THIRDS (1¾ CUPS)

DRESSING

2 CLOVES GARLIC, PEELED, CRUSHED, AND CHOPPED FINE (1 TEASPOON)

2 TEASPOONS DIJON-STYLE MUSTARD

½ TEASPOON SALT

½ TEASPOON FRESHLY GROUND BLACK PEPPER

1½ TABLESPOONS SHERRY VINEGAR

1½ TABLESPOONS VIRGIN OLIVE OIL

1 TABLESPOON CANOLA OIL

1 TABLESPOON UNSALTED BUTTER

⅛ TEASPOON SALT

⅛ TEASPOON FRESHLY GROUND BLACK PEPPER

1½ TEASPOONS CHOPPED FRESH TARRAGON

1½ TEASPOONS CHOPPED FRESH PARSLEY

1 HEAD ESCAROLE (8 TO 10 OUNCES), AS WHITE AS POSSIBLE INSIDE, TRIMMED AND CUT INTO 1½-INCH PIECES, THEN WASHED AND SPUN DRY (ABOUT 4 CUPS)

1. Wash the potatoes, and place them in a saucepan with enough water to cover them by 1 inch. Bring the water to a boil over high heat, then reduce the heat to low, and boil the potatoes gently for 25 to 35 minutes, until they are tender when pierced with the point of a sharp knife. Drain off the water and cool the potatoes to lukewarm.

2. When the potatoes are lukewarm, peel them, and cut them into 1-inch cubes. Place them in a bowl with the garlic, mustard, ½ teaspoon each salt and pepper, vinegar, and the olive and canola oils. Toss the potatoes well, and set them aside until cooled to room temperature.

3. At serving time, heat the butter in a skillet. When the butter is hot but not smoking, add the shrimp and the ⅛ teaspoon each salt and pepper, and sauté the shrimp for 1½ to 2 minutes. Stir in the tarragon and parsley.

4. Add the escarole to the room-temperature potato salad, and mix well. Divide the mixture among four salad plates, and sprinkle the shrimp on top. Serve immediately.

Carrots with Orange and Dill

I like to season carrots with different herbs. Here, I cook carrots in orange juice, which sweetens them and imparts a mild orange taste, and serve them with fresh dill. This dish can be made up to a day ahead, but don't add the dill until the last moment, as it tends to lose its flavor and darken if added too soon.

1 POUND CARROTS, PEELED AND CUT INTO
  1-INCH DICE (3 CUPS)

¾ CUP FRESHLY SQUEEZED ORANGE JUICE

1 TABLESPOON UNSALTED BUTTER

½ TEASPOON SALT

½ TEASPOON FRESHLY GROUND BLACK PEPPER

¼ CUP LOOSELY PACKED FRESH DILL LEAVES

1. Place all the ingredients except the dill in a stainless-steel saucepan.

2. Bring the mixture to a boil and boil it, uncovered, over medium to high heat for 15 to 20 minutes, until the carrots are tender, all the liquid has evaporated, and the carrots are beginning to glaze in the butter.

3. Sprinkle on the dill and serve immediately.

TOTAL TIME

About 30 minutes

YIELD

4 servings

NUTRITION

97 calories

2 g protein

3 g fat

1 g saturated fat

8 mg cholesterol

332 mg sodium

17 g carbohydrate

2 g dietary fiber

The carrots in this recipe provide enough beta-carotene to supply 300% of the daily value for vitamin A.

Petits Filets Mignons of Pork in Port Wine

In this recipe, a fillet of pork — very low in both fat and cholesterol — is cut into tiny *filets mignons*, briefly sautéed, and served with a rich port wine sauce flavored with thyme.

TOTAL TIME

20 to 30 minutes

YIELD

4 servings

NUTRITION

297 calories

33 g protein

10 g fat

3 g saturated fat

97 mg cholesterol

266 mg sodium

6 g carbohydrate

2 g dietary fiber

1 LARGE PORK FILLET, TRIMMED OF ALL SURROUNDING FAT (ABOUT 1 POUND, 6 OUNCES)

1 TABLESPOON UNSALTED BUTTER

1 TABLESPOON VIRGIN OLIVE OIL

¼ TEASPOON SALT

¼ TEASPOON FRESHLY GROUND BLACK PEPPER

⅓ CUP PORT WINE

½ CUP CHICKEN STOCK

1½ TABLESPOONS KETCHUP

1 TEASPOON CHOPPED FRESH THYME

1. Preheat the oven to 180 degrees.

2. Cut the trimmed fillet crosswise into 8 small pork steaks or *petits filets mignons*, each about 1¼ inches thick.

3. Heat the butter and oil in a large saucepan. Meanwhile, sprinkle the steaks with the salt and pepper. When the butter and oil are hot, arrange the steaks in one layer in the saucepan, and cook them over high heat for 2½ minutes on each side.

4. Transfer the steaks from the saucepan to a gratin dish, and place them in the 180-degree oven to keep warm while you finish the recipe.

5. Meanwhile, add the port wine to the drippings in the saucepan, bring the mixture to a boil, and cook it over high heat for about 1 minute. Add the chicken stock and ketchup, and cook the mixture over high heat for 2 to 3 minutes. (It should not be too thick.) Add the thyme and mix well.

6. At serving time, place two small pork steaks on each of four plates, and spoon some sauce around them. Serve immediately.

Petits Filets Mignons *of Pork (this page) and Carrots with Orange and Dill (page 177)*

Phyllo Tart with Fruit Salpicon

TOTAL TIME

About 45 minutes

YIELD

4 servings

NUTRITION

271 calories

3 g protein

8 g fat

2 g saturated fat

8 mg cholesterol

116 mg sodium

50 g carbohydrate

2 g dietary fiber

CLAUDINE

———

I would probably make this beautiful phyllo tart with bananas (because I love bananas). Phyllo dough has such an elegant taste and consistency to it, this is a special dessert no matter what fruit you use.

This dish consists of two recipes: one is for a flavored fruit mixture, the other for a different and interesting phyllo dough shell on which to serve the fruit. Phyllo dough, available frozen in most supermarkets, is rolled and cut into strips here. Tossed with butter, oil, and sugar, these strips are patted lightly into a tart shell and baked. The shell can be baked ahead, and the fruit — which can be varied based on quality and market availability — also can be prepared several hours before serving.

SALPICON

⅓ CUP APRICOT PRESERVES, BEST POSSIBLE QUALITY

1½ TABLESPOONS LEMON JUICE

12 OUNCES LARGE DAMSON OR BURBANK PLUMS (ABOUT 3), PEELED IF THE SKIN IS TOUGH, PITTED, AND THE FLESH CUT INTO ½-INCH DICE

1 CUP BLUEBERRIES

4 SHEETS (14 BY 18 INCHES) THAWED PHYLLO DOUGH (ABOUT 3 OUNCES TOTAL), ROLLED TOGETHER INTO A SCROLL AND CUT CROSSWISE INTO ¼-INCH STRIPS (ABOUT 3 CUPS SHREDDED PHYLLO)

1 TABLESPOON UNSALTED BUTTER, MELTED

1 TABLESPOON CANOLA OIL

2 TABLESPOONS SUGAR

4 SMALL SPRIGS FRESH MINT, OR STRIPS OF LEMON ZEST, FOR GARNISH

1. *For the* Salpicon: Mix the apricot preserves and lemon juice together in a bowl large enough to accommodate all the fruit. Add the diced plums and blueberries, and mix well. Cover, and place in a cool place (not the refrigerator) until serving time.

2. Preheat the oven to 350 degrees.

3. Roll the sheets of phyllo together into a scroll, and cut them crosswise into ¼-inch strips. (You should have about 3 cups of shredded phyllo.)

4. Place the shredded phyllo dough on a nonstick cookie sheet. Add the butter, oil, and sugar, and mix gently until all the strands of dough are coated with the fat and sugar. Gather up the phyllo strips and press them into an 8-inch tart pan or ring set on a cookie sheet.

5. Bake the phyllo shell in the 350-degree oven for 15 to 18 minutes, until nicely browned and crisp. Cool the crust on a rack in the tart shell, then transfer it to a serving platter.

6. At serving time, spoon the *salpicon* of fruit on top of the phyllo crust, decorate the dessert with the mint sprigs or lemon zest, and cut it into slices at the table. Serve immediately.

Cuisine Surprise

RICE NOODLE STICKS
WITH DRIED MUSHROOM STEW

NEW ZEALAND GREEN MUSSELS
STUFFED ALEXANDRE

SAUTÉED TURNIP GREENS

TOP-CRUST CHERRY PIE

———

This menu brings together an unusual assortment of dishes to create a very unconventional meal. ✔ The first course, often served at our house as a main dish, is a combination of chewy and elastic Chinese rice noodle sticks with shiitake mushrooms, garlic, and oyster sauce. ✔ Our main course features New Zealand green mussels. Enormous, tender, and beautiful, this mussel variety is available in most fish stores around the country. Our recipe uses them in a south of France—inspired dish: each mussel is stuffed with a mixture of bread, eggs, onion, and sausage meat, and the stuffed mussels are cooked in a tomato sauce. ✔ The next dish in this unorthodox menu is made with turnip greens. Cooked with bacon and a dash of sugar and salt, the greens also could be served as an accompaniment to roasted poultry or meat. ✔ We finish our "cuisine surprise" meal with a top-crust cherry pie. For this recipe, large pitted Bing cherries are mixed with a little potato starch and sugar and baked in a gratin dish with a layer of dough on top — thereby eliminating the problem of a soggy bottom crust, a common occurrence with this type of pie. For serving, the crusty top layer of dough is broken into pieces and arranged on plates with a large spoonful of the cherry filling on top.

White
TRIMBACH,
PINOT BLANC

Red dessert
KWV, RED
MUSCADEL

Rice Noodle Sticks with Dried Mushroom Stew

TOTAL TIME

*About 30 minutes,
plus soaking time
for mushrooms
and noodles*

YIELD

4 servings

NUTRITION

*282 calories
8 g protein
5 g fat
.4 g saturated fat
0 mg cholesterol
441 mg sodium
53 g carbohydrate
3 g dietary fiber*

This Asian pasta dish is a favorite at our house. The dried shiitake mushrooms go well with the wide rice noodle sticks, which are reconstituted in warm water, then finished on the stove with all the seasonings. An excellent first course, this makes a great vegetarian main course or side dish as well.

4 OUNCES MIXED DRIED SHIITAKE AND TREE EAR MUSHROOMS

4 CUPS HOT TAP WATER

5 OUNCES MEDIUM-SIZE RICE NOODLE STICKS

1½ TABLESPOONS CANOLA OIL

1 SMALL ONION (3 OUNCES), PEELED AND CHOPPED (ABOUT ½ CUP)

3 CLOVES GARLIC, PEELED, CRUSHED, AND FINELY CHOPPED (2 TEASPOONS)

1 SMALL PIECE GINGER, PEELED AND CHOPPED FINE (1 TEASPOON)

½ TEASPOON SEEDED AND CHOPPED JALAPEÑO PEPPER

1 TABLESPOON OYSTER SAUCE

4 TEASPOONS SOY SAUCE

2 TABLESPOONS RICE WINE (OR IF UNAVAILABLE, DRY WHITE WINE)

1. Soak the dried shiitake and tree ear mushrooms in the hot water for 45 minutes. Drain, reserving 1 cup of the soaking liquid for later use in this recipe. (If desired, freeze the remainder for use in soup or stock.)

2. Cut off and discard the stems of the shiitake mushrooms. Cut the caps into ½-inch slices. Remove any roots or dirt from the tree ear mushrooms, and cut them into ½-inch strips. You should have about 2 cups of reconstituted mushrooms.

3. Place the noodles in a large bowl and cover them with hot tap water. Soak the noodles for 20 minutes, then drain them in a colander. If you prefer shorter noodles, cut them into shorter pieces with scissors.

4. Heat the oil in a saucepan. Add the onion and cook it for 1 minute over high heat. Add the garlic, ginger, jalapeño pepper, oyster sauce, soy sauce, rice wine, and the reserved cup of mushroom soaking liquid.

5. Add the mushrooms to the saucepan and mix well. Bring the mixture to a boil over high heat, then reduce the heat to medium, cover, and cook for 10 to 12 minutes. Most of the liquid will have evaporated, but there still will be some moisture in the pan.

6. Add the drained noodles to the mushroom mixture, mix well, and cook for about 1 to 2 minutes, stirring constantly, until the noodles soften and become transparent. Divide among four plates and serve.

New Zealand Green Mussels Stuffed Alexandre

Beautiful, very large mussels from New Zealand are available all year round in most fish stores. My inspiration for this recipe is a similar dish I enjoyed in the south of France on a recent visit. This variation features mussels stuffed with sausage meat, bread, onion, and garlic and cooked in a light tomato sauce.

2 POUNDS (ABOUT 16) NEW ZEALAND MUSSELS

8 OUNCES SWEET ITALIAN SAUSAGE MEAT

2 OUNCES BREAD, PREFERABLY A COUNTRY-STYLE VARIETY, COARSELY CHOPPED IN A FOOD PROCESSOR (¾ CUP)

1 LARGE EGG

⅓ CUP CHOPPED ONION

2 SMALL CLOVES GARLIC, PEELED, CRUSHED, AND FINELY CHOPPED (1 TEASPOON)

½ TEASPOON FRESHLY GROUND BLACK PEPPER

½ CUP COARSELY MINCED FRESH CHIVES

SAUCE

2 TOMATOES (12 OUNCES), QUARTERED

3 CLOVES GARLIC, PEELED AND CRUSHED

¼ CUP DRY WHITE WINE

¼ TEASPOON SALT

½ TEASPOON *HERBES DE PROVENCE*

1. Cut between the mussel shells to sever the hinge or abducting muscle, and pull the mussel shells open. Set the mussels, still in their open shells, aside while you make the stuffing.

2. In a bowl, mix together the sausage meat, bread, egg, onion, garlic, pepper, and chives. Divide the mixture into 16 equal portions, and arrange a portion on top of each mussel. Close the mussel shells to conceal the stuffing, and arrange the mussels in one layer in a large 12-inch saucepan.

(CONTINUED)

TOTAL TIME

45 minutes to
1 hour

YIELD

4 servings

NUTRITION

334 calories
24 g protein
17 g fat
5 g saturated fat
129 mg cholesterol
932 mg sodium
17 g carbohydrate
1 g dietary fiber

186

*Mussels are gener-
ally a very good
source of selenium,
which may protect
against cancer.
Tomatoes are rich
in vitamin C and
lycopene, a potent
antioxidant.*

3. *For the Sauce:* Place the tomatoes, garlic, wine, salt, and *herbes de Provence* in the bowl of a food processor, and process the mixture for 10 to 15 seconds, until it is partially liquefied. Pour the sauce on top of the stuffed mussels in the pan.

4. Bring the contents of the pan to a rolling boil, uncovered, on top of the stove. Then cover the pan, reduce the heat to low, and cook the mussels gently for 18 to 20 minutes. Using a slotted spoon, transfer the mussels to a platter, and boil the sauce in the pan for 3 to 4 minutes, until it is reduced to 1 cup.

5. Pour the sauce over the mussels, and serve immediately, four mussels per person with some of the sauce.

*New Zealand
Green Mussels
Stuffed Alexandre
(page 185)*

Sautéed Turnip Greens

TOTAL TIME

30 to 40 minutes

YIELD

4 servings

NUTRITION

133 calories

8 g protein

9 g fat

2 g saturated fat

18 mg cholesterol

615 mg sodium

6 g carbohydrate

2 g dietary fiber

Turnip greens are a good source of vitamins A, C, and folate, as well as carotenoids and calcium. They also contain phyto-chemicals, natural plant substances that may protect against cancer.

A number of different greens — from kale to mustard greens — can be prepared in the same manner as these turnip greens. I use a minimum amount of bacon, one slice per person, to give the desired taste and texture to the greens.

4 SLICES BACON (3 OUNCES), CUT INTO ¼-INCH PIECES

1½ POUNDS TURNIP GREENS, TOUGH STEMS AND DAMAGED LEAVES REMOVED, AND REMAINDER CUT INTO 2-INCH PIECES (ABOUT 1¼ POUNDS TRIMMED)

2 TEASPOONS SUGAR

¼ TEASPOON SALT

½ TEASPOON FRESHLY GROUND BLACK PEPPER

1. Place the bacon pieces in a large sauce-pan and cook them over medium heat until all the pieces are well browned, about 6 minutes.

2. Meanwhile, wash the trimmed turnip greens in cool water (several times, if necessary, to clean) and drain them in a colander. Add the greens, still wet from washing, to the bacon pieces in the saucepan, and sprinkle on the sugar, salt, and pepper.

3. Cook the greens, covered, over high heat for 3 to 5 minutes, until they begin to wilt. Mix them well with the bacon and bacon fat, then reduce the heat to low, cover, and continue cooking for 15 to 20 minutes, until all the moisture is gone and the greens become glazed with the sugar and bacon fat. (If there is still moisture remaining in the pan after 20 minutes, remove the lid and cook, uncovered, for a few additional minutes to evaporate any remaining moisture.) The greens should be tender but not mushy.

4. Add additional salt to taste, as needed, depending on the saltiness of the bacon, and serve immediately.

Top-Crust Cherry Pie

This is an easy way of making a large cherry pie, with the sweetened cherries baked in a gratin dish with a layer of dough on the top only. Serve the pie by cutting out pieces of the brown, crisp crust, inverting them onto dessert plates, and piling the baked cherries on top. If fresh cherries are not available, substitute unsweetened, individually quick frozen (IQF) cherries.

2 POUNDS LARGE BING CHERRIES, PITTED, OR A MIXTURE OF BING, RAINIER (GOLDEN BING), OR MONTMORENCY CHERRIES, PITTED (ABOUT 5½ CUPS, 1 POUND, 10 OUNCES PITTED WEIGHT)

⅔ CUP SUGAR

2 TABLESPOONS POTATO STARCH

1 TEASPOON PURE VANILLA EXTRACT

½ TEASPOON PURE ALMOND EXTRACT

DOUGH

¾ CUP ALL-PURPOSE FLOUR

2 TABLESPOONS UNSALTED BUTTER

1½ TABLESPOONS SUGAR

PINCH OF SALT

6 TABLESPOONS COTTAGE CHEESE

ICE CREAM, SOUR CREAM, OR PLAIN YOGURT (OPTIONAL)

YIELD

6 servings

NUTRITION

233 calories

3 g protein

3 g fat

2 g saturated fat

9 mg cholesterol

96 mg sodium

48 g carbohydrate

1 g dietary fiber

1. Preheat the oven to 375 degrees.

2. Place the cherries, sugar, starch, vanilla, and almond extract in a bowl. Mix well, and transfer the mixture to a round or oval gratin dish with a capacity of about 5 cups.

3. Place the flour, butter, sugar, salt, and cottage cheese in the bowl of a food processor. Process the dough mixture for 15 to 20 seconds, until it begins to come together.

4. Transfer the dough to a piece of plastic wrap 3 to 4 inches larger than the gratin dish, and form the dough into a ball in the center of the wrap. Place another piece of plastic wrap (of about the same size as the first piece) on top of the dough, then roll the dough out to form a circle or an oval (depending on the shape of your gratin dish) about 1 inch larger than the dish.

(CONTINUED)

190

5. Peel the top piece of plastic wrap from the surface of the dough, and, holding the edges of the remaining piece of wrap, invert the dough over the gratin dish so it hangs down about 1 inch beyond the sides of the dish. Peel off the remaining piece of plastic wrap.

6. Carefully lift the dough overhang with your fingers, and roll it onto itself to create a thicker layer of dough all around the edge of the dish. Then, using your thumb and fingers, press on the thick dough edge to seal it to the dish and create a decorative border.

7. Prick the dough in the center a few times with a sharp knife, to enable steam to escape, and place the gratin dish on a cookie sheet. Bake the pie in the 375-degree oven for 45 minutes, covering it with aluminum foil the last 10 minutes, if necessary, to prevent the dough from becoming too brown. Cool the pie to room temperature on a rack.

8. To serve, break through the crust with a spoon, and arrange a section of the crust with a portion of the filling on top or alongside it on each of six plates. Serve, if desired, with a small ball of ice cream or a tablespoon of sour cream or plain yogurt.

Top-Crust Cherry Pie (page 189)

Contemporary French Cooking

POACHED TROUT IN VEGETABLE BROTH

BRAISED RABBIT WITH
MORELS AND PEARL ONIONS

POTATO SLABS RACLETTE

PEARS IN CHOCOLATE

———

The first course in this menu is designed to show Claudine how to poach trout in a light vegetable broth. The trout is cooked whole in this recipe, with the skin and bones removed at the table or in the privacy of the kitchen just before the trout is served. ↴ The main dish features rabbit prepared in two distinct ways: the front and back legs are braised in a stew with morels and pearl onions; the elongated tender part of the back, called the saddle, is roasted with a topping of bread crumbs flavored with horseradish and mustard. The two dishes can be served at different meals, or they can be served together, as they are in this menu. ↴ Potato slabs raclette, a classic winter dish in France, makes a great accompaniment for the rabbit. For this recipe, large potatoes are cooked in water, then sliced and broiled with a topping of raclette cheese. If raclette, a beautifully melting cheese from Switzerland or France, is unavailable, substitute cheddar, Gruyère, or even fontina. ↴ The meal ends with pears in chocolate. After quartered pears are cooked in a light syrup, some chocolate is added to the cooking syrup to create a chocolate sauce that is very good served with the pieces of pear.

White
COMTE LA
FOND,
LADOUCETTE
SANCERRE

Red
STONESTREET,
PINOT NOIR

Poached Trout in Vegetable Broth

In this recipe, trout are poached whole in a mixture of onions, carrots, scallions, and herbs. Then, their skin is removed, their meat is slid off the bone, and the boneless fillets are returned to the stock and finished with a little butter and oil. This light, elegant fish also could be served whole if guests don't mind removing the skin and bones themselves at the table.

TOTAL TIME

About 45 minutes

YIELD

4 servings

NUTRITION

291 calories

17 g protein

9 g fat

3 g saturated fat

78 mg cholesterol

363 mg sodium

26 g carbohydrate

3 g dietary fiber

½ POUND ALL-PURPOSE POTATOES (ABOUT 2 POTATOES)

½ CUP SLICED ONIONS

1 CARROT (2 OUNCES), PEELED AND THINLY SLICED (⅓ CUP)

1 SCALLION, PEELED AND CUT INTO 1-INCH PIECES (2 TABLESPOONS)

1 BAY LEAF

1 SPRIG FRESH THYME

2 STRIPS LIME PEEL, REMOVED WITH A VEGETABLE PEELER

½ TEASPOON COARSELY GROUND BLACK PEPPER (*MIGNONNETTE*)

¼ TEASPOON SALT

⅓ CUP DRY, FRUITY WHITE WINE

¾ CUP WATER

2 TROUT, GUTTED AND HEADS REMOVED (ABOUT 1 POUND)

1½ TEASPOONS UNSALTED BUTTER

1½ TEASPOONS VIRGIN OLIVE OIL

1. Preheat the oven to 180 degrees.

2. Place the potatoes in a saucepan, cover them with water, and bring the water to a boil over high heat. Reduce the heat to low, and boil the potatoes, uncovered, for 25 to 30 minutes, until they are tender. Drain off the water, and set the potatoes aside until they are cool enough to handle. Peel the potatoes and cut them into ¾-inch slices. Arrange the slices in an ovenproof receptacle and keep them warm in the 180-degree oven.

3. Place all the remaining ingredients except the trout, butter, oil, and chives in a large saucepan, preferably stainless steel. Bring the mixture to a boil, then reduce the heat to low, cover, and boil gently for 3 minutes. Add the trout, return the mixture to a boil, then reduce the heat to low, cover, and cook for 5 minutes.

(CONTINUED)

196

4. Using a slotted spoon, lift the trout from the stock, and place them on a plate. Remove and discard the skin from the trout, then remove the two fillets from the central bone of each fish, and discard the bones. Arrange the fillets in an oven-proof receptacle and keep them warm in the preheated 180-degree oven while making the sauce.

5. Add the butter and oil to the stock and vegetables in the saucepan. Bring the mixture to a strong boil. Arrange 2 or 3 slices of potato in the bottom of each soup plate, and place 1 trout fillet on top of the potato in each plate. Spoon some of the stock and vegetables on top and serve immediately.

Braised Rabbit with Morels and Pearl Onions

I use dried morels in this stew, 1½ ounces of which are equivalent to about 1 pound of fresh morels. The dried morels have more taste than fresh ones, and the water obtained from reconstituting them is added to the sauce, giving it more intense flavor.

TOTAL TIME

1½ hours

YIELD

4 servings

NUTRITION

BRAISED RABBIT

369 calories

33 g protein

14 g fat

4 g saturated fat

89 mg cholesterol

587 mg sodium

21 g carbohydrate

5 g dietary fiber

RABBIT SADDLE

289 calories

31 g protein

15 g fat

3 g saturated fat

85 mg cholesterol

95 mg sodium

4 g carbohydrate

.3 g dietary fiber

1½ OUNCES DRIED MORELS

2 CUPS HOT TAP WATER

1 RABBIT, CLEANED, WITH LIVER REMOVED
   (2¾ POUNDS)

¾ TEASPOON SALT

1 TEASPOON *HERBES DE PROVENCE*

¼ TEASPOON FRESHLY GROUND BLACK PEPPER

1 TABLESPOON UNSALTED BUTTER

1 TABLESPOON VIRGIN OLIVE OIL

16 PEARL ONIONS (ABOUT 12 OUNCES), PEELED

2 TABLESPOONS CHOPPED SHALLOTS

1 TABLESPOON ALL-PURPOSE FLOUR

⅓ CUP DRY, FRUITY WHITE WINE

1. Rinse the morels for a few seconds under running tap water, then place them in a bowl. Pour the hot tap water over them. Place a small saucepan on top of the morels in the bowl to push them down into the water, and set them aside for 30 minutes to reconstitute in the water.

2. Meanwhile, cut the two back legs from the body of the rabbit, and halve each of the legs at the joint. Next, remove the rabbit's front legs and the front part of the body containing the rib cages. Cut this rib portion in half. These cut portions, 8 in all, weighing about 1¾ pounds, will be used in our rabbit stew; the saddle or back, left in one long, narrow piece weighing from 14 to 16 ounces, will be cooked separately and can be served with the stew or on its own (see recipe below).

3. In a small bowl, mix together ½ teaspoon of the salt, the *herbes de Provence*, and the pepper. Sprinkle the saddle and the rabbit pieces with the mixture.

4. Heat the butter and oil until hot in a large, sturdy casserole dish or dutch oven. Add the rabbit saddle and pearl onions, and sauté them over medium to high heat, turning them occasionally, for 10 minutes, until they are browned on all sides. Remove the saddle and set it aside for use in another recipe (see below). Remove the onions and set them aside in a bowl.

(CONTINUED)

198

CLAUDINE

*When I was young
we had a little
bunny that we got
from friends of
my parents, and it
was my pet. One
day I asked my
mother, "When is
the rabbit going
to get big enough
to eat?" This
freaked my mother
out tremendously—
she was just
appalled. She gave
the rabbit back.
My father, on
the other hand,
was very proud
that I had such
French genes that
I understood the
entire food cycle:
people have
rabbits, they raise
rabbits, and then
they eat rabbits.*

5. Add the rabbit pieces in one layer to the drippings in the casserole, and brown them on all sides over medium to high heat for 10 minutes.

6. Meanwhile, remove the morels from the soaking water (reserving the water), and press on them lightly to remove some of the liquid. Cut each morel in half lengthwise, and rinse off any dirt you see in the hollow center. Slowly pour the soaking liquid into a clean bowl, leaving behind any sandy residue. (You should have 1½ to 1¾ cups of liquid.)

7. When the rabbit stew pieces have browned for 10 minutes, add the shallots and flour, mix gently, and cook for about 1 minute. Then add the wine, mushroom liquid, and remaining ¼ teaspoon salt, and mix well. Bring the mixture to a boil, reduce the heat to low, cover, and cook gently for 45 minutes. Add the reserved morel pieces and pearl onions, and cook, covered, over low heat for 15 additional minutes.

8. Serve the stew of rabbit with some of the morels and pearl onions. If desired, serve with the saddle, finishing and serving it as indicated below.

TO FINISH THE SADDLE

1 TABLESPOON DIJON-STYLE MUSTARD

1 SLICE BREAD (¾ OUNCE)

1 PIECE FRESH HORSERADISH, PEELED AND CUT INTO ½-INCH PIECES (2 TEASPOONS)

2 TEASPOONS VIRGIN OLIVE OIL

1. Preheat the oven to 425 degrees.

2. Place the browned saddle of rabbit on a jelly roll pan lined with aluminum foil, and brush the top and sides of it with the mustard. Place the bread and horseradish in the bowl of a food processor and process until the mixture is finely ground. Transfer the mixture to a bowl, add the olive oil, and mix just enough to combine and moisten the bread. (Do not overmix; the mixture should be light and fluffy.) Pat the mixture lightly over the top and sides of the saddle, making it adhere to the mustard coating.

3. At cooking time, place the saddle in the 425-degree oven and bake it for 20 minutes. Remove the saddle from the oven and let it rest for at least 15 minutes before serving. To serve, cut into 4 pieces, and arrange one piece alongside the stew on each of the four dinner plates, or serve as a separate main dish at another meal.

Braised Rabbit with Morels and Pearl Onions (page 197) and Potato Slabs Raclette (page 200)

Potato Slabs Raclette

TOTAL TIME

About 1 hour

YIELD

4 servings

NUTRITION

285 calories

14 g protein

14 g fat

9 g saturated fat

45 mg cholesterol

273 mg sodium

26 g carbohydrate

2 g dietary fiber

Raclette cheese comes from both Switzerland and France, but the name raclette comes from the French *racler*, meaning "to scrape." This reference reflects the traditional practice of exposing a chunk of raclette cheese to heat — often an open fire — then scraping it off as it melts and eating it on boiled potato slices. In this recipe, the cheese is sliced, melted under a broiler atop thick slices of boiled potato, and served with cornichons, small sour pickles. If raclette cheese is not available, cheddar, Gruyère, or fontina can be substituted.

2 LARGE RUSSET OR IDAHO POTATOES (1¼ POUNDS)

1 PIECE RACLETTE CHEESE (OR, IF NOT AVAILABLE, CHEDDAR OR GRUYÈRE), ABOUT 6 OUNCES

¼ TEASPOON FRESHLY GROUND BLACK PEPPER

¼ TEASPOON PAPRIKA

CORNICHONS (FRENCH-STYLE GHERKINS) (OPTIONAL)

1. Preheat a broiler.

2. Place the potatoes in a saucepan, and add enough water so that the water covers them by about 1 inch. Bring the water to a boil, reduce the heat to low, and boil gently for 40 to 45 minutes, until the potatoes are tender but not mushy. Drain off the water.

3. When the potatoes are cool enough to handle, peel them, and cut each of them lengthwise into 3 slices. Arrange the slices on a baking sheet.

4. Cut the cheese into 12 slices, and cover each potato slab with 2 slices of the cheese. Sprinkle with the pepper and paprika.

5. Place the slabs under the preheated broiler, about 10 inches from the heat source, and cook them for about 5 to 6 minutes, until the cheese is nicely browned and bubbly. Eat, if desired, with cornichons.

Pears in Chocolate

In this easy, flavorful recipe, pears are cooked simply with sugar, water, and vanilla. Then, when they are tender, cocoa powder and bittersweet chocolate are added to the cooking liquid to create a sauce.

⍗   ⍗   ⍗   ⍗   ⍗   ⍗   ⍗   ⍗

4 RIPE ANJOU PEARS (ABOUT 2 POUNDS), PEELED, QUARTERED, AND CORED

¼ CUP SUGAR

¾ CUP WATER

½ TEASPOON PURE VANILLA EXTRACT

2 OUNCES BITTERSWEET CHOCOLATE

1 TABLESPOON UNSWEETENED COCOA POWDER

4 SPRIGS FRESH MINT

4 COOKIES (OPTIONAL)

1. Place the pear pieces in a stainless-steel saucepan. Add the sugar, water, and vanilla. Bring the mixture to a boil over high heat, then reduce the heat to low, cover, and cook the pears for 10 to 12 minutes, or until they are very tender when pierced with the pointed tip of a sharp knife.

2. Using a slotted spoon, transfer the pears to a bowl. (You should have about ½ cup of cooking liquid in the pan. If you have more, boil it until reduced to ½ cup; if you have less, add water to bring it to ½ cup.) Add the bittersweet chocolate and the cocoa powder to the liquid in the pan. Mix with a whisk over low heat, until the chocolate has melted and the mixture is smooth.

3. Transfer the chocolate sauce to a bowl. Cool it to room temperature. It should thicken to a syruplike consistency. (Yield: 1 cup.)

4. Divide the sauce among four dessert plates, and arrange the pear pieces on top of the sauce. Decorate each serving with a sprig of mint, and serve, if desired, with a cookie.

TOTAL TIME

About 30 minutes

YIELD

4 servings

NUTRITION

246 calories

2 g protein

5 g fat

3 g saturated fat

0 mg cholesterol

4 mg sodium

53 g carbohydrate

6 g dietary fiber

CLAUDINE
———
Cooked pears have to be tender when you poke them with a knife — that's how you know when they are done.

A Food Lover's Delight

SEA BASS WITH GREEN OLIVES

CHICKEN LEG "SAUSAGE"
WITH MUSHROOM SAUCE

ESSENCE OF TOMATO "PETALS"
WITH TARRAGON OIL

APRICOT AND HAZELNUT BISCOTTI

———

This menu starts with sea bass served with green olives. Both the large sea bass, usually from Chile, and the small sea bass, prized by Chinese cooks, are available from fishmongers. We use small sea bass in our recipe, although it could be prepared with fillet steaks cut from large sea bass. If sea bass isn't available at all, red snapper, striped bass, and even catfish can be used instead in this recipe.   ↓   Our main course is chicken leg "sausages." I explain and demonstrate to Claudine how to skin, bone, and stuff chicken legs, then how to enclose these stuffed legs in waxed paper and aluminum foil to create chicken sausages. Baked first, these sausages are finished in a mushroom sauce.   ↓   A summer favorite, our tomato side dish should be prepared only when tomatoes are really ripe and flavorful. The skin and seeds of the tomatoes are removed,

and the tomato flesh segments are partially dried in the oven to concentrate their flavor. They are served with a sprinkle of tarragon oil on top.   ↓   The dessert for this menu is biscotti made with apricot and hazelnuts. Biscotti is one of Claudine's favorite snacks, so I devised a simple, easy recipe that she can make herself.

White
BOISSET,
MEDITERRANEE
CHARDONNAY

Red
EDMEADES,
ZINFANDEL

Dessert
MICHELE
CHIARLO
NIVOLE,
MOSCATO
D'ASTI

Sea Bass with Green Olives

TOTAL TIME

About 30 minutes

YIELD

4 servings

NUTRITION

290 calories

32 g protein

17 g fat

2 g saturated fat

70 mg cholesterol

797 mg sodium

1 g carbohydrate

.1 g dietary fiber

Like the large sea bass from Chile, available from most fishmongers, smaller sea bass — widely used in Chinese restaurants — are beautifully white, flaky, and flavorful. I use small bass fillets with the skin left on in this recipe, cooking them quickly in a skillet, then serving them with a mixture of chopped green olives, scallions, garlic, and olive oil. No salt is added here because of the natural saltiness of the olives.

2 SEA BASS, GUTTED (EACH ABOUT 1½ POUNDS)

4 OUNCES LARGE GREEN OLIVES WITH PITS

2 TABLESPOONS MINCED ONION

2 CLOVES GARLIC, PEELED, CRUSHED, AND FINELY CHOPPED (1 TEASPOON)

¼ TEASPOON FRESHLY GROUND BLACK PEPPER

3 TABLESPOONS VIRGIN OLIVE OIL

1 TABLESPOON LEMON JUICE

1. Bone the sea bass to have 4 fillets, each about 6 ounces. Arrange the fillets, skin side up, in one layer on a plate, and cut 2 or 3 horizontal or diagonal slits no more than ¼ inch deep in the skin of each fillet.

2. Crush the olives lightly, and remove and discard the pits. Cut the olive flesh into thin pieces. (You should have about ¾ cup.) Place the olives in a bowl with the onion, garlic, pepper, 2½ tablespoons of the olive oil, and the lemon juice.

3. When ready to cook the fish, rub the skin of the fillets with the remaining ½ tablespoon of olive oil. Heat a large nonstick skillet until hot. Place the fish fillets skin side down in the skillet. Cook the fillets, uncovered, over high heat for 2½ minutes. Cover the pan, and continue to cook the fish over high heat for 1½ to 2 minutes longer, depending on the thickness of the fillets.

4. Remove the skillet from the heat and set it aside, covered, for 1 to 2 minutes longer so the fillets continue to cook in their own residual heat.

5. Arrange the fillets skin side up on a serving plate. Spoon the olive mixture on top, and serve immediately.

Sea Bass with Green Olives (this page) and Essence of Tomato "Petals" with Tarragon Oil (page 209)

Chicken Leg "Sausage" with Mushroom Sauce

In this recipe, chicken legs are skinned, boned, then stuffed with a mixture of portobello mushrooms, garlic, shallots, scallions, and cheese. Wrapped securely in waxed paper and aluminum foil, the resulting "sausages" are cooked in the oven long enough for them to hold their shape. Then, they are unwrapped and finished in a light sauce.

❧   ❧   ❧   ❧   ❧   ❧   ❧   ❧

4 CHICKEN LEGS (ABOUT 2½ POUNDS)

1½ TABLESPOONS VIRGIN OLIVE OIL

2 LARGE SHALLOTS, PEELED AND COARSELY CHOPPED (ABOUT ½ CUP)

1 SMALL BUNCH SCALLIONS (6), CLEANED AND CUT INTO ½-INCH PIECES (ABOUT ½ CUP)

3 PORTOBELLO MUSHROOM CAPS (6 OUNCES), WASHED AND CUT INTO ½-INCH PIECES (3½ CUPS)

2 LARGE CLOVES GARLIC, PEELED, CRUSHED, AND CHOPPED (2 TEASPOONS)

½ TEASPOON SALT

¼ TEASPOON FRESHLY GROUND BLACK PEPPER

3 TABLESPOONS GRATED PARMESAN CHEESE

½ CUP DRY WHITE WINE

¼ CUP KETCHUP

¼ CUP WATER

2 TABLESPOONS CHOPPED FRESH PARSLEY (OPTIONAL)

1. Cut off the tip of the drumstick of each chicken leg. Then, using a towel to firmly grip the skin, pull it off. Remove the thigh bone, drumstick bone, and any visible fat from each leg. (Reserve the bones, if desired, for use in stock.) You should have about 1½ pounds of skinless, boneless chicken.

2. Heat the oil in a sturdy saucepan, and add the shallots and scallions. Cook over medium heat for 1 minute. Add the mushrooms, garlic, salt, and pepper, and cook over medium heat for 5 minutes, or until the mixture is dry and lightly browned.

3. Remove ¾ cup of the mushroom mixture, and place it in bowl. Add the cheese to the mixture in the bowl, mix well, and set aside until cool. Meanwhile, add the wine, ketchup, and water to the remaining mushroom mixture in the pan, and set it aside.

(CONTINUED)

TOTAL TIME

About 1 hour

YIELD

4 servings

NUTRITION

463 calories

50 g protein

22 g fat

5 g saturated fat

161 mg cholesterol

628 mg sodium

6 g carbohydrate

1 g dietary fiber

4. Preheat the oven to 425 degrees.

5. Place each of the 4 boned chicken legs boned side up on a piece of waxed paper 10 by 12 inches. Divide the cooled mushroom cheese mixture among the legs. Then, using the waxed paper, roll each leg into a tight "sausage" about 5½ inches long and 1½ inches in diameter. Place each wrapped sausage in the center of a 10- by 12-inch piece of aluminum foil, and fold the foil tightly around it.

6. Arrange the foil-wrapped packages on a tray, and bake them in the 425-degree oven for 30 minutes. Let cool for 5 minutes while you bring the reserved sauce in the pan to a boil.

7. Carefully unwrap the chicken sausages, and place them seam side down in the pan of hot sauce. Bring the sauce back to a boil, reduce the heat to low, cover, and cook the sausages gently in the sauce for 10 minutes.

8. Serve one chicken sausage per person with some of the sauce and, if desired, a sprinkling of parsley on top.

Essence of Tomato "Petals" with Tarragon Oil

This recipe can be served as an accompaniment to fish, poultry, or meat, but it also is good on its own. Segments of skinned, seeded tomato are cooked in the oven until the tomato dries out a little and its taste becomes concentrated. Moistened with a little olive oil and seasoned with tarragon, the tomato "petals" are served at room temperature.

4 LARGE, FIRM, RIPE TOMATOES (2¼ POUNDS)

⅓ TEASPOON SALT

2 TABLESPOONS EXTRA VIRGIN OLIVE OIL

¼ TEASPOON FRESHLY GROUND BLACK PEPPER

1 TABLESPOON CHOPPED FRESH TARRAGON

1. Preheat the oven to 400 degrees.

2. Bring 3 cups of water to a boil in a medium saucepan. Submerge the tomatoes in the boiling water for 1 minute. Drain off the water, and peel the skin from the tomatoes.

3. Cut each tomato from top to base into 4 segments. Remove the juice, seeds, and some of the ribs from the segments with your fingers. (My tomatoes yielded 1¾ cups of skin, juice, flesh, and seeds.)

4. Arrange the tomato petals rib side down on a nonstick pan, and sprinkle them with the salt. Place in the 400-degree oven for 30 minutes. Remove the petals from the oven and arrange them on a platter.

5. Mix the oil, pepper, and tarragon together in a small bowl. When the tomato petals have cooled to room temperature, sprinkle them with the tarragon oil. Serve.

TOTAL TIME

45 minutes

YIELD

4 servings

NUTRITION

91 calories

2 g protein

7 g fat

.9 g saturated fat

0 mg cholesterol

519 mg sodium

5 g carbohydrate

1 g dietary fiber

Tomatoes are rich in vitamin C and lycopene, a natural plant chemical that is a potent antioxidant.

Apricot and Hazelnut Biscotti

TOTAL TIME

About 1 1/2 hours

YIELD

24 biscotti

NUTRITION

237 calories

4 g protein

9 g fat

.8 g saturated fat

18 mg cholesterol

168 mg sodium

36 g carbohydrate

2 g dietary fiber

CLAUDINE

I love biscotti: imagine how cool it would be to be able to tell your friends that you made your own biscotti. I think I'd dunk at least half of mine in chocolate.

Biscotti, which keep for a long time, are great for snacks or desserts on their own or with fresh fruit. This recipe is easy. All the ingredients are mixed together for a few seconds in a food processor, shaped into a loaf, cooked in the oven for 30 minutes, then sliced and returned to the oven for 20 minutes more to dry out further. The addition of dried apricots lends tangy taste and chewiness to the biscotti.

2 CUPS ALL-PURPOSE FLOUR

¾ CUP SUGAR

¼ TEASPOON SALT

1 TEASPOON BAKING POWDER

1 LARGE EGG

3 TABLESPOONS MILK

2 TABLESPOONS CANOLA OIL

1½ TEASPOONS VANILLA

¾ CUP SHELLED HAZELNUTS OR CASHEW NUTS

4 OUNCES DRIED APRICOTS, CUT INTO ¼-INCH SLICES (⅔ CUP)

1. Preheat the oven to 375 degrees.

2. Place the flour, sugar, salt, and baking powder in the bowl of a food processor and process for 5 seconds. Add the egg, milk, oil, and vanilla and process for 10 seconds, or just until the mixture begins to hold together.

3. Transfer the mixture to a bowl, add the nuts and apricots, and mix by hand until the mixture is thoroughly combined.

4. Line a cookie sheet with parchment paper. Place the dough in a mound on top of a piece of plastic wrap about 18 inches long, and press on it to form it into a log about 12 inches long by 3 inches wide by 1 inch high. Invert the dough log onto the parchment paper–lined sheet, and peel off the plastic wrap. Place in the 375-degree oven and bake for 30 minutes, until lightly browned on all sides and cracked on top. Cool for about 10 minutes. Meanwhile, reduce the oven heat to 350 degrees.

5. Using a serrated knife, cut the log crosswise into ½-inch slices. (You should have about 24 slices.) Arrange the slices on the parchment paper–lined cookie sheet, and bake the biscotti for 20 minutes, until nicely browned on both sides. (There is no need to turn the biscotti over halfway through the baking time, as many biscotti recipes instruct; these brown nicely on both sides without turning.)

6. Cool the biscotti thoroughly on a wire rack, then store them in a dry place (or wrap well and freeze).

Cooking for Tonton Richard

FILLET OF SOLE IN ARTICHOKE BOTTOMS

HORSERADISH AND COTTAGE CHEESE DIP

SPICY RIB ROAST

SKILLET LETTUCE "PACKAGES"

APRICOT *FEUILLETÉ*

———

This menu is special for both Claudine and me. It is dedicated to my brother, her *tonton*, or uncle, and we prepared food that we know he would love if he could be with us. ⩗ There is a great deal of technique demonstrated in these dishes. The first one, for example, provides a lesson on how to trim artichokes to obtain artichoke bottoms, which we use here as receptacles. Shallots and mushrooms, cooked and transformed into a puree called *duxelles*, are used to line the bottom of a gratin dish. The artichoke receptacles are arranged on top of the *duxelles*, and, eventually, partially cooked sole fillets are rolled and placed in the artichoke bottoms, which then are baked and served with a sauce. ⩗ Our main course is a spicy rib roast. When selecting a roast for this recipe, be sure to buy three ribs from near the saddle, which have much less fat than ribs from close to the shoulder. Before it is cooked, the top of the roast is trimmed of all fat and coated with a rub. While our rub contains garlic, ginger, soy, cayenne, and dry mustard, you can create your own rub with a different assortment of herbs and spices. The roast is cooked at a high temperature, then left to rest — a very important step — in a low-temperature oven. We serve the roast with a horseradish sauce or dip made with horseradish, garlic, and cottage cheese. ⩗ A classic accompaniment for roast beef, and one that I know my brother would like, is braised lettuce. For this dish, we use red leaf lettuce, cooking it in a skillet until tender. ⩗ Our dessert for this menu is a *feuilleté* of apricot, which we make with a fast puff pastry. This recipe shows Claudine that in winter, when fresh, ripe apricots are not available, canned apricots can be used with very good results.

White
JOSEPH
DROUHIN,
RULLY BLANC

Red
HARTFORD
COURT,
PINOT NOIR

White Dessert
CHATEAU
RAYMOND-
LAFON,
SAUTERNES

Fillet of Sole in Artichoke Bottoms

This recipe is composed of several subrecipes, one addressing the preparation of artichoke bottoms, another the making of mushroom *duxelles*, and a third the poaching of fish fillets in a tomato and wine mixture that is ultimately transformed into a creamy sauce. Each of these subrecipes could be served independently, but when combined as they are here, into a single dish, the result is elegant party fare.

TOTAL TIME
About 1 hour

YIELD
4 servings

NUTRITION
251 calories
25 g protein
11 g fat
1 g saturated fat
60 mg cholesterol
658 mg sodium
9 g carbohydrate
1 g dietary fiber

ARTICHOKES

4 ARTICHOKES, ABOUT 2 POUNDS

1 TABLESPOON LEMON JUICE

1 CUP WATER

¼ TEASPOON SALT

MUSHROOM *DUXELLES*

3 TABLESPOONS PEELED AND FINELY CHOPPED SHALLOTS

1 TABLESPOON VIRGIN OLIVE OIL

6 OUNCES CREMINI MUSHROOMS, WASHED AND COARSELY CHOPPED

¼ TEASPOON SALT

¼ TEASPOON FRESHLY GROUND BLACK PEPPER

SOLE

1 POUND LEMON SOLE FILLETS (4 FILLETS)

1 LARGE RIPE TOMATO (8 OUNCES), CUT INTO 1-INCH PIECES

¼ TEASPOON SALT

¼ TEASPOON FRESHLY GROUND BLACK PEPPER

¼ CUP FRUITY DRY WHITE WINE (LIKE A SAUVIGNON BLANC)

2 TABLESPOONS VIRGIN OLIVE OIL

1 TABLESPOON CHOPPED FRESH PARSLEY

1. *For the Artichokes:* Remove the stems from the artichokes, cutting them off at the base of each artichoke. Peel the stems and place them in a saucepan. Cut off the top of each artichoke, and trim the leaves of the artichokes so that you are left only with artichoke bottoms or hearts. Place the bottoms in the saucepan with the stems, and add the lemon juice, water, and the ¼ teaspoon salt. Bring the mixture to a boil, cover, reduce the heat to low, and cook gently for 18 to 20 minutes, until the artichoke bottoms and stems are tender. Using a slotted spoon, transfer the bottoms and stems to a plate and allow them to cool to lukewarm. Discard the cooking liquid.

2. When the artichoke bottoms are cool enough to handle, remove and discard the chokes from each. Cut the stems into 1-inch pieces and set them aside with the bottoms.

3. Preheat the oven to 180 degrees.

(CONTINUED)

216

CLAUDINE
———
*We did an
awesome menu
this time. For me
these are foods
from my child-
hood. My mom is
usually not too
crazy about beef,
but she will eat
it if it's cooked
this way because
she really likes
the spice rub and
the horseradish.
So her chance to
eat both of those
is to have them
with the beef.*

4. *For the* Duxelles: Place the shallots in a skillet with the tablespoon of olive oil, and cook them for 2 minutes over medium heat. Add the mushrooms and the ¼ teaspoon each salt and pepper. Sauté over medium to high heat for about 5 minutes, until the moisture from the mushrooms is gone and the mushrooms are lightly browned.

5. Arrange the artichoke bottoms in a 6-cup gratin dish, and divide the mush-room mixture among the artichokes, filling them lightly. Surround with the artichoke stem pieces. (Alternatively, spoon the mushroom mixture into the gratin dish, and arrange the artichoke bottoms on top and the stem pieces around them.) Keep warm in the 180-degree oven while you cook the sole, or cool and reheat when needed.

6. *For the Sole:* Fold in the ends of each fillet (as you would fold a letter) to create a somewhat square three-layered "package," and arrange the packages seam side down in a skillet. Place the tomato pieces around the sole, and sprinkle the fish and the tomatoes with the ¼ teaspoon each salt and pepper. Add the white wine.

7. Bring the mixture to a boil over high heat and boil it for about 30 seconds. Then, turn the sole "packages" with a fork so they are seam side up, cover, reduce the heat to medium, and cook for 2½ minutes. The fillets should be slightly undercooked in the center at this point.

8. Arrange one sole fillet in each artichoke bottom. Return the gratin dish to the 180-degree oven while you prepare the sauce.

9. Place the cooking liquid with the tomato pieces in a 2-cup glass measuring cup, and add the 2 tablespoons olive oil. Using a handheld immersion blender, emulsify the mixture for 30 to 40 seconds, until it is smooth and creamy.

10. Pour the sauce over the sole fillets, and sprinkle the parsley on top. Serve immediately.

Horseradish and Cottage Cheese Dip

This is a classic garnish for rib roast, although it is very often made by combining horseradish, garlic, and seasonings with whipped cream instead of our lighter substitute, cottage cheese. The dip goes well, too, with cold leftovers of most any roast meat, from pork to goose. For a decorative touch, serve the dip in a hollowed-out yellow, red, or green bell pepper.

TOTAL TIME
10 minutes

YIELD
1 ¼ cups

NUTRITION
55 calories
4 g protein
.6 g fat
.3 g saturated fat
2 mg cholesterol
216 mg sodium
8 g carbohydrate
.7 g dietary fiber

1 PIECE FRESH HORSERADISH (ABOUT 1½ OUNCES), PEELED AND CUT INTO ½-INCH PIECES

1 LARGE CLOVE GARLIC, PEELED

⅓ TEASPOON SALT

¼ TEASPOON SUGAR

1 CUP COTTAGE CHEESE

2 TO 3 TABLESPOONS MILK

1. Place all the ingredients except the milk in the bowl of a food processor. Process the mixture briefly, then add the milk 1 tablespoon at time while continuing to process, until the dip is smooth and the consistency of a light mayonnaise.

2. Refrigerate until serving time.

Spicy Rib Roast

My wife is not an aficionado of roast beef, but she loves this recipe. I think the spicy mixture — a combination of garlic, ginger, a dash of sugar, some soy, cayenne, dry mustard, and paprika — that I rub on the roast before cooking it is the reason why. ❧ The roast should be from the smaller and less fatty end of the rib section. Totally cleaned of the layer of fat on top, the meat is roasted in a hot oven, then allowed to rest for at least 20 minutes in a warm oven before serving, so it is totally pink throughout.

YIELD

6 to 8 servings

NUTRITION

401 calories

47 g protein

21 g fat

8 g saturated fat

136 mg cholesterol

388 mg sodium

2 g carbohydrate

.1 g dietary fiber

RUB

3 LARGE CLOVES GARLIC, PEELED

1 PIECE OF GINGER (ABOUT THE SAME SIZE AS THE COMBINED GARLIC GLOVES), PEELED

2 TEASPOONS SUGAR

2 TABLESPOONS SOY SAUCE

½ TEASPOON CAYENNE PEPPER

1 TEASPOON DRY MUSTARD

1 TEASPOON PAPRIKA

1 3-RIB BEEF RIB ROAST (ABOUT 7 POUNDS), WITH ALL VISIBLE FAT TRIMMED FROM TOP (ABOUT 6 POUNDS TRIMMED)

½ CUP WATER

1 SMALL BUNCH WATERCRESS, CLEANED, FOR GARNISH (OPTIONAL)

1. Preheat the oven to 400 degrees.

2. Place all the rub ingredients in a blender, and blend them until smooth. Rub the mixture on the top and sides of the roast.

3. Place the roast meat side up in a small roasting pan, and cook it in the 400-degree oven for 30 minutes. Turn the meat so it is bone side up and cook it for another 30 minutes. Remove the roast from the oven, and leave the oven door open to cool the oven to about 180 degrees.

4. Place the roast on a platter, and discard all the fat that has accumulated in the roasting pan. Add the water to the drippings in the pan, and stir to mix them together well.

5. Place the roast, bone side up, back in the roasting pan with the juices, and place the pan in the 180-degree oven to rest for at least 20 to 30 minutes (but as long as 2 hours) before carving. Serve, if desired, on watercress.

Spicy Rib Roast (this page), Horseradish and Cottage Cheese Dip (page 217), and Skillet Lettuce "Packages" (page 220)

Skillet Lettuce "Packages"

TOTAL TIME
10 to 15 minutes

YIELD
4 servings

NUTRITION
82 calories
2 g protein
7 g fat
1 g saturated fat
0 mg cholesterol
306 mg sodium
4 g carbohydrate
2 g dietary fiber

CLAUDINE

If you have more lettuce than you're going to eat raw, this is a good alternative. You can also put it in soup.

We often don't take advantage of lettuce as a cooked vegetable, but this recipe is a classic that I have updated. Instead of braising lettuce in wine with pork rind and ham in the rich way it was prepared traditionally, I lighten the dish by cooking lettuce segments, still wet from washing, in a little olive oil until they are limp, then season and sauté them until they are lightly browned. Folded into "packages," they make a delightful garnish for the Spicy Rib Roast (page 219).

2 HEADS RED LEAF LETTUCE (ABOUT 12 OUNCES EACH)

2 TABLESPOONS VIRGIN OLIVE OIL

½ TEASPOON SALT

¼ TEASPOON FRESHLY GROUND BLACK PEPPER

1. Cut the lettuce heads lengthwise into quarters so that the leaves of each quarter remain attached together at the root end. Wash the lettuce quarters under cool tap water, and drain them in a colander.

2. Heat the 2 tablespoons olive oil in a large skillet. When the oil is hot, add the lettuce (still damp from washing), laying the pieces side by side and slightly overlapping in the skillet. Cook the lettuce, covered, over medium to high heat for 3 to 4 minutes, until the leaves are wilted. Season with the salt and pepper, then turn the lettuce pieces over (they will have shrunk considerably),

arrange them side by side in the skillet, and cook, covered, for 4 to 5 minutes longer, until the pieces are soft and lightly browned on both sides. Set the skillet aside off the heat, covered, until serving time. (The lettuce will hold like this for 15 to 20 minutes; if holding it longer, reheat it before serving.)

4. To serve, fold each lettuce piece (eight in all) into a neat package. Serve two lettuce packages alongside each serving of Spicy Rib Roast (page 219).

Apricot Feuilleté

The dough base for this dessert is what I call "mock" puff paste. Made with instant Wondra flour, it is prepared rapidly in a food processor and the butter incorporated in far fewer steps than is generally required to create the multilayered effect that is characteristic of conventional puff pastry. ❧ This is a recipe I prepare quite often, especially in the winter, with canned apricots, which are appealingly sweet and often give me better results than fresh apricots – unless I can find them ripe from the tree. Apricot halves are dried first in a hot oven to concentrate their flavor, then arranged on a rectangle of the puff pastry and cooked. You will find that the number of apricots per can varies widely – some 16-ounce cans contain as few as 8 apricots, others as many as 16. Use larger apricots, if possible, but follow the same procedures whatever the size of the fruit.

TOTAL TIME

About 2 hours

YIELD

8 servings

NUTRITION

226 calories

2 g protein

8 g fat

5 g saturated fat

23 mg cholesterol

50 mg sodium

37 g carbohydrate

2 g dietary fiber

MOCK PUFF PASTRY

1 CUP INSTANT WONDRA FLOUR (ABOUT 4½ OUNCES) PLUS ¼ CUP WONDRA FLOUR FOR USE IN ROLLING THE DOUGH

⅛ TEASPOON SALT

¼ TEASPOON SUGAR

¾ STICK COLD UNSALTED BUTTER, CUT INTO 6 SLICES (3 OUNCES)

¼ CUP ICE-COLD WATER

2 CANS (16 OUNCES EACH) APRICOT HALVES, DRAINED, JUICE RESERVED

1. *For the Mock Puff Pastry:* Place the cup of flour in the bowl of a food processor with the salt, sugar, butter, and water. Process for 5 seconds. (The dough will not begin to gather together at this point, and pieces of butter will be visible throughout the mixture.)

2. Transfer the mixture to a cold surface (preferably marble). Using plastic wrap, gather it together, pressing it into a rough mass. Sprinkle the dough and the rolling surface generously with some of the remaining ¼ cup of flour, and roll the dough into a rectangle about 14 inches by 5 inches.

3. Fold in the two narrow ends of the dough so they meet in the middle, then fold the dough again on this center meeting line to have a rectangle about 5 inches by 3½ inches.

(CONTINUED)

222

Apricots are made orange by the beta-carotene in them. Each serving has enough beta-carotene to provide more than 20% of the daily value for vitamin A.

4. Using more of the remaining flour, place the rectangle of dough so one of the narrow ends faces you, and roll it again into a 14-by 5-inch rectangle. Repeat the folding procedure explained in step 3, wrap the resulting 5-by 3½-inch rectangle of dough in plastic wrap, and refrigerate it for at least 1 hour before proceeding.

5. Meanwhile, preheat the oven to 350 degrees.

6. Arrange the drained apricot halves, cut side down, on a jelly roll pan lined with parchment paper, and place them in the 350-degree oven for about 40 minutes. Set the apricots aside to cool until cooking time.

7. About 20 minutes before cooking time, preheat the oven to 400 degrees.

8. At cooking time, sprinkle the rolling surface with the remaining flour, roll the dough into a thin rectangle measuring 16 by 6 inches, and transfer it to a nonstick cookie sheet or a cookie sheet lined with a nonstick baking mat or parchment paper.

9. Arrange the apricot halves skin side up and side by side in rows on the pastry rectangle so they are about ¾ inch from the pastry edge on all sides. Then, bring the pastry edges back over the apricots at the edge to create a dough "container."

10. Place the *feuilleté* in the 400-degree oven for about 40 minutes, until the surface of the apricots is lightly browned and the dough is dark brown and crisp. Let the *feuilleté* cool for at least 15 minutes.

11. Meanwhile, bring the reserved 1½ cups of juice from the apricots to a boil over high heat in a small saucepan. Boil the syrup until it is reduced to ⅓ cup.

12. Slide the cooled *feuilleté* onto a serving platter and, using a pastry brush, glaze the apricots with the reduced syrup. Cool to room temperature, cut into slices, and serve.

Apricot Feuilleté
(page 221)

A Menu for all Seasons

HALIBUT *ANTIBOISE*

POULET AU RIZ

BEET SALAD WITH PECANS

PECAN-AND-ARMAGNAC-STUFFED DATES

———

We start this menu with halibut prepared in the style of Antibes, a small town in the south of France. ↡ The chicken with rice dish that follows is intended to teach Claudine how to poach a chicken properly; boiling it gently to start, then setting it aside off the heat to continue cooking slowly in the hot stock makes the flesh very moist and tender. To make the dish as lean as possible, the skin is removed from the chicken before it is served, and as much fat as can be retrieved from the stock is discarded. The chicken flesh and vegetable garnish are served on jasmine rice, which has a flavor I particularly like. If jasmine is not available, however, substitute another variety of rice. ↡ As a bonus to our chicken and rice recipe, we make a sturdy soup from the leftovers. Extra chicken, vegetables, rice, and stock are combined for this satisfying soup, which serves as another meal when accompanied by crusty bread and cheese. ↡ The chicken with rice main course is followed by a beet salad. For this recipe, fresh beets are cooked, cut into sticks, and tossed with Chinese garlic sauce, a dash of sugar, salt, diced onions, and pecans, and the mixture is served on salad greens. ↡ Our meal for all seasons ends with pecan-and-Armagnac-stuffed dates. A great dessert during the holiday season — especially if you can find the very large Medjool dates — the recipe includes crushed cookies as a major ingredient in the stuffing.

White
CAMBRIA,
CHARDONNAY
RESERVE

Red
QUINTA DO
CRASTO,
DOURO RED

Halibut Antiboise

TOTAL TIME

About 20 minutes

YIELD

4 servings

NUTRITION

317 calories

35 g protein

16 g fat

3 g saturated fat

66 mg cholesterol

1110 mg sodium

6 g carbohydrate

1 g dietary fiber

This halibut is served with a fresh olive and tomato sauce in the style of Antibes. While the sauce can be made ahead, the halibut is broiled at the last moment, then coated with the sauce and served.

ANTIBOISE SAUCE

2 TABLESPOONS VIRGIN OLIVE OIL

½ CUP CHOPPED ONION

1 TEASPOON CHOPPED FRESH THYME LEAVES

2 TOMATOES (12 OUNCES TOTAL), PEELED, SEEDED, AND CUT INTO ½-INCH PIECES (1½ CUPS)

¼ CUP WATER

½ TEASPOON SALT

¼ TEASPOON FRESHLY GROUND BLACK PEPPER

24 KALAMATA OLIVES, PITTED AND CUT INTO ½-INCH PIECES (½ CUP)

2 TABLESPOONS SHREDDED BASIL

4 PIECES HALIBUT, SKIN REMOVED AND TOTALLY CLEANED OF SINEWS, EACH ABOUT 6 OUNCES AND ¾ INCH THICK (1½ POUNDS)

½ TEASPOON SALT

1 TEASPOON VIRGIN OLIVE OIL

1. *For the Sauce:* Heat the 2 tablespoons olive oil in a skillet. Add the onion and thyme. Cook over medium heat for 1½ minutes, then add the tomatoes, water, ½ teaspoon salt, and pepper. Cook for 1 minute longer, then set the sauce aside. (The sauce can be prepared to this point up to 2 hours ahead.) Reserve the olives and basil in separate bowls for last minute addition to the sauce.

2. About 15 minutes before serving time, preheat a broiler.

3. At serving time, sprinkle both sides of the halibut steaks with the ½ teaspoon salt and brush them with the teaspoon of olive oil. Arrange the steaks on a cookie sheet (lined, if desired, with aluminum foil), and place the sheet under the hot broiler so the steaks are about 4 inches from the heat. Cook the steaks for 2½ minutes on each side.

4. Arrange a steak on each of four warmed dinner plates. Add the reserved olives and basil to the sauce, and bring the mixture to a boil. Pour the sauce over the steaks and serve immediately.

Poulet au Riz

This recipe reminds me of similar dishes my mother used to prepare when I was a child. Where she would use a hen, cooking it for hours and hours, I simplify the dish and shorten the cooking time by using a regular roasting chicken. ↯ I like flavorful rice and have selected the jasmine variety. Feel free, however, to substitute basmati or another rice of your choosing. I cook quite a lot of rice for this recipe – more than we need – but use it in a soup I make with *Poulet au Riz* leftovers (see Note at end of recipe).

TOTAL TIME
About 1 ¾ hours

YIELD
4 servings

NUTRITION
583 calories
55 g protein
10 g fat
2 g saturated fat
143 mg cholesterol
1286 mg sodium
66 g carbohydrate
6 g dietary fiber

↯   ↯   ↯   ↯   ↯   ↯   ↯   ↯

CHICKEN

1 LARGE OR 2 SMALL LEEKS (12 OUNCES), TRIMMED (WITH MOST OF THE GREEN LEFT ON), SPLIT, AND WASHED

1 LARGE ONION, PEELED AND HALVED

4 CARROTS (12 OUNCES), PEELED AND HALVED

3 PARSNIPS (6 OUNCES), PEELED AND HALVED

4 WHITE TURNIPS (12 OUNCES), PEELED AND HALVED

1 BOUQUET GARNI (ABOUT 12 PARSLEY STEMS, 1 LARGE SPRIG ROSEMARY, 1 LARGE SPRIG SAGE, 2 BAY LEAVES, AND 1 RIB CELERY, ALL TIED TOGETHER WITH KITCHEN TWINE)

2¼ TEASPOONS SALT

4 QUARTS WATER

1 CHICKEN (ABOUT 4 POUNDS) WITH NECK AND GIZZARD (LIVER RESERVED FOR ANOTHER USE)

RICE

1½ CUPS JASMINE RICE, OR ANOTHER RICE OF YOUR CHOICE (1 POUND)

3 CUPS CHICKEN STOCK (FROM THE COOKING OF THE CHICKEN, ABOVE)

1 BUNCH SCALLIONS (7 OR 8), TRIMMED (WITH MOST OF THE GREEN LEFT ON), CLEANED, AND COARSELY CHOPPED (¾ CUP)

½ TEASPOON SALT

OPTIONAL ACCOMPANIMENTS: CORNICHONS (SMALL FRENCH GHERKINS), FRENCH MUSTARD, GRATED SWISS CHEESE, COUNTRY BREAD

1. *For the Chicken:* Place all the ingredients in a large, narrow stock pot and bring the mixture to a boil over high heat. Cover, reduce the heat to low, and boil gently for 30 minutes. Set the covered pot off the heat, and let the chicken poach in the hot liquid for 30 minutes.

2. Using a large skimmer, remove the chicken and vegetables from the pot, and place them on a platter. Reserve the stock. (You should have about 4 quarts, or 16 cups, of stock. Skim off and discard as much fat from the surface of the stock as possible. Set aside 3 cups for the chicken and vegetables and 5 cups for the rice. Freeze the remaining 8 cups of stock or refrigerate it for use in making soup from the *Poulet au Riz* leftovers, as instructed in the Note at the end of recipe.)

(CONTINUED)

228

This poulet au riz is something that I've had since the dawn of time at my grandmother's house. I like it nowadays especially because you can make two dishes in one: first the chicken itself, then the soup with the leftovers. You can freeze the soup and save it for another day.

3. When the chicken is cool enough to handle, remove and discard the skin, and pick the meat in large pieces from the bones. Place the meat in a large, deep gratin dish, and arrange the vegetables around it (discarding the bouquet garni). Pour the 3 cups of reserved stock over the meat and vegetables in the dish. Cover, and set aside while you make the rice.

4. *For the Rice:* Place all the ingredients for the rice in a medium saucepan. Bring the mixture to a boil over high heat, stirring occasionally. Cover, reduce the heat to low, and cook for 25 minutes, stirring occasionally.

5. Reheat the chicken and vegetables until warmed through. Mound some of the rice in the center of each of four dinner plates, and arrange a few pieces of chicken on top. Place some vegetables around the chicken and rice, and spoon on some of the stock from the gratin dish. Serve, if desired, with cornichons, French mustard, grated Swiss cheese (sprinkled on the rice), and chunks of country bread.

Note: To make soup with the *Poulet au Riz* leftovers: Place the reserved 2 quarts (8 cups) stock in a large saucepan. Coarsely chop any remaining chicken and vegetables, and add them to the stock along with any leftover rice. (If there are not enough vegetables and/or rice, add some grated raw carrot, sliced scallion, or even leftover salad greens to the pan along with a little pastina or cornmeal.) Cook for 5 minutes, and serve, if desired, with the optional accompaniments listed in step 5.

Poulet au Riz (page 227) and Beet Salad with Pecans (page 230)

Beet Salad with Pecans

TOTAL TIME

About 1 ½ hours

YIELD

4 servings

NUTRITION

226 calories

3 g protein

15 g fat

1 g saturated fat

0 mg cholesterol

679 mg sodium

21 g carbohydrate

5 g dietary fiber

Beets are a good source of vitamin C, folate, and fiber.

This refreshing beet salad is excellent as an accompaniment for meat and great on its own as a first course. In the summer, when I have fresh beets, I bake them or boil them in water for recipes as I do here; if you want to save some time, however, you can cook them in a microwave oven. For this unusual dish, I combine sticks of cooked beets with vinegar and chili sauce and serve them on salad greens.

4 OR 5 RED BEETS (1¼ POUNDS)

2 TABLESPOONS RED WINE VINEGAR

1 TABLESPOON CHINESE CHILI GARLIC SAUCE (AVAILABLE IN ASIAN MARKETS, SPECIALTY FOOD STORES, AND SOME SUPERMARKETS)

1½ TEASPOONS SUGAR

¾ TEASPOON SALT

2 TABLESPOONS CANOLA OIL

1 MEDIUM ONION (4 OUNCES), PEELED AND CUT INTO A ¼-INCH DICE (⅔ CUP)

½ CUP PECAN PIECES

8 BOSTON LETTUCE LEAVES, WASHED AND SPUN DRY (OPTIONAL)

1. Place the beets in a saucepan, cover them with cold water, and bring the water to a boil over high heat. Reduce the heat to low, cover, and cook the beets gently for 1 to 1¼ hours, until they are tender. Drain and cool.

2. When the beets are cool enough to handle, peel them, and cut them into ½-inch sticks about 2 inches long. (If you are concerned about staining, wear plastic gloves and cover your cutting board with plastic wrap.) Place the beet sticks in a serving bowl.

3. In a small mixing bowl, combine the vinegar, chili sauce, sugar, salt, and oil. Add this mixture to the beets along with the diced onion and pecans. Mix well.

4. Serve the salad at room temperature on its own or, if you prefer, on top of lettuce leaves.

Pecan-and-Armagnac-Stuffed Dates

These dates are an appealing dessert or a welcome snack at any hour of the day. I like to use the very large Medjool dates when they are available, but regular dates are fine for this recipe. The stuffing mixture is mostly cookies, and any type of cookies you have on hand can be used.

❧ ❧ ❧ ❧ ❧ ❧ ❧ ❧

20 REGULAR-SIZE DRIED, PITTED DATES, OR
   12 VERY LARGE MEDJOOL PITTED DATES

3 OUNCES COOKIES (I USED GINGERSNAPS, BUT
   CHOCOLATE CHIP, TUILES, OR EVEN GRAHAM
   CRACKERS CAN BE SUBSTITUTED)

1½ TABLESPOONS LEMON JUICE

1½ TABLESPOONS ARMAGNAC OR COGNAC
   (OR, FOR A NONALCOHOLIC ADDITION,
   SUBSTITUTE ORANGE JUICE)

⅓ CUP COARSELY CHOPPED PECANS

1 TABLESPOON MINCED FRESH MINT

20 SMALL SPEARMINT OR PEPPERMINT LEAVES,
   FOR USE AS DECORATION

1. Using a sharp knife, split the dates, stopping before cutting them in half entirely, and open each one like a book. Crush the cookies coarsely in a small bowl, and lightly mix in the lemon juice and Armagnac. Add the nuts and minced mint, and mix until the ingredients are well combined.

2. *To Fill Regular Dates:* spoon about 1 teaspoon of the cookie mixture onto each open date, then gently fold the date to partially close it around the stuffing. Follow the same procedure to fill Medjool dates, but use about 2 teaspoons of the cookie mixture for each date.

3. Decorate the dates by inserting the stem end of a small mint leaf in the center of the stuffed edge. Arrange the dates on a platter, and refrigerate them until serving time.

TOTAL TIME
15 minutes

YIELD
4 servings

NUTRITION
282 calories
3 g protein
8 g fat
.8 g saturated fat
0 mg cholesterol
209 mg sodium
51 g carbohydrate
4 g dietary fiber

The Adventurous Cook

SALTED CODFISH FARO

EXOTIC ROAST OF PORK

SPICY CELERY WITH GARLIC

PLUM COBBLER

———

The more adventurous and lovers of the exotic will enjoy the different taste sensations in this spicy, flavorful menu. ↯ We start with a salted codfish recipe that I have named "Faro" after the town in Portugal's Algarve region that provided the inspiration for this dish (and after my dog, Faro, whom I found there as a lost puppy on the beach and brought back home with me). Although salted codfish is rich, cooking it with vegetables, as we do here, tones down its intense taste. ↯ The codfish is followed by a roast of pork cooked with several exotic seasonings, among them five-spice powder, ginger, and sherry vinegar. For this recipe, use knuckle or sirloin tip, both lean, moist cuts from the animal's back leg. ↯ The roast is served with a spicy celery dish. Available year round, celery isn't served cooked as often as it should be. Here, we cook it in a little hot salsa, available in all markets, and serve it either hot or at room temperature. ↯ Finally, as a dessert for this adventurous menu, we make a plum cobbler with a baked-on topping of old-fashioned oats, a little flour, pecans, and cinnamon. This dessert is best served lukewarm or at room temperature.

White
AS LAXAS

Red
ALLANDALE
MATTHEW,
SHIRAZ

Salted Codfish Faro

TOTAL TIME

About 50 minutes,
plus soaking time

YIELD

4 servings

NUTRITION

552 calories
50 g protein
22 g fat
3 g saturated fat
107 mg cholesterol
6440 mg sodium
34 g carbohydrate
6 g dietary fiber

The salted codfish I usually buy at the supermarket comes from Canada in little wooden boxes, each holding a pound. When buying salt cod packaged in this manner, try to look inside several of the boxes, and choose one that contains a thick fillet instead of small pieces of fish. ↓ If you are fortunate enough to be in an area where there are Italian, Spanish, or Portuguese markets, you may find large fillets of salted, dried codfish hanging in the markets. Purchased this way, the cod – often called *bacalao* – may be drier and saltier and may require longer soaking (up to 24 hours) in more changes of water than the boxed fillets, but the quality is much better.

1 POUND SALT COD (SALTED AND DRIED CODFISH)

2 TO 3 MEDIUM RED POTATOES (1 POUND)

3 TABLESPOONS VIRGIN OLIVE OIL

1 GREEN PEPPER (12 OUNCES), SEEDED AND CUT INTO 1-INCH PIECES (2 CUPS)

6 SCALLIONS, TRIMMED, CLEANED, AND COARSELY MINCED (ABOUT ¾ CUP)

1 SMALL ONION (ABOUT 3 OUNCES), PEELED AND CHOPPED (ABOUT ½ CUP)

5 CLOVES GARLIC, PEELED AND THINLY SLICED (2 TABLESPOONS)

½ CUP DRY SHERRY

½ TEASPOON FRESHLY GROUND BLACK PEPPER

1 CUP UNPITTED MIXED OLIVES (KALAMATA, GREEN, OIL-CURED, ETC.), RINSED IN COLD WATER

2 TABLESPOONS CHOPPED FRESH PARSLEY

1. Place 8 cups of cold water in a large bowl. Add the salt cod, and soak it in the water for 2 to 3 hours. Drain off the water, add 8 cups of fresh water to the bowl, and soak the cod for 9 to 10 hours longer, for a total of 12 hours. Drain. (Note: If using thicker *bacalao* from an ethnic market, soak it longer – up to 24 hours – changing the water three to four times during the soaking process.)

2. Bring 6 cups of water to a boil in a medium saucepan, add the pieces of fish to the water, and bring the mixture back to a boil. Boil very gently, uncovered, for 10 minutes. Drain off the water, and place the fish in a bowl of cold water. Using your fingers, separate the fish into flakes, removing and discarding the bones and skin pieces. (You should have 2 cups of flaked fish.) Set the fish aside.

3. Place the potatoes in a medium sauce-pan, cover them with cold water, bring the water to a boil, and boil the potatoes gently until very tender, 30 to 40 minutes. Drain the potatoes. When they are cool enough to handle, peel them, and cut them into ¾-inch slices. Set the potatoes aside.

4. Heat the olive oil in a sturdy saucepan, and add the green pepper, scallions, onion, and garlic. Cook over low heat for 5 minutes. Add the flaked fish pieces, sherry, and pepper. Cover and cook over low heat for 15 minutes. (This recipe can be made to this point up to 2 hours ahead.)

5. At serving time, add the olives, and mix them in gently. Arrange the potato slices on top, and heat the mixture for a few minutes until it is hot throughout.

6. Arrange a couple of potato slices on each of four dinner plates, and ladle some of the fish mixture on top. Sprinkle with the chopped parsley, and serve immediately.

Exotic Roast of Pork

TOTAL TIME

About 1½ hours

YIELD

4 to 6 servings

NUTRITION

333 calories

37 g protein

17 g fat

6 g saturated fat

94 mg cholesterol

680 mg sodium

4 g carbohydrate

.1 g dietary fiber

CLAUDINE

I personally like the exotic roast of pork because the whole thing is done on the stovetop. Doing the whole thing on the stovetop makes me feel more confident about how it's going to turn out.

This dish is especially good if you use pork top knuckle, a lean, solid muscle from the upper hind leg that becomes very tender and remains juicy when braised. Made with the loin, this roast will not be as moist; made with the shoulder, it will be quite moist but much less lean. ❧ Leftover roast is excellent sliced (not too thin) and served with some of its cold meat juices on top of a garlicky salad of bitter greens, like curly endive, as a lunch or light supper entree the following day.

1 TABLESPOON UNSALTED BUTTER

1 PORK ROAST (1¾ POUNDS), PREFERABLY THE TOP KNUCKLE OR SIRLOIN TIP PART OF THE UPPER HIND LEG, COMPLETELY TRIMMED OF ALL SURROUNDING FAT

¼ TEASPOON SALT

1 TABLESPOON PEELED GINGER PIECES

1 TABLESPOON PEELED GARLIC PIECES (3 TO 4 CLOVES)

1½ TABLESPOONS SOY SAUCE

½ TEASPOON FIVE-SPICE POWDER

2 TABLESPOONS SHERRY VINEGAR

3 TABLESPOONS KETCHUP

¼ CUP WATER

1. Heat the butter in a dutch oven or *cocotte* (the French name for a heavy-duty, high-sided, enameled cast-iron pot). Sprinkle the roast with the salt, and sauté it over medium heat, uncovered, for 15 to 20 minutes, turning it occasionally so it browns nicely on all sides.

2. While the roast is browning, place the remaining ingredients in a blender, and blend them until smooth.

3. When the roast is browned, add the sauce mixture from the blender to the pot. Bring to a boil, cover, reduce the heat to very low, and cook, covered, for 1 hour, turning the roast in the sauce every 15 minutes.

4. Let the roast rest in the sauce for 10 minutes, then cut it into ¼-inch slices, and serve the slices with the sauce.

Exotic Roast of Pork (this page) and Spicy Celery with Garlic (page 238)

Spicy Celery with Garlic

TOTAL TIME
35 to 40 minutes

YIELD
4 servings

NUTRITION
125 calories
3 g protein
10 g fat
1 g saturated fat
1 mg cholesterol
418 mg sodium
7 g carbohydrate
3 g dietary fiber

A large bunch of celery is the main ingredient in this vegetable accompaniment. I peel the outer ribs of the celery stalks first, then cut them into pieces and cook them gently in a little chicken stock flavored with hot red salsa to give the celery a spicy taste. Most of the liquid evaporates in the cooking, leaving the celery moist and flavorful.

1 BUNCH CELERY (1½ POUNDS), WITH INNER STALKS AS WHITE AS POSSIBLE

3 TO 4 CLOVES GARLIC, PEELED AND THINLY SLICED (1½ TABLESPOONS)

½ CUP HOMEMADE CHICKEN STOCK OR CANNED CHICKEN BROTH

¼ CUP HOT RED SALSA

3 TABLESPOONS VIRGIN OLIVE OIL

¼ TEASPOON SALT

1. Using a vegetable peeler, peel the outside of the outer ribs of celery to remove the tough, fibrous strings from the surface. Cut the celery into 2-inch pieces. You should have 6 to 7 cups.

2. Place the celery pieces in a large bowl, cover them with cold water, and wash them thoroughly.

3. Lift the celery from the water and place it, still wet, in a large saucepan with the remainder of the ingredients. Bring the mixture to a boil, uncovered, then reduce the heat, cover, and cook gently for about 25 minutes, until most of the liquid is gone and the celery pieces are tender.

4. Serve immediately. (For later use, cool, cover, refrigerate, and reheat briefly in a microwave oven or in a saucepan on top of the stove.)

Plum Cobbler

The old-fashioned dough topping for this classic dessert is quick and easy to make in a food processor. Assembly requires simply sprinkling the topping over pitted plums and baking the dish in a hot oven. Always reliable and good, this is one of my favorites.

❧   ❧   ❧   ❧   ❧   ❧   ❧   ❧

DOUGH TOPPING

⅓ CUP OLD-FASHIONED ROLLED OATS

⅓ CUP ALL-PURPOSE FLOUR

⅓ CUP SUGAR

⅓ CUP PECAN HALVES

½ TEASPOON GROUND CINNAMON

3 TABLESPOONS UNSALTED BUTTER

1 TABLESPOON CANOLA OIL

1¼ POUNDS (ABOUT 7) RIPE PLUMS (SANTA ROSA, FRIAR, OR ANOTHER VARIETY)

⅓ CUP SLICED DRIED APRICOTS

½ CUP PLAIN YOGURT OR SOUR CREAM

1. Preheat the oven to 400 degrees.

2. *For the Dough Topping:* Place all the dough ingredients in the bowl of a food processor, and process the mixture for 15 to 20 seconds, until it is crumbly.

3. Quarter the plums, and pit them. Place the plums in a 6-cup gratin dish, and distribute the apricots around them. Sprinkle the crumbly dough mixture on top.

4. Bake the cobbler in the 400-degree oven for 40 minutes. Serve lukewarm with 1 rounded tablespoon of yogurt or sour cream per serving.

TOTAL TIME

About 1 hour

YIELD

4 servings

NUTRITION

286 calories

4 g protein

13 g fat

4 g saturated fat

17 mg cholesterol

124 mg sodium

41 g carbohydrate

3 g dietary fiber

This dish is a good source of fiber. Plums are rich in vitamin C, providing 20% of the daily value per serving.

The Classic Cook

COD IN BASIL AND ALMOND SAUCE
ON ZUCCHINI-POTATO BED

STUFFED QUAIL WITH GRAPE SAUCE

GRATIN OF LEEKS

PEACHES IN RED WINE

———

To begin this menu, we poach fresh cod in the classic manner and serve it on a puree of potatoes and zucchini with a basil and almond sauce. The portions that we serve, each 4½ to 5 ounces, are the perfect size for a first course, but you can serve the same recipe as a main course by increasing the portions of fish to about 7 ounces each. ✧ We follow with boned, stuffed quail, a recipe that provides a good lesson for Claudine on how to bone these tiny, delicate birds. The quail are stuffed with a mixture of diced vegetables – leeks, carrots, and celery – and are served with a garnish of fresh grapes in a savory sauce. ✧ As a vegetable side dish, we prepare a gratin of leek. Not covered with a cream sauce as it is conventionally, the gratin is baked with a mixture of bread crumbs, garlic, cheese, salt, and pepper on top. ✧ The dessert for this classic menu is peaches in red wine. Easy and delicious, this recipe can be made with either ripe yellow or white peaches.

White
BOISSET, CLASSIC
POUILLY FUISSE

Red
CAMBRIA, PINOT
NOIR RESERVE

Cod in Basil and Almond Sauce on Zucchini-Potato Bed

TOTAL TIME

About 1 hour

YIELD

4 servings

NUTRITION

430 calories

31 g protein

22 g fat

6 g saturated fat

90 mg cholesterol

773 mg sodium

26 g carbohydrate

3 g dietary fiber

Since I use fresh basil in this recipe, I use the water in which I first blanch the basil as the agent for cooking the potatoes and zucchini (although the zucchini-potato mixture also can be cooked in plain water if basil water is not available). These vegetables ultimately are pureed, and this puree is used as a bed for the cod, which then is coated with basil and almond sauce and served.

2 CUPS WATER

2 CUPS (LIGHTLY PACKED) BASIL LEAVES

ZUCCHINI-POTATO MIXTURE

2 POTATOES (1 POUND), PEELED AND CUT INTO 1-INCH PIECES

1 ZUCCHINI (10 OUNCES), TRIMMED AND CUT INTO 1-INCH PIECES

2 CLOVES GARLIC, PEELED

½ TEASPOON SALT

⅓ CUP HEAVY CREAM

BASIL AND ALMOND SAUCE

BLANCHED BASIL, FROM ABOVE

3 TABLESPOONS VIRGIN OLIVE OIL

3 TABLESPOONS WATER

2 TABLESPOONS GRATED PARMESAN CHEESE

½ TEASPOON SALT

¼ TEASPOON TABASCO HOT PEPPER SAUCE

3 TABLESPOONS COARSELY CHOPPED ALMONDS

DASH OF SALT

4 PIECES COD, EACH ABOUT 1 INCH THICK AND WEIGHING 4½ TO 5 OUNCES (1¼ POUNDS TOTAL)

1. Bring the 2 cups of water to a boil in a medium saucepan. Add the basil and cook it for about 1 minute, just until it is wilted. Using a skimmer, remove the basil from the hot water, and refresh it under cold running water. Drain the basil and set it aside.

2. *For the Zucchini-Potato Mixture:* Add the potatoes, zucchini, garlic, and ½ teaspoon salt to the basil cooking water in the saucepan, and bring the water to a boil. Cover the saucepan, reduce the heat to low, and boil the mixture for 30 minutes, until the vegetables are tender and very little water remains in the pan. Add the cream, and, using a handheld immersion blender, mash the mixture into a coarse puree. Set the zucchini-potato mixture aside in a warm place.

3. *For the Basil and Almond Sauce:* Place the reserved blanched basil leaves in the bowl of a conventional blender, add the olive oil, 3 tablespoons water, Parmesan cheese, ½ teaspoon of salt, and Tabasco, and blend until very smooth. Transfer the basil mixture to a small bowl, stir in the almonds, and set the sauce aside.

4. About 10 minutes before serving time, bring 2 cups water to a boil in a large saucepan, and add the dash of salt. Drop the cod pieces into the boiling water, and bring the water back to a boil over high heat (which will take about 2 minutes). Immediately cover the pan, set it off the heat, and let the fish steep in the hot water for 4 to 5 minutes, depending on the thickness of the pieces.

5. To serve, divide the zucchini-potato puree among four warm plates. Using a skimmer, remove the fish pieces from the cooking liquid, and blot them well with paper towels to remove excess moisture.

6. Arrange one cod piece on top of the puree on each plate. Coat the fish with the basil and almond sauce, and pour a few drops of the sauce around the fish as a decorative touch and for taste. Serve immediately.

The combination of potato, zucchini, and basil lends more than 50% of the daily value for vitamin C.

Stuffed Quail with Grape Sauce

TOTAL TIME
About 2 hours

YIELD
4 servings

NUTRITION
353 calories
27 g protein
17 g fat
5 g saturated fat
96 mg cholesterol
1320 mg sodium
21 g carbohydrate
3 g dietary fiber

This is a classic dish prepared in a modern way. The quail are boned, and a stock is made from the bones. Stuffed with a vegetable mixture, the boned birds are roasted, then finished under the broiler. A delicious sauce is created from their cooking juices, the previously made stock, a little thickening, and white grapes.

1 LEEK (6 OUNCES), TRIMMED, THOROUGHLY WASHED, AND CUT INTO 1-INCH PIECES

2 CARROTS (4 OUNCES), PEELED AND CUT INTO 1-INCH PIECES

2 STALKS CELERY (5 OUNCES), CLEANED AND CUT INTO 1-INCH PIECES

1 TABLESPOON PLUS 1 TEASPOON UNSALTED BUTTER

2 CLOVES GARLIC, PEELED, CRUSHED, AND FINELY CHOPPED

¼ CUP WATER

1 TEASPOON SALT

¼ TEASPOON FRESHLY GROUND BLACK PEPPER

4 LARGE QUAIL (7 OUNCES EACH)

2 TEASPOONS VEGETABLE OIL

4 CUPS WATER

1½ TABLESPOONS SOY SAUCE

1 TEASPOON HONEY

1 CUP WHITE SEEDLESS GRAPES (6 OUNCES)

½ TEASPOON CORNSTARCH DISSOLVED IN 1 TEASPOON WATER

1 TABLESPOON MINCED FRESH PARSLEY OR CHIVES (OPTIONAL)

1. Place the leek, carrots, and celery in the bowl of a food processor and chop them coarsely. (Yield: 3 cups.)

2. Melt the tablespoon of butter in a skillet, and add the processed vegetables and garlic to the skillet along with the water. Cook the mixture, covered, over medium heat for 10 minutes, or until the vegetables are soft and tender and the water is gone. Add the salt and pepper, mix well, and set aside to cool.

3. Bone the quail by cutting through the joint of the shoulders of each and pulling the carcass out without cutting open the skin. Cut off the ends of the drumsticks and remove the wing tips, leaving the first and second joint of the wings attached to the shoulder. Remove the thigh bones. (All the bones together should weigh about 8 ounces.) The only bones remaining in the quail should be the bones in the drumsticks and attached wings.

4. Place the bones in a skillet with the remaining teaspoon of butter and the oil, and brown them over low heat, covered, turning them occasionally, for 20 minutes. Add the water and 1 tablespoon of the soy sauce to the skillet, and bring the mixture to a boil. Reduce the heat, cover, and boil gently for 30 minutes, maintaining the gentle boil throughout. Strain the mixture through a fine strainer set over a saucepan, and discard the bones. Boil the strained liquid in the saucepan to reduce it to 1 cup, then set this stock aside in the pan.

5. Preheat the oven to 425 degrees.

6. Using a pastry bag, stuff the quail with the cooled vegetable mixture. Arrange the stuffed quail on a plate, and place them in a steamer set over boiling water. Steam, covered, for 5 minutes.

7. Mix the remaining ½ tablespoon of soy sauce with the honey in a small bowl. Transfer the quail to a small ovenproof skillet and brush them with the soy mixture. Place them in the 425-degree oven and cook them for 10 minutes, then baste them with the liquid that has accumulated in the skillet. Heat the broiler, and broil the quail 6 to 8 inches from the heat source for 5 minutes, until they are nicely browned.

8. Meanwhile, add the grapes to the cup of reserved stock in the saucepan, bring the mixture to a boil, and boil for 1 minute. Add the dissolved cornstarch and stir to thicken the mixture.

9. When the quail are cooked, remove them from the skillet, and arrange them on a serving plate. Strain any accumulated juices in the skillet into the sauce containing the grapes. Pour the sauce over the quail on the serving plate. Sprinkle if desired with the parsley or chives. Serve immediately, one quail per person.

245

This menu is classical and impressive, but really useful, too. We made cod in this beautiful green sauce, which I'm convinced I'm going to be using for pasta. And boning a quail is not the easiest technique, but once you know how to do it, you can bone any poultry. I'm going to practice it a lot.

Gratin of Leeks

For this simple, flavorful gratin, leeks are cooked in just enough water so that by time they are tender, the water has evaporated, leaving behind precious nutrients that would have been lost had the leeks required draining. Arranged in a gratin dish and topped with a mixture of bread crumbs, Swiss cheese, a bit of garlic, and olive oil, the leeks are finished in a hot oven or under a hot broiler.

TOTAL TIME

About 30 minutes

YIELD

4 servings

NUTRITION

356 calories

13 g protein

17 g fat

9 g saturated fat

42 mg cholesterol

546 mg sodium

39 g carbohydrate

3 g dietary fiber

4 LARGE LEEKS (ABOUT 1¾ POUNDS),
    DARK GREEN LEAF TIPS AND TOUGH OUTER
    GREEN LEAVES REMOVED

1 CUP WATER

3 SLICES BREAD (4 OUNCES)

3 LARGE CLOVES GARLIC

1 PIECE SWISS CHEESE, PREFERABLY EMMENTALER
    (4 OUNCES)

½ TEASPOON SALT

½ TEASPOON FRESHLY GROUND BLACK PEPPER

1½ TEASPOONS VIRGIN OLIVE OIL

2 TABLESPOONS UNSALTED BUTTER

1. Split the trimmed leeks in half lengthwise, and wash them well under cold tap water to remove any sand and dirt.

2. Bring the 1 cup of water to a boil in a large skillet, then place the leek halves in one layer in the skillet. Bring the water to a boil again over high heat, then cover the skillet, reduce the heat to medium high, and cook for 10 to 12 minutes, until the leeks are tender and most of the moisture has evaporated. (If there is any water remaining in the skillet, boil the leeks, uncovered, for about a minute to eliminate this moisture.)

3. Remove the leeks from the skillet, place them on a cutting board, and cut them horizontally into 3-inch lengths. Arrange the leek pieces (alternating white, light green, and dark green pieces) in one layer in a 4- to 5-cup gratin dish.

(CONTINUED)

*Stuffed Quail
with Grape Sauce
(page 244) and
Gratin of Leeks
(this page)*

248

Leeks, along with onions, garlic, and chives, belong to the Allium *genus of vegetables. These vegetables contain substances that show promise in protecting against heart disease and cancer, and that may act as anti-bacterials and anti-inflammatories in the body.*

4. Preheat the oven to 475 to 500 degrees, or preheat a broiler until it is very hot.

5. Place the bread, garlic, cheese, salt, and pepper in the bowl of a food processor, and process the mixture until it is finely chopped, then transfer it to a bowl. Add the oil, and mix gently with your hands to lightly coat the bread mixture with the oil. (Caution: Don't overmix or it will become pasty.)

6. Spread the bread mixture on top of the leeks. Break the butter into small pieces, and dot the top of the gratin with the butter.

7. At serving time, place the gratin in the preheated oven, or place it under the hot broiler, positioning it so it is 9 to 10 inches from the heat. Cook for 7 to 8 minutes, until heated through and nicely browned on top.

Peaches in Red Wine

In full summer, when peaches are ripe, soft, and juicy, I make this dessert often. I prepare it here with a little black currant liqueur and red wine, but the recipe can be made with white wine and a little honey or with champagne and a dash of framboise (raspberry brandy). At times of the year when fresh peaches are not available, substitute unsweetened individually quick frozen (IQF) peaches, defrosting them slowly in the refrigerator overnight.

❧   ❧   ❧   ❧   ❧   ❧   ❧   ❧

4 RIPE YELLOW PEACHES (ABOUT 1½ POUNDS)

3 TABLESPOONS SUGAR

3 TABLESPOONS CASSIS (BLACK CURRANT LIQUEUR)

½ CUP FRUITY, ACIDIC RED WINE, LIKE A BEAUJOLAIS OR ZINFANDEL

4 SPRIGS FRESH MINT

1. Using a vegetable peeler, peel the peaches, and cut each of them into 6 wedges, discarding the pits and skin. (You should have about 3 cups of peach wedges.)

2. Place the peaches in a bowl with the sugar, cassis, and wine. Mix well, and refrigerate for up to 8 hours.

3. To serve, divide the peaches and surrounding juice among four wine goblets. Top each dessert with a mint sprig.

TOTAL TIME

20 minutes

YIELD

4 servings

NUTRITION

159 calories

1 g protein

.2 g fat

0 g saturated fat

0 mg cholesterol

3 mg sodium

30 g carbohydrate

3 g dietary fiber

The Fish Connection

ARUGULA SALAD WITH
SALMON CRACKLING AND GARLIC CHIPS

ENDIVE WITH TARRAGON OIL

BAKED SALMON IN GREEN HERB SAUCE

TARRAGON OIL

QUICK ALMOND AND PLUM CAKE

———

We start this menu with an arugula salad garnished and flavored with the skin of the salmon we use in the main course. The salmon skin is cut into strips and cooked in a skillet until crisp. At serving time, this salmon crackling is sprinkled on the arugula greens as a garnish along with "chips" of thinly sliced, lightly browned garlic. ❧ The main-course salmon is baked and served in a green herb sauce made with ingredients that include the salmon cooking liquid, spinach, chives, parsley, and tarragon. This sauce, which is a beautiful bright green color initially, should be served as soon as possible since the acidity of the white wine – a component of the salmon cooking liquid – tends to turn the herbs and spinach a yellowish-green color after a few hours. ❧ As a vegetable for this meal, we serve wedges of endive

that are cooked simply in a dash of water and sugar, then served with a little tarragon oil on top. ❧ Our menu concludes with a flavorful and attractive almond and plum cake. Whole, pitted plums are submerged and baked in a cake batter, and the cake is glazed with a mixture of plum jam and brandy.

Red
LA CREMA
SONOMA COAST,
PINOT NOIR

White
ST. ROMAIN,
SOUS ROCHE,
BURGUNDY

Arugula Salad with Salmon Crackling and Garlic Chips

TOTAL TIME
20 minutes

YIELD
4 servings

NUTRITION
127 calories
4 g protein
11 g fat
1 g saturated fat
8 mg cholesterol
88 mg sodium
3 g carbohydrate
.2 g dietary fiber

Although the skin of salmon tends to hold much of its fat, most of it is cooked out in this recipe. What remains is predominantly protective omega-3 fatty acids.

It is always nice to be able to use things that, conventionally, a cook throws out. In this recipe, I use salmon skin, a delicacy in Japanese cooking, cutting it into strips and sautéing it until crisp and brown. These strips and lightly sautéed, thinly sliced garlic are used as garnishes on a salad made with spicy arugula leaves.

1 TABLESPOON CANOLA OIL

8 LARGE CLOVES GARLIC, PEELED AND VERY THINLY SLICED (⅓ CUP)

1 4-OUNCE PIECE SALMON SKIN (FROM BAKED SALMON IN GREEN HERB SAUCE, PAGE 254), CUT CROSSWISE INTO ¼-INCH STRIPS

DASH OF SALT

1 TABLESPOON SHERRY VINEGAR

¼ TEASPOON SALT

¼ TEASPOON FRESHLY GROUND BLACK PEPPER

2 TABLESPOONS EXTRA VIRGIN OLIVE OIL

6 CUPS (LIGHTLY PACKED) ARUGULA, WASHED AND DRIED

1. Heat the canola oil in a skillet until it is hot but not smoking. Add the garlic slices, and cook them for about 2 minutes over medium heat, stirring occasionally, until the garlic is light blond in color. (Do not let the garlic brown in the oil or it will taste bitter.) Remove the garlic with a slotted spoon and set it aside.

2. Add the salmon skin strips to the skillet with the dash of salt, and immediately cover the skillet with a splash guard (to prevent splattering). Cook the strips over medium heat, stirring carefully a few times to separate the pieces, for about 4 minutes, until the skin is crisp and brown. Remove the skin with a slotted spoon and set it aside. Discard the fat in the skillet.

3. In a bowl large enough to hold the arugula, mix together the vinegar, ¼ teaspoon each salt and pepper, and olive oil. Add the arugula and toss it with the dressing. Divide the salad among four plates. Sprinkle the salmon skin and garlic chips on top of the salad. Serve immediately.

Endive with Tarragon Oil

This is a very simple and flavorful way of preparing and serving endive. Cut into wedges and cooked with a little sugar, salt, and water, the endive is served with tarragon oil on top, or, if you prefer, plain virgin olive oil.

❖   ❖   ❖   ❖   ❖   ❖   ❖   ❖

4 BELGIAN ENDIVES (ABOUT 1¼ POUNDS)

¼ TEASPOON SALT

¼ TEASPOON SUGAR

1 TEASPOON LEMON JUICE

1 TABLESPOON VIRGIN OLIVE OIL

¼ CUP WATER

4 TABLESPOONS TARRAGON OIL OR PASTE
(SEE TARRAGON OIL, PAGE 256) OR EXTRA VIRGIN
OLIVE OIL

1. Wash the endives in cool water, then halve each of them lengthwise. Taking care to keep the leaves attached at the root end, cut each half into 5 or 6 lengthwise wedges.

2. Place the endive wedges in a large stainless-steel saucepan, and add the salt, sugar, lemon juice, olive oil, and water. Bring to a boil over high heat, then cover, reduce the heat to medium, and cook for 8 to 10 minutes, until no liquid remains and the endive wedges begin to brown.

3. Divide the endive wedges among four plates. Top with the tarragon oil or paste. Serve immediately.

TOTAL TIME

15 to 20 minutes

YIELD

4 servings

NUTRITION

195 calories

2 g protein

14 g fat

1 g saturated fat

0 mg cholesterol

213 mg sodium

17 g carbohydrate

4 g dietary fiber

Baked Salmon in Green Herb Sauce

TOTAL TIME

About 30 minutes

YIELD

4 servings

NUTRITION

337 calories

29 g protein

19 g fat

2 g saturated fat

80 mg cholesterol

527 mg sodium

2 g carbohydrate

.5 g dietary fiber

The sauce for this dish is best made at the last moment. Before the spinach and herbs are pureed in a blender, they are blanched in the salmon cooking liquid, which contains wine. While the mixture is a beautiful dark green color when fresh from the blender, the color begins to fade after an hour or so (although the taste is not affected) because of the acidity in the wine. An ideal dish for a large party, the salmon is best served lukewarm or at room temperature.

3 SHALLOTS, PEELED AND CHOPPED (⅓ CUP)

1 CUP DRY, FRUITY WHITE WINE

¾ TEASPOON SALT

½ TEASPOON FRESHLY GROUND BLACK PEPPER

1¼ POUNDS CENTER CUT SKINLESS SALMON FILLET (WITH SKIN RESERVED FOR ARUGULA SALAD WITH SALMON CRACKLING AND GARLIC CHIPS, PAGE 252)

1½ CUPS (LOOSELY PACKED) SPINACH LEAVES (ABOUT 3 OUNCES)

1¼ CUPS (LOOSELY PACKED) CLEANED HERBS (A MIXTURE OF FRESH CHIVES, PARSLEY, AND TARRAGON)

2 TABLESPOONS MAYONNAISE

DASH OF CAYENNE PEPPER

1 TABLESPOON WHITE WINE VINEGAR

⅓ CUP EXTRA VIRGIN OLIVE OIL

1. Preheat the oven to 350 degrees.

2. Place the shallots, wine, half the salt, and the pepper in an ovenproof stainless steel or other nonreactive metal skillet.

3. Place the salmon on top of the shallots in the skillet, and bring the mixture to a boil over high heat. Place the skillet in the 350-degree oven, and bake the salmon for 12 minutes, until it is medium rare. Remove the salmon from the liquid in the skillet, and place it on a platter.

4. Sprinkle the spinach and herbs into the liquid in the skillet, and cook the mixture over high heat for about 2 minutes, until the herbs are wilted and soft.

5. Transfer the mixture to a blender, and blend it into a smooth puree. Add the mayonnaise, cayenne, and vinegar and blend for a few seconds. Add the oil and continue processing the mixture for about 10 seconds.

6. Spoon the lukewarm sauce onto a large platter, and arrange the lukewarm salmon on top. Serve the fish with some of the sauce.

Baked Salmon in Green Herb Sauce (this page) and Arugula Salad with Salmon Crackling and Garlic Chips (page 252)

Tarragon Oil

It is important to retain the bright green color of the tarragon leaves in this preparation. Blanching the leaves before pureeing them in a blender (much better than a food processor for this purpose) locks in their vibrant color.

TOTAL TIME
About 10 minutes

YIELD
2 cups

NUTRITION
122 calories
0 g protein
13 g fat
1 g saturated fat
0 mg cholesterol
37 mg sodium
0 g carbohydrate
0 g dietary fiber

1 CUP (LIGHTLY PACKED) FRESH TARRAGON LEAVES
¼ TEASPOON SALT
1 CUP CANOLA OIL

1. Bring 1 cup of water to a boil in a small saucepan. Add the tarragon leaves and mix well. Return the water to a boil, and boil the tarragon leaves for 10 seconds. Drain the leaves in a sieve, spraying cold water on them as you do so to cool them quickly.

2. Place the drained leaves in a blender with the salt and ½ cup of the oil. Blend the mixture for 30 seconds, then scrape down any of the mixture that is clinging to the sides of the blender. Add the remaining ½ cup of oil, and blend the mixture for another 30 seconds. (Yield: 1 cup.)

1. Transfer the contents of the blender bowl to a glass jar with a tight-fitting lid and store the mixture in the refrigerator for use within two weeks. If any of the mixture is left at that point, pour the oil on top into another container (the tarragon will have settled to the bottom of the jar by then and be starting to discolor). Discard the tarragon leaves. Cover the container of tarragon oil, and use it as needed over the next several weeks, keeping the oil in the refrigerator between uses.

Quick Almond and Plum Cake

This is a very fast cake to make, requiring only a few seconds to process the flour and almonds together, creating a coarse powder to which you add the remaining cake ingredients. The batter can be baked in a springform mold, or in a regular loaf pan for a type of pound cake. ✱ If baked without the fruit garnish, the cake freezes well. (It is best not to freeze it with the fruit garnish as the fruit becomes soggy and mushy when the dessert is defrosted.) For best results, wrap the cake carefully in plastic wrap and aluminum foil before freezing it, and defrost it in the refrigerator while still wrapped.

TOTAL TIME
About 1 hour

YIELD
6 to 8 servings

NUTRITION
581 calories
9 g protein
27 g fat
7 g saturated fat
93 mg cholesterol
219 mg sodium
79 g carbohydrate
4 g dietary fiber

CAKE

1 CUP ALL-PURPOSE FLOUR (5½ OUNCES)

1 CUP WHOLE ALMONDS (5½ OUNCES)

⅔ CUP SUGAR

1 TEASPOON DOUBLE-ACTING BAKING POWDER

1 TEASPOON VANILLA EXTRACT

½ STICK (2 OUNCES) UNSALTED BUTTER, SOFTENED (WITH ¼ TEASPOON RESERVED FOR BUTTERING THE MOLD)

2 TABLESPOONS CANOLA OIL

2 EGGS

⅓ CUP MILK

GARNISHES

4 TO 6 RIPE PLUMS, PREFERABLY BLACK FRIAR OR SANTA ROSA (1¼ POUNDS)

3 TABLESPOONS SUGAR

½ CUP PLUM JAM

1 TABLESPOON PLUM BRANDY OR COGNAC

1. Preheat the oven to 350 degrees.

2. *For the Cake:* Place the flour, almonds, ⅔ cup sugar, and baking powder in the bowl of a food processor, and process until the mixture is a coarse powder. Add the baking powder, vanilla, butter (minus ¼ teaspoon), oil, and eggs and process for a few seconds, just until incorporated. Add the milk and process for an additional few seconds, until the mixture is smooth. Use the reserved ¼ teaspoon of butter to coat the inside of a 9-inch springform mold. Pour in the batter. (It should be about ¾ inch thick in the mold.)

(CONTINUED)

QUICK ALMOND AND PLUM CAKE *(CONTINUED)*

Almonds and plums are a terrific combination. I'd like to try it with the plums cut up into pieces rather than left whole, though. I wonder if that would work…

3. *For the Garnishes:* Using the point of a sharp knife, remove the pit from the stem end of each plum. (If the plums are not fully ripened and feel hard, prick them all over with the point of a sharp knife to soften them.) Rinse the whole pitted plums well in cold water. While the plums are still wet, roll them in the 3 tablespoons of sugar. Arrange the plums on top of the cake, spacing them evenly, and push them down into the batter until the bottom half of each is immersed.

4. Place the cake on a cookie sheet, and bake it in the center of the 350-degree oven for 50 to 60 minutes, or until puffy and nicely browned on top. Cool on a rack until lukewarm.

5. Mix the plum jam and the brandy together in a small bowl, and brush the top of the lukewarm cake with the mixture. Remove the cake from the mold and cut it into six wedges so that each serving contains one plum. Serve while still lukewarm or just at room temperature.

Quick Almond and Plum Cake (page 257)

JACQUES PÉPIN'S KITCHEN: ENCORE WITH CLAUDINE

A Graduation Party

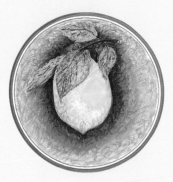

SHRIMP *PANÉ* ON WATERCRESS

ROAST RACK OF LAMB WITH LAMB TIMBALES

SPINACH WITH PIGNOLA NUTS AND CROUTONS

BERRIES *RAFRAÎCHIS*

BERRY JAM

———

This is a rich and elegant menu for a very special occasion. Yet, it teaches notions of economy and demonstrates many important cooking techniques. ⬇ The menu begins with a shrimp pané on watercress. The shrimp are peeled and deveined, and their tails, along with a few of the smaller shrimp, are transformed into a mousse. The remaining shrimp, about four per person, are lined up in portions on a cookie sheet and coated on both sides with the mousse. The resulting patties are cooked and served on top of watercress for a delightful and original first course. ⬇ The main dish is a roast rack of lamb. Although rack of lamb is expensive, we use only one rack for this recipe. While, conventionally, this would be considered too little for four people, it is enough because we extend the dish by creating timbales from the defatted lamb trimmings to serve with the chops. Packed into individual ramekins, the timbales are cooked until well done and served with the medium-rare rack. ⬇ A classic garnish for rack of lamb is spinach. Here, we sauté spinach in olive oil and add croutons and pignola nuts to give some texture and crunchiness to the dish, which we garnish with chopped hard-cooked eggs. ⬇ This elegant graduation party menu finishes with a berry *rafraîchi*, a mixture of strawberries, blueberries, and raspberries cooked with red wine and jam. This dessert is served in soup plates with little pieces of brioche or cookies. As a special bonus, we transform leftover *rafraîchis* into a delicious berry jam that will keep for months in the refrigerator.

SUGGESTED WINES

Aperitif and Dessert
KRISTONE BRUT ROSE

White
LITTLE'S SEMILLON-CHARDONNAY

Red
STONESTREET LEGACY

Shrimp Pané on Watercress

TOTAL TIME
30 to 40 minutes

YIELD
4 servings

NUTRITION
338 calories
27 g protein
20 g fat
4 g saturated fat
233 mg cholesterol
581 mg sodium
11 g carbohydrate
1 g dietary fiber

In this recipe, the tails of shelled shrimp and a few whole shrimp are transformed into a mousse or puree. Then, for each serving, four shrimp are coated with the puree, and the resulting "patty" is breaded and sautéed in oil with a dash of butter. The flavorful patties are served on watercress salad.

20 EXTRA LARGE SHRIMP (16 TO 20 COUNT PER POUND), SHELLED, DEVEINED, WASHED AND DRIED (16 OUNCES)

1 LARGE EGG

1 SMALL CLOVE GARLIC, PEELED

¼ TEASPOON SALT

¼ TEASPOON FRESHLY GROUND BLACK PEPPER

1 TABLESPOON FRESH PARSLEY LEAVES

3 SLICES BREAD (2½ OUNCES), PROCESSED INTO CRUMBS IN A FOOD PROCESSOR (1 CUP)

2 TABLESPOONS CANOLA OIL

1 TABLESPOON UNSALTED BUTTER

WATERCRESS SALAD

1 BUNCH WATERCRESS (8 OUNCES)

1 TABLESPOON SHERRY VINEGAR

2 TABLESPOONS EXTRA VIRGIN OLIVE OIL

¼ TEASPOON SALT

¼ TEASPOON FRESHLY GROUND BLACK PEPPER

1. Cut off the lower tail pieces of each shrimp and reserve these pieces for the mousse. Place these tail pieces with the 4 smallest shrimp (total weight about 6 ounces) in the bowl of a food processor along with the egg, garlic clove, and the ¼ teaspoon each salt and pepper, and process for about 20 seconds. Scrape down the sides of the bowl, add the parsley, and process for another 15 to 20 seconds, until the mixture is smooth. Transfer the mixture to a bowl. (You should have about 1 cup of mousse.)

2. Divide the 16 remaining shrimp into four portions. Arrange these portions on a tray so that each portion of 4 shrimp is clustered together to form a flat patty measuring about 3 by 2 inches. Coat the top surface of each of these patties with about 1½ tablespoons of the shrimp mousse, using up half of the mixture. Then, sprinkle half the fresh bread crumbs over the mousse on the patties, and press the crumbs gently into the mousse.

3. Using a spatula, gently turn the patties over so they are breaded side down on the tray. Spread the remaining mousse on the shrimp patties and coat as before with the remaining bread crumbs. Cover and refrigerate until ready to cook.

4. At cooking time, heat the canola oil and butter in a large skillet. Transfer the patties carefully from the tray to the skillet, arranging them in one layer, and cook them gently for 3 minutes on that side. Turn carefully (as they are delicate) and cook for 3 minutes on the other side. Cover and set aside while you prepare the salad.

5. *For the Watercress Salad:* Cut off the bottom 2½ inches from the watercress stems, reserving them, if you desire, in the refrigerator or freezer for use in soup. (You should have about 5 ounces of watercress or 4 cups remaining.) Wash the watercress well, and dry it in a salad spinner.

6. Combine the sherry vinegar, olive oil, and ¼ teaspoon each salt and pepper in the bowl in which you will serve your salad. Just before serving, add the watercress to the bowl. Toss the greens to coat them with the dressing.

7. Divide the salad among four plates, and serve each with a shrimp *pané* on top.

Watercress is rich in vitamins A and C, providing more than 30% of the daily value for each.

263

Roast Rack of Lamb with Lamb Timbales

For this recipe, one rack of well-trimmed lamb is roasted with a coating of flavored bread crumbs. In addition, to extend the lamb rack and make it more elegant as well as economical, meat from the trimmings is transformed into timbales. The timbales are cooked in ½-cup molds, and each person is served a small timbale along with a large lamb chop from the rack. If the 6 to 8 ounces of meat needed for the timbales cannot be obtained from the rack trimmings, buy an extra lamb shoulder chop or a few pieces of lamb stew to get the 6 to 8 ounces of meat.

❧   ❧   ❧   ❧   ❧   ❧   ❧   ❧   ❧

1 RACK LAMB (ABOUT 3 POUNDS), COMPLETELY TRIMMED OF FAT AND 6 TO 8 OUNCES OF MEAT REMOVED FOR THE TIMBALES (ABOUT 1¼ POUNDS TRIMMED RACK WEIGHT)

TIMBALES

6 TO 8 OUNCES MEAT FROM RACK (SEE ABOVE)

1½ SLICES BREAD (1½ OUNCES), CUT INTO A ½-INCH DICE (1¼ CUPS)

1 EGG, LIGHTLY BEATEN

¼ CUP DRY WHITE WINE

2 TABLESPOONS CHOPPED SHALLOTS

1 TABLESPOON CHOPPED FRESH MINT

1 TEASPOON CHOPPED FRESH THYME

½ TEASPOON SALT

½ TEASPOON FRESHLY GROUND BLACK PEPPER

LAMB RACK

1 TRIMMED LAMB RACK, FROM ABOVE (1¼ POUNDS)

¼ TEASPOON SALT

½ TEASPOON FRESHLY GROUND BLACK PEPPER

2 SLICES BREAD (2 OUNCES)

1 TABLESPOON MINT LEAVES

1 TEASPOON THYME OR LEMON THYME LEAVES

1 TABLESPOON CHOPPED SHALLOTS

2 TEASPOONS VIRGIN OLIVE OIL

Roast Rack of Lamb with Lamb Timbales (this page) and Spinach with Pignola Nuts and Croutons (page 267)

1. Preheat the oven to 350 degrees.

2. *For the Timbales:* Remove and discard any remaining fat and sinews from the lamb trimmings, and cut the trimmings into ½-inch pieces. Chop the meat trimmings coarsely in a food processor. Place the bread, egg, wine, shallots, mint, thyme, and the ½ teaspoon each salt and pepper in a mixing bowl along with the chopped meat, and mash the mixture well with a fork or with your hands.

3. Divide the timbale mixture among four small ramekins (½ cup capacity), spooning about ⅓ cup of the mixture into each mold. Place the molds in a saucepan, and surround them with 1 cup of luke-warm water.

(CONTINUED)

TOTAL TIME

About 1½ hours

YIELD

4 servings

NUTRITION

LAMB TIMBALES

333 calories

34 g protein

15 g fat

5 g saturated fat

105 mg cholesterol

645 mg sodium

12 g carbohydrate

.7 g dietary fiber

RACK OF LAMB

228 calories

23 g protein

11 g fat

3 g saturated fat

73 mg cholesterol

274 mg sodium

7 g carbohydrate

.4 g dietary fiber

CLAUDINE

These lamb timbales have a wonderful texture which contrasts well with the meat on the rack of lamb. This dish is very smart in that it's elegant but economical: you really do use everything.

4. Bring the water in the saucepan to a boil over high heat on top of the stove, then cover with a lid, reduce the heat to low, and cook the timbales gently for 10 to 12 minutes, until they are set and the lamb mixture is cooked through. (Note: The timbales can be cooked up to a few hours ahead and reheated in a skillet, surrounded by water, on top of the stove at serving time.)

5. Preheat the oven to 425 degrees.

6. *For the Rack of Lamb:* Heat a large nonstick skillet on top of the stove. Meanwhile, sprinkle the lamb with the ¼ teaspoon salt and ¼ teaspoon of the pepper. Place the rack flat in the hot skillet. Cook the rack, turning it occasionally, for 4 to 5 minutes, until it is seared on all sides. Transfer the lamb rack to a small roasting pan, placing it flesh side up in the pan.

7. Place the bread, remaining ¼ teaspoon of pepper, mint, and thyme in the bowl of a food processor, and process the mixture until it is chopped but still fluffy. Transfer the processed mixture to a bowl, add the chopped shallots and oil, and mix gently to moisten the bread but not make it pasty or wet. Lightly press the bread mixture over the top of the rack. (Note: This can be done a few hours ahead.)

8. At cooking time, place the rack with the bread topping in the 425-degree oven, and cook it for 15 minutes for medium-rare meat. Let rest in a warm place (a 160-degree oven, if possible) for 10 minutes before carving.

9. Serve a double chop per person with a lamb timbale.

Spinach with Pignola Nuts and Croutons

I love spinach and usually serve it sautéed with a bit of olive oil or butter, salt, and pepper. Here, to make it special, I combine it with croutons and nuts after it is sautéed and serve it with a sprinkling of chopped hard-cooked egg.

❧   ❧   ❧   ❧   ❧   ❧   ❧   ❧

3 TABLESPOONS VIRGIN OLIVE OIL

2 OUNCES DAY-OLD BAGUETTE, CUT INTO
¾-INCH PIECES (1¼ CUPS)

2 TABLESPOONS PIGNOLA NUTS

4 TO 5 LARGE CLOVES GARLIC, PEELED AND
THINLY SLICED (3 TABLESPOONS)

2 BUNCHES (20 OUNCES) FRESH SPINACH,
TRIMMED OF LARGE STEMS AND DAMAGED
LEAVES, AND WASHED

⅓ TEASPOON SALT

¼ TEASPOON FRESHLY GROUND BLACK PEPPER

1 HARD-COOKED EGG, PEELED AND COARSELY
CHOPPED, OR CUT WITH AN EGG CUTTER
INTO SLICES, THEN TURNED 90 DEGREES IN
THE CUTTER AND CUT AGAIN INTO A DICE

1. Heat 1½ tablespoons of the olive oil in a skillet. Add the bread pieces and cook, stirring, for 2 minutes. Add the nuts and garlic and cook, stirring, for 1 minute, until the bread, nuts, and garlic are nicely browned. Transfer the mixture to a bowl.

2. Place the spinach, still wet from washing, into the same skillet you used to cook the bread mixture, and add the salt, pepper, and remaining 1½ tablespoons of oil. Cover, and cook for about 4 minutes, until the spinach is wilted and soft. Just before serving, add the crouton mixture, and combine well.

3. Arrange the spinach on a serving platter, sprinkle with the chopped egg, and serve immediately.

TOTAL TIME
About 10 minutes

YIELD
4 servings

NUTRITION
203 calories
8 g protein
14 g fat
2 g saturated fat
53 mg cholesterol
389 mg sodium
13 g carbohydrate
4 g dietary fiber

Spinach is a good source of vitamins A and C, folate, and calcium.

Berries Rafraîchis

TOTAL TIME
About 20 minutes,
plus cooling time

YIELD
4 servings

NUTRITION
175 calories
1 g protein
.6 g fat
0 g saturated fat
0 mg cholesterol
19 mg sodium
45 g carbohydrate
4 g dietary fiber

Rafraîchir means "to refresh," which is what this beautiful, summer berry dish does for those who consume it. I double the quantity of berries to have enough for another recipe (see Berry Jam, page 270.)

1 CUP FRUITY RED WINE (LIKE A BEAUJOLAIS)

¼ CUP SUGAR

1 CUP JAM OR PRESERVES (CHERRY, STRAWBERRY, RASPBERRY, APRICOT, OR A MIXTURE OF THESE AND/OR OTHER JAMS)

2 SPRIGS FRESH MINT, TIED TOGETHER WITH TWINE

1 POUND STRAWBERRIES, WASHED, HULLED, AND HALVED (4 CUPS)

12 OUNCES BLUEBERRIES, WASHED (2 CUPS)

6 OUNCES RASPBERRIES (1 CUP)

OPTIONAL GARNISHES: CAKE SLICES, SOUR CREAM, AND MINT SPRIGS

1. Place the wine, sugar, jam, and mint in a large saucepan, and bring the mixture to a boil. Mix well. Add the strawberries, blueberries, and raspberries, and bring the mixture back to a boil over high heat, stirring and shaking the pan occasionally to mix the liquid with the fruit.

2. When the whole mixture is boiling (this will take about 5 minutes), cover the pan, reduce the heat to medium, and boil it gently for 1 minute. Transfer the mixture to a bowl, and cool it to room temperature. (Yield: 5 cups.)

3. To serve, spoon about ⅔ cup of the berry mixture onto each of four dessert plates. Serve, if desired, with cake and garnishes of sour cream and mint. (Note: The remaining 2½ cups of berries can be refrigerated for serving the following day or used to make Berry Jam, page 270.)

Berry Jam

TOTAL TIME

About 5 hours

YIELD

1 ¾ cups

NUTRITION

50 calories

0 g protein

.2 g fat

0 g saturated fat

0 mg cholesterol

6 mg sodium

13 g carbohydrate

1 g dietary fiber

Whatever is left over from Berries *Rafraîchis*, page 268, is placed in a low oven for a few hours and transformed into this delicious jam. As good spooned over ice cream as it is spread on toast, it will keep for weeks in the refrigerator.

❧   ❧   ❧   ❧   ❧   ❧   ❧   ❧

2½ CUPS LEFTOVER BERRY MIXTURE FROM BERRIES *RAFRAÎCHIS*, PAGE 268

1. Preheat the oven to 200 degrees.

2. Pour the berry mixture into an oven-proof glass dish or stainless-steel pan large enough so that the mixture is about 1 inch deep in the pan.

3. Place the pan in the 200-degree oven, and bake the berries for about 5 hours to evaporate the moisture surrounding them and concentrate the flavor of the fruit.

4. Transfer the jam to a jar, cool, cover, and refrigerate. Use within one month as a topping for toast, over ice cream, with pancakes, etc.

Once there was a particularly trying day in the studio when everyone was having difficulty getting on the same page, so to speak. Finally we were ready to shoot, and Jacques picked up the knife he was going to use; it was second nature for him to check the blade. Finding it to be somewhat less than perfect, he walked off the set, found a steel and proceeded to sharpen the knife. It took a few minutes. He thought nothing of the fact that forty-two people were all finally ready and were now waiting for him; he was not going to begin until the knife was sharp enough. Period. After that, whenever he was ready and we were not, he would say, "What are we waiting for?" and I'd reply, "We're sharpening our knives."

The standard of excellence that Jacques set with that one sharp knife has been in place ever since. Camera operators who are used to capturing everything from a right field pop fly to the track of a tear down a cheek lovingly followed each lemon slice, each trip to the oven, each perfectly placed chive. Food purveyors sent their most succulent goods, manufacturers their finest wares. Of course a company wants the public to see Jacques Pépin using their product; what is less obvious is the fact that his delight in a great oven, a fine sauté pan, an excellent vegetable peeler is infectious. He appreciates quality in all spheres and imparts that appreciation to all those who work with him. It makes everyone rise to their best self, and that attention to quality shows in all facets of the show.

In addition, this year saw the rising star of Claudine Pépin, no longer just the apple of Jacques' eye but a fine talent in her own right. She was funny and willing to try anything, and she brought a lot to the table with her wit, candor, and upbeat attitude.

My deepest appreciation goes to the following crew members for their excellent work: to floor directors Jean Tuckerman and Squire Alligator; camera operators Harry Betancourt, Brad Cochrane, Mike Ratusz, Marcial Lopez, and Nick Utley; lighting designer Greg King; audio engineer Birrell Walsh; video operator Eric Shackelford; technical director djovida; video tape engineers Helen Silvani and Richard Schiller; studio supervisor Walt Bjerke; editors Dawn Logsdon and John Andreini; production manager Gigi Lee; unit manager Jolee Hoyt; and last but never least, production support from Carolyn Abate, Eugene Kim, Sasha Petrosky, Katie Price, and Charlotte Zyskowski.

Very special thanks go to the Viking Range Corp. for supplying our set and back kitchen with magnificent appliances, and to Eddie Bauer for their impeccable wardrobe and set furnishings. Accommodations were generously provided by the Clift Hotel in San Francisco for Jacques, Claudine, and our director Brian Murphy; their famous Redwood Room was home to many late-night schmooze fests.

In addition, we thank Sue Conley and Peggy Smith of Tomales Bay Foods and the Cowgirl Creamery for their hospitality in allowing us to shoot on their premises (I've never eaten so much cheese in one day in my life!) and to Jeff Dawson who hosted Claudine at the Kendall-Jackson Vineyards and gardens. He taught us all a thing or two about wine. Jacques' level of excellence is one to which we would all like to become accustomed. There is nothing like getting to work with the best, and he is it.

— *PEGGY LEE SCOTT*

SPECIAL THANKS

Apple Computer	*Gene Schick Co.*	*Sarah Stocking*
Biordi Art Imports	*Kendall-Jackson Winery*	*Silver Terrace Nurseries*
Bourgeat USA, Inc.	*Lamson & Goodnow Mfg. Co.*	*Sur La Table*
Couzon, USA	*Lunt Silversmiths*	*Tomales Bay Foods*
Draeger's Market	*Oscartielle Equip., Calif.*	*Villeroy & Boch*
Emile Henry USA Corp	*Persian Mercantile Co.*	

FOOD PROVIDED BY	WINE PROVIDED BY	
Andronico's Market	*Ausvin U.S.A., Inc.*	*Kendall-Jackson Vineyards & Winery*
Birite Foodservice Distributors	*Balzac Communications*	*Kobrand Corporation*
The Fresh Fish Company	*Bedford International Ltd.*	*Maisons Marques & Domaines USA, Inc.*
Golden Gate Meats	*Boisset Wines, U.S.A.*	*Martin Sinkoff Wines, Inc.*
Greenleaf Produce	*Broadbent Selections, Inc.*	*Rosemount Estate*
Melissa's	*Diamond Wine Merchants*	*S.A. Wine Company / Cape Ventures*
Modesto Poultry	*Dreyfus, Ashby & Co.*	
Napa Valley Kitchens	*French Prestige Wines, Inc.*	
Osprey Seafood	*Frontier Wine Imports*	
Peet's Coffee & Tea	*Jackson Family's Artisans & Estates Wineries*	
Provimi Veal		
Straus Family Creamery		
Superior Farms		
Vanilla, Saffron Imports		

KQED gratefully acknowledges the generous support from these companies

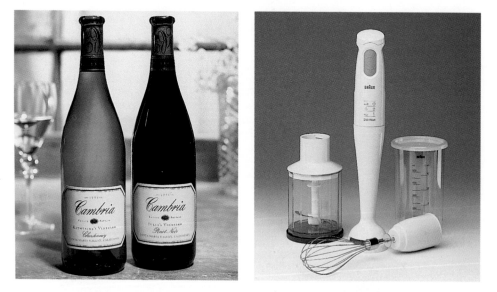

Cambria

BRAUN